THE BERLITZ

"Aimed at educated, experienced travellers, the [Berlitz Travellers] Guides capture the flavor of foreign lands."

—*Entrepreneur*

"Filling a needed niche in guidebooks . . . designed to eliminate the cumbersome lists of virtually every hotel and restaurant . . . . Special out-of-the-way places are detailed. . . . The books capture the personality and excitement of each destination."

—*Los Angeles Times*

"There's a different tone to these books, and certainly a different approach . . . information is aimed at independent and clearly sophisticated travellers. . . . Strong opinions give these books a different personality from most guides, and make them fun to read."

—*Travel & Leisure*

"Aimed at experienced, independent travellers who want information beyond the nuts-and-bolts material available in many familiar sources. Although each volume gives necessary basics, the series sends travellers not just to 'sights,' but to places and events that convey the personality of each locale."

—*The Denver Post*

"Just the right amount of information about where to stay and play."

—*Detroit Free Press*

"The strength of the [Berlitz Travellers Guides] lies in remarks and recommendations by writers with a depth of knowledge about their subject."

—*Washington Times*

"The most readable of the current paperback lot."

—*New York Post*

"Highly recommended."

—*Library Journal*

"Very strong on atmosphere and insights into local culture for curious travellers."

—*Boston Herald*

"The [Berlitz Travellers Guides] eliminate cumbersome lists and provide reliable information about what is truly exciting and significant about a destination. . . . [They] also emphasize the spirit and underlying 'vibrations' of a region—historical, cultural, and social—that enhance a trip."

—*Retirement Life*

"Information without boredom. . . . Good clear maps and index."

—*The Sunday Sun* (Toronto)

CONTRIBUTORS

BUDDY MAYS, a freelance writer and photographer who specializes in travel and natural history, has travelled extensively in the rain forests of Central and South America. He is the author of several books, and his work has appeared in such publications as *Travel & Leisure, The National Geographic, Audubon, Sunset, Forbes,* and *Travel Holiday* magazines. A contributor to *The Berlitz Travellers Guide to the American Southwest,* he lives in Hot Springs, Arkansas. He has been a special consultant for this guidebook.

RICHARD CARROLL, based in Shadow Hills, California, has travelled extensively in Mexico and Central America in his VW camper, and is the author of *The Motor Camper's Guide to Mexico and Baja* and *A Photo Journey to Los Angeles,* and the coauthor of *Hidden Mexico* (3rd edition). He is also a regular contributor to the Copley News Service and to *Family Living* and *Motorhome* magazines, and has won four international writing awards.

TONY TEDESCHI's articles and photographs have appeared in more than 100 publications, including *Travel Holiday, Caribbean Travel & Life,* and *Penthouse* magazines and the *New York Times, Washington Post, Boston Globe,* and *Baltimore Sun.* He writes a special section on eco-tourism twice a year for *Audubon* magazine that focuses on the natural and cultural attractions of the Caribbean and of Central and South America. He travels extensively throughout Costa Rica, particularly the national parks of the Pacific coast.

THE BERLITZ TRAVELLERS GUIDES

THE AMERICAN SOUTHWEST

AUSTRALIA

BERLIN

CANADA

THE CARIBBEAN

COSTA RICA

ENGLAND & WALES

FRANCE

GERMANY

GREECE

HAWAII

IRELAND

LONDON

MEXICO

NEW ENGLAND

NEW YORK CITY

NORTHERN ITALY AND ROME

PORTUGAL

SAN FRANCISCO &
NORTHERN CALIFORNIA

SOUTHERN ITALY AND ROME

SPAIN

TURKEY

THE BERLITZ TRAVELLERS GUIDE TO COSTA RICA

ALAN TUCKER
General Editor

BERLITZ PUBLISHING COMPANY, INC.
New York, New York

BERLITZ PUBLISHING COMPANY LTD.
Oxford, England

THE BERLITZ TRAVELLERS GUIDE
TO COSTA RICA

Published by Berlitz Publishing Company, Inc.
257 Park Avenue South, New York, New York 10010, U.S.A.

Distributed in the United States by
the Macmillan Publishing Group

Distributed elsewhere by Berlitz Publishing Company Ltd.
Berlitz House, Peterley Road, Horspath, Oxford OX4 2TX, England

ISBN 2-8315-1702-8
ISSN 1067-7135

Designed by Beth Tondreau Design
Cover design by Dan Miller Design
Cover photograph © Kevin Schafer
Maps by Mark Stein Studios
Illustrations by Bill Russell
Copyedited by Patricia Fogarty
Fact-checked by Sara Maneiro
Edited by Alan Tucker

Printed in the United States of America
1 3 5 7 9 10 8 6 4 2

THIS GUIDEBOOK

The Berlitz Travellers Guides are designed for experienced travellers in search of exceptional information that will enhance the enjoyment of the trips they take.

Where, for example, are the interesting, out-of-the-way, fun, charming, or romantic places to stay? The hotels described by our expert writers are some of the special places, in all price ranges except for the very lowest—not just the run-of-the-mill, heavily marketed places in advertised airline and travel-wholesaler packages.

We are *highly* selective in our choices of accommodations, concentrating on what our insider contributors think are the most interesting or rewarding places, and why. Readers who want to review exhaustive lists of hotel and resort choices as well, and who feel they need detailed descriptions of each property, can supplement the *Berlitz Travellers Guide* with tourism industry publications or one of the many directory-type guidebooks on the market.

We indicate the approximate price level of each accommodation in our description of it (no indication means it is moderate in local, relative terms), and at the end of every chapter we supply more detailed hotel rates as well as contact information so that you can get precise, up-to-the-minute rates and make reservations.

The Berlitz Travellers Guide to Costa Rica highlights the more rewarding parts of the country so that you can quickly and efficiently home in on a good itinerary.

Of course, this guidebook does far more than just help you choose a hotel and plan your trip. *The Berlitz Travellers Guide to Costa Rica* is designed for use *in* Costa Rica. Our writers, each of whom is an experienced travel journalist who either lives in or regularly tours the city or region of Costa Rica he covers, tell you what you really need to know, what you can't find out so easily on your own. They identify and describe the truly out-of-the-ordinary resorts, restaurants, shops, activities, tours, and sights, and tell you the best way to "do" your destination.

Our writers are highly selective. They bring out the significance of the places they *do* cover, capturing the personality and the underlying cultural and historical resonances of a city or region—making clear its special appeal.

The Berlitz Travellers Guide to Costa Rica is full of reliable information. We would like to know if you think we've left out some very special place. Although we make every effort to provide the most current information available about every destination described in this book, it is possible too that changes have occurred before you arrive. If you do have an experience that is contrary to what you were led to expect by our description, we would like to hear from you about it.

A guidebook is no substitute for common sense when you are travelling. Always pack the clothing, footwear, and other items appropriate for the destination, and make the necessary accommodation for such variables as altitude, weather, and local rules and customs. Of course, once on the scene you should avoid situations that are in your own judgment potentially hazardous, even if they have to do with something mentioned in a guidebook. Half the fun of travelling is exploring, but explore with care.

ALAN TUCKER
General Editor
Berlitz Travellers Guides

Root Publishing Company
350 West Hubbard Street
Suite 440
Chicago, Illinois 60610

CONTENTS

This Guidebook v

Overview 5

Useful Facts 21

Bibliography 34

San José 37
Getting Around 49
Accommodations 51
Dining 56
Nightlife 64
Shops and Shopping 68

Around San José 73
EAST AND SOUTH
Irazú Volcano 78
Cartago 79
The Orosí Valley 80
The Turrialba Valley 83
The Saints' Route 86
NORTHWEST
Butterfly Farm 88
Zoo-Ave 89
Alajuela 89
Poás Volcano 90
Sarchí 91
The Britt Coffee Tour 93
NORTH
Barva Cloud Forest and Volcano 95
Braulio Carrillo National Park 98

The Caribbean Coast 105
The Pacific Coast 134
North-Central Costa Rica 181

Historical Chronology 201
Index 205

MAPS

Costa Rica 2
San José 40
Around San José 74
The Caribbean Coast 106
The Southern Pacific Coast 137
The Northern Pacific Coast 160
North-Central Costa Rica 183

THE BERLITZ TRAVELLERS GUIDE TO COSTA RICA

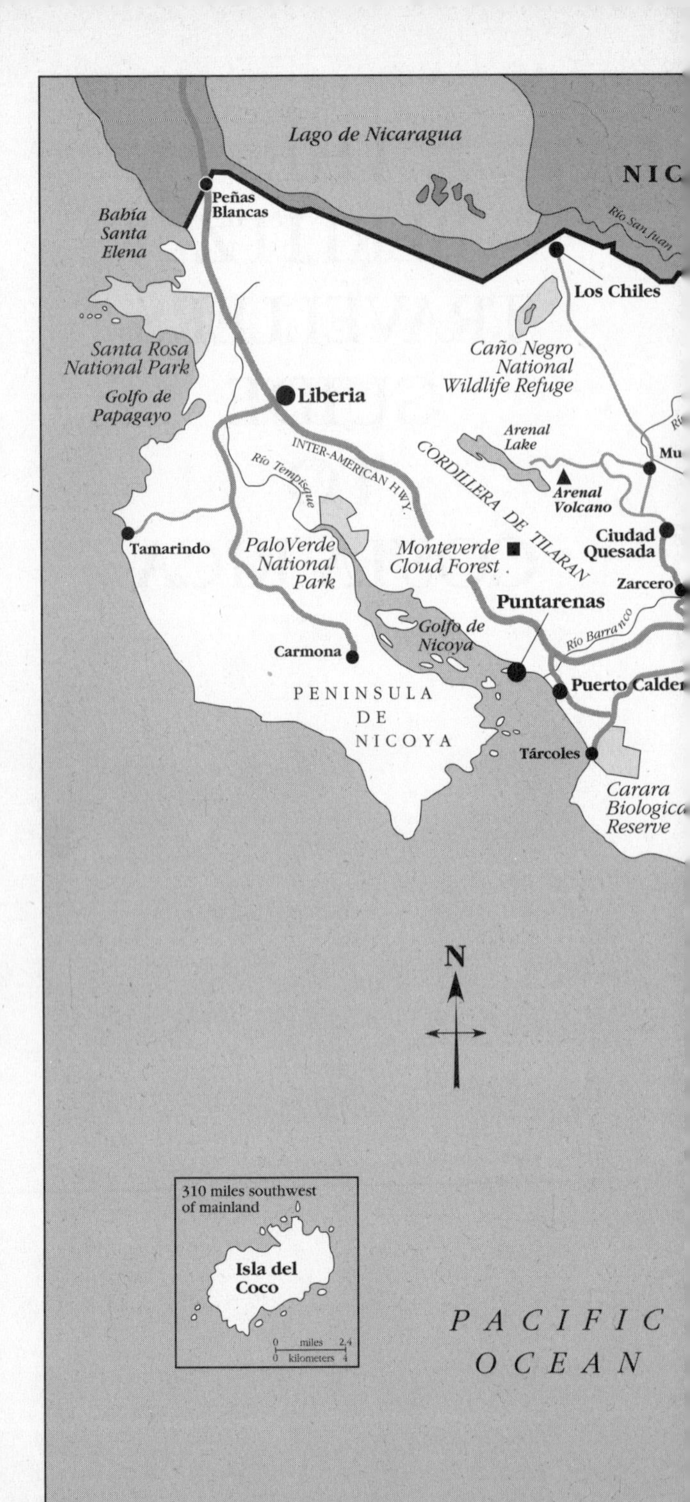
Lago de Nicaragua
NIC
Peñas Blancas
Bahía Santa Elena
Río San Juan
Los Chiles
Santa Rosa National Park
Caño Negro National Wildlife Refuge
Golfo de Papagayo
Liberia
Arenal Lake
INTER-AMERICAN HWY.
CORDILLERA DE TILARAN
Río Tempisque
Arenal Volcano
Mu
Tamarindo
Palo Verde National Park
Monteverde Cloud Forest
Ciudad Quesada
Zarcero
Puntarenas
Golfo de Nicoya
Río Barranco
Carmona
PENINSULA DE NICOYA
Puerto Calder
Tárcoles
Carara Biologica Reserve
N
310 miles southwest of mainland
Isla del Coco
0 miles 2.4
0 kilometers 4
PACIFIC OCEAN

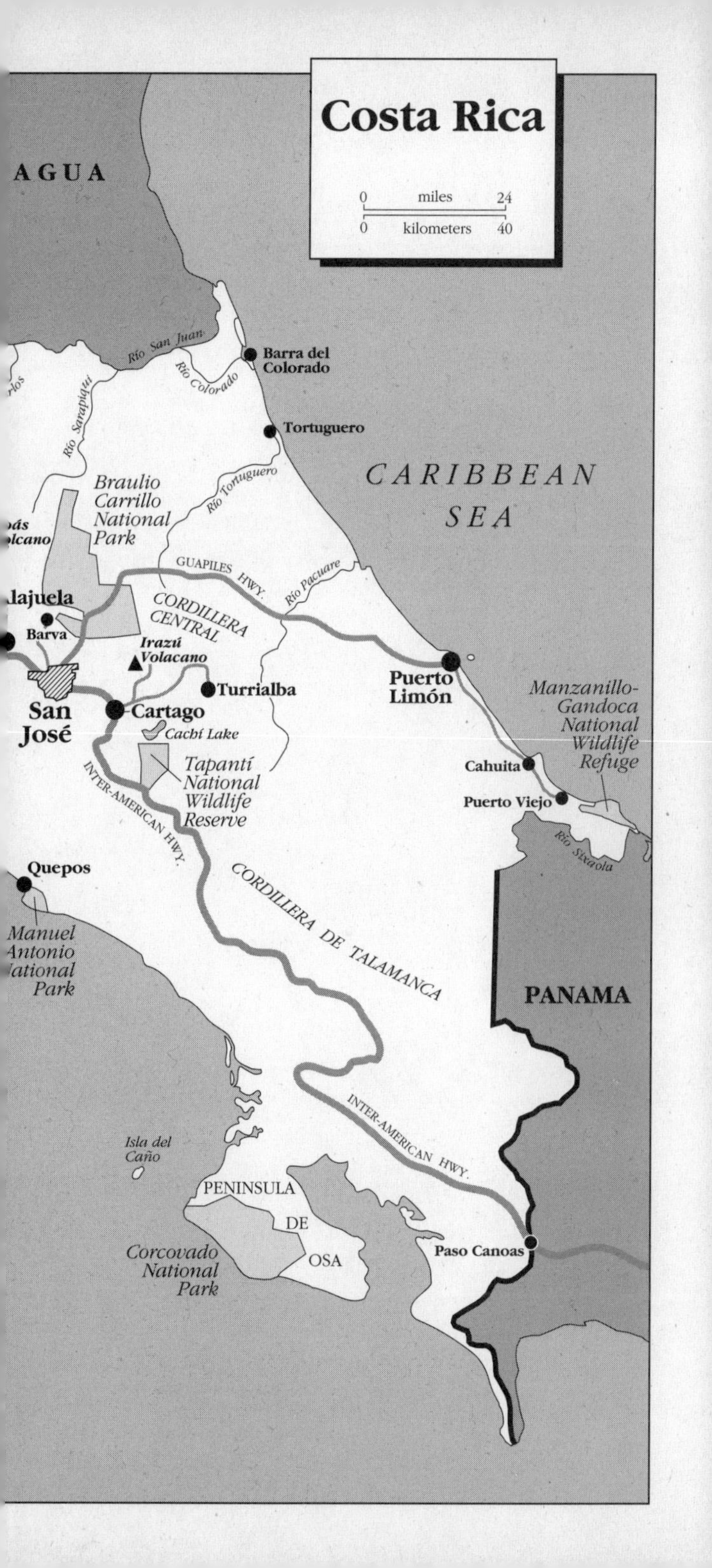

Costa Rica
0 miles 24
0 kilometers 40
AGUA
Río San Juan
Barra del Colorado
Río Colorado
Río Sarapiquí
Tortuguero
Río Tortuguero
CARIBBEAN SEA
Braulio Carrillo National Park
GUAPILES HWY.
Río Pacuare
CORDILLERA CENTRAL
Barva
Irazú Volacano
Turrialba
Puerto Limón
San José
Cartago
Cachí Lake
Tapantí National Wildlife Reserve
Manzanillo-Gandoca National Wildlife Refuge
Cahuita
Puerto Viejo
Río Sixaola
INTER-AMERICAN HWY.
Quepos
Manuel Antonio National Park
CORDILLERA DE TALAMANCA
PANAMA
INTER-AMERICAN HWY.
Isla del Caño
PENINSULA DE OSA
Corcovado National Park
Paso Canoas

OVERVIEW

By Tony Tedeschi

Tony Tedeschi's articles and photographs have appeared in more than 100 publications, including Travel Holiday, Caribbean Travel & Life, *and* Penthouse *magazines and the* New York Times, Washington Post, Boston Globe, *and* Baltimore Sun. *He writes a special section on eco-tourism twice a year for* Audubon *magazine that focuses on the natural and cultural attractions of the Caribbean and of Central and South America. He travels extensively throughout Costa Rica, particularly the national parks of the Pacific coast.*

Among those who favor nature travel—or, as it has come to be known, eco-travel—Costa Rica is the "must see" destination in the Western Hemisphere, if not the world. National parks, preserves, reserves, and refuges are scattered throughout the country, along both the Caribbean and Pacific coasts and up the Central Valley and the inland mountain ranges. Within these areas visitors are exposed to some of the most exotic flora and fauna in the world, and in a variety and quantity found nowhere else. Because of a compact geography that places the gateway San José metropolitan area within a few hour's striking distance of most of the rest of the country, the traveller is presented with a cornucopia of choices. The sheer abundance of the wildlife, and the ability of visitors to get to it, and then—if they choose—to move back into the cosmopolitan environment of the Central Valley, make Costa Rica one of the most attractive experiences in travel today.

WHY COSTA RICA IS DIFFERENT

Other key elements set Costa Rica apart from its neighbors in Central America and from other Latin American countries. Perhaps more than anything else it is a place of stability in a region known for its turmoil. Part of the reason is Costa Rica's history, which is unique to Spanish America in a number of ways and which has had an impact not only upon what the country has become but upon why it is a repeat destination for many visitors.

The first Europeans to explore the land that is now Costa Rica were those who accompanied Columbus when he sailed along the Caribbean coast of Central America from Honduras to Panamá during his fourth and final voyage, from 1502 to 1504. Columbus spent two and a half weeks on the Caribbean shore near what is now Puerto Limón, and during that time he noted the gold jewelry worn by a few local natives. A half century of Spanish colonization began in 1506, but climate and disease forced the principal settlement away from the coast—where the seafaring Spaniards were wont to set up their base camps—and into the more accommodating Central Valley, where a lasting settlement was established at Cartago in 1563. However, since the anticipated riches never materialized, and there was no great native civilization to exploit, Spanish interest waned and the settlement became all but isolated. In the 18th century an expanding population flowed into new communities at Heredia, San José, and Alajuela. Today the country's population is still concentrated in the Central Valley.

Costa Rica, along with much of continental New Spain, gained independence from the mother country in the 1820s. Although independence ushered in a period of political instability, including various grabs for power by a series of strongmen, problems were local and resolved by the local citizenry. Costa Rica has never suffered an extended invasion or occupation by a major power. Shortly after its independence from Spain, the country began attracting immigrants—mostly from Western Europe—who saw in Costa Rica's rich soil and accommodating climate the opportunity to live off the results of their hard work in an atmosphere of rare tranquillity. Unlike much of the rest of Spanish America, Costa Rica did not develop a social structure centered around large landholdings. Consequently farms and plantations here are much smaller than those in the rest of Latin America, and the more general land distribution has helped to create a large middle class.

The country's only major international military crisis occurred in 1856, when William Walker, a soldier of fortune from the United States, decided that the countries of Central America were weakly governed and ripe for exploitation. His far-fetched plan was to subdue them, then use the enforced labor of their people to build a canal connecting the Pacific with the Caribbean. He was successful in Nicaragua, then pushed south into Costa Rica, where he and his band dug in at the hacienda Casona Santa Rosa in the far northwestern part of the country. But here Walker and company fell under the fire of a quickly organized militia of 9,000 citizens, who drove them back toward Nicaragua. Pursued by the Costa Ricans, Walker sought shelter in a fort at the town of Rivas, where a young drummer boy from Alajuela named Juan Santamaría volunteered to torch the wooden fort. Santamaría accomplished the mission, which led to the defeat of Walker, but was killed in the battle. The international airport near San José is named in honor of his sacrifice for his country.

THE TICOS

Ticos, as Costa Ricans refer to themselves, are perhaps as ethnically diverse as the citizens of any country in Latin America. Although the original inhabitants of the country were Indian, today full-blooded native people make up less than 1 percent of the country's three million inhabitants. Spanish settlers arrived in the 16th century, but the influx of other Europeans, particularly British, Germans, and Italians, which escalated during the 19th century, has significantly altered the demographic composition of the country. Today, while many citizens are direct descendants of the original Spanish, or claim at least some Spanish ancestry, it is not unusual to see the heritage of fair skin, light hair, and light eyes from the other immigrants among people throughout Costa Rica.

The army was outlawed in 1948, and much of the money that might have been spent on military personnel, equipment, and infrastructure was subsequently redirected into education and medical services. The country has acquired a reputation for its peace-loving nature; in

1987 its president, Oscar Arias Sánchez, was awarded the Nobel Peace Prize for helping to broker peace in Central America.

Costa Rica today boasts one of the most highly educated populations in the world. Because of its literate and largely middle-class society—and its wonderful climate and natural beauty—the country is a favorite for expatriates and retirees, many from the United States and Western Europe.

Costa Rica's official language is Spanish, although many of its citizens are multilingual; in particular, many speak English. Because of the strong Caribbean islands influence on the east coast, many of the locals there speak a Creole patois. They are often difficult to understand, but slowing down, a word of Spanish here and there, and a lot of gesturing will work for you here, as it does in most places. Although Catholicism claims 90 percent of the country's population, the Costa Rican people are free to practice any religion.

THE ECOLOGICAL DILEMMA

While Costa Rica's large middle-class society sets it apart from the rest of Latin America, this is not to say that the country's economic problems are minimal; quite the contrary. Its export base is principally agricultural—mostly bananas and coffee and, to a lesser degree, pineapples and other tropical fruits—so it is vulnerable to price swings in farm products in a world marketplace in which it does not have the leverage of its larger competitors. The result has been a great deal of borrowing that has saddled the country with one of the world's highest per-capita foreign debts. The consequent need to generate revenue has placed Costa Rica in conflict with itself. To meet the demands of its economy it is faced with the prospect of clearing more land for farming and ranching, and cutting more of its great variety of trees for export. But in Costa Rica you do not simply "clear land," for in the process you destroy some of the most biologically rich territory on earth.

While Costa Rica has as great a percentage of its territory set aside as protected areas as any country in the world—more than 25 percent—it also has one of the highest deforestation rates, 4 percent per annum. There is the impression that designating national parks, much of which has occurred during the last quarter century, was, at least to a degree, a stop-the-bleeding fix. The tension between the environmental and business sectors of the community adds a sense of urgency to a visit here. Whatever your motivation, however, during a trip to this remarkable country and an exploration into its hinterlands you will see things that you have never seen before, and perhaps could not see anywhere else.

Local biologists will tell you that the great biodiversity in their country is a result of the fact that it is the transition zone between the flora and fauna of North and South America. The habitats of species from both directions overlap in Costa Rica. They live in, around, and among native species—or at least come to stay for the winter or stop off en route to other destinations.

The visitor to Costa Rica will be plopped down in the middle of this richness. Evidence of it will be all around you. If you are alert, you will even see examples off the edges of the principal highways, where a toucan sings on a limb over a canyon, a capuchin monkey swings through the canopy, or crocodiles sun themselves in the river beneath a concrete bridge. If you go looking for the natural treasures, especially if you do so with the assistance of local experts, you will find them—and to do that you can point yourself in just about any direction.

Costa Rica for Travellers

Costa Rica splits neatly into three principal regions: the Caribbean coast, the Central Valley and adjacent mountains, and the Pacific coast. The capital, San José, and a cluster of adjacent cities form a major subdivision within the central region. Because the country is quite compact—it's only a few hours' drive between many of its major attractions—you can see quite a lot of it without necessarily having to relocate constantly. However, merely getting from A to B or C should not be an end in itself. There is much to see in many of the places, be they urban metropolis or vast natural preserve, and you would be wise not to try to see all of this living museum in one visit. The natural riches of the country alone have kept biologists busy for decades.

Travel wisdom dictates first a careful consideration of what you expect to get out of a visit to Costa Rica, then the design of an appropriate itinerary. Those interested in the hot, steamy environment of the Caribbean rain forests, and the animal and plant life that thrives in this environment, can easily spend a week or two exploring there. The Pacific coast's assortment of rain, cloud, and dry forests offers an incredible smorgasbord of flora and fauna spread across a wide range of habitat. Again, you could easily spend a week or two there as well. Even for the hard-core trekker some time in and around the capital, with exposure to its historical, anthropological, and artistic attractions, is well worth the time spent.

This guidebook is divided along geographical lines into the three principal regions—central, Caribbean, and Pacific—with subdivisions within those categories. (Our final chapter, North-Central Costa Rica, spoils this neat division somewhat.) It is inadvisable even to try to cover in one visit all that Costa Rica has to offer. Some areas, while differentiated for various reasons by local authorities, are not, in reality, all that different from other areas. Realizing that you probably have to make choices, we present, when confronted with duplication, what we feel are the best attractions.

Some areas, such as many of the offshore islands, are not covered because they are very difficult to get to and often do not provide a unique experience. One that does—Caño Island Biological Reserve—is included. Accessibility to specific areas can be a problem on the mainland as well. For example, vast stretches of the giant Corcovado National Park on the southern Pacific coast are very difficult to get to and are therefore not covered, because the more accessible areas of the park provide the opportunity to see much of what the inaccessible areas offer.

As most visitors to Costa Rica begin their journey with a flight into the international airport near San José, the capital city is the logical jumping-off point for us as well. It is also the best place for an introduction to what Costa Rica has to offer, and for getting acquainted with the Costa Rican people.

SAN JOSE

The capital city is the urban counterweight to Costa Rica's natural wonders. San José and environs—including Heredia and Alajuela to the north and west, and

Cartago to the southeast—make up the only true metropolitan area in the country. The other "cities" scattered about the remainder of the landscape—Liberia in the northwest, Puntarenas on the west coast, and Puerto Limón on the Caribbean—are little more than towns that owe their existence to some logistical imperative. The greatest concentration of population lives in the Central Valley around the capital; the principal public- and private-sector business offices are here, as well as the leading hotels, the best and greatest concentration of restaurants, and most of the country's principal cultural attractions.

Metropolitan San José is only a few hours' drive from either coast and less than a day's drive from anywhere in the country. Visitors who choose to locate in or around San José can make day trips to the Pacific or the Caribbean, visit any of a half dozen national parks or wildlife refuges within striking distance of the city center, and be home for dinner at a downtown restaurant and a night on the town. Those who choose to do the reverse can hole up on either coast and make a day trip into the capital for lunch and a visit to one of the many museums or other cultural attractions in town, with a bit of time left over to shop.

The city radiates outward from the Plaza de la Cultura, where you can stop at the Café Parisienne in front of the Gran Hotel, sip a cup of coffee or a cool drink, and people-watch while fantasizing that you are a character in a Lost Generation novel about Europe between the wars. This plaza is the core of things cultural in Costa Rica. In or around it are the national theater and a series of fascinating museums that feature beautiful examples of the pre-Columbian gold that obsessed the *conquistadores,* wonderful samples of New World jade, archaeological artifacts from ancient cultures, and beautiful paintings, sculpture, and murals created by Costa Rica's artists.

While daytime may find you strolling down European-style boulevards and surveying relics of the country's past, nighttime in San José is decidedly modern, with fashionably dressed Ticos enjoying a candlelit dinner or the pleasing strains of a cabaret act or a hot time on the dance floor. If you seek variety in your nightlife activities, you will find it at the Centro Comercial El Pueblo, where you can choose from a dozen night spots and restaurants in a Spanish-style setting of courtyards, fountains, and gardens. Or, downtown at La Esmeralda, you can enjoy some of the finest mariachi music south of Mexico City.

While dining may not be as interesting in Costa Rica as in other parts of Latin America, there are some rewarding culinary experiences nonetheless, particularly in some of the smaller hotels and quiet inns: tasty soups, savory meats, fresh seafood, tangy chicken, and spicy rice-and-bean dishes. As a country heavily influenced by an influx of immigrants, Costa Rica has adopted the various cuisines of many of its adopted people, including Spanish, Italians, Argentines, Mexicans, North Americans, and Asians. Restaurants specializing in foreign food are found throughout San José and the surrounding communities; some are built into the hills and offer wonderful views of the night-lit Central Valley.

The best shopping in and around the capital focuses on special local attractions. A must is a bag of the rich coffee that is a staple of Costa Rica's economy. Others include hammocks—a Costa Rican tradition—gold, silver, and jade jewelry, and wood carvings. The colorful art of Costa Rica in oils and watercolors is available at galleries throughout the Central Valley. Among the most unusual items are the Sarchí oxcarts. Once the principal method of hauling agricultural freight, the carts are now made in replica as decorative pieces, beautifully finished in highly polished wood and striking enamel colors. They make wonderful freestanding pieces and can be purchased in sizes from tiny desktop models to cocktail-cart size, in prices that run from a few dollars to more than $700. They disassemble and reassemble easily, and so can be shipped back home.

For visitors who choose to locate in the Central Valley there is a range of accommodations, from large downtown hotels to small inns and guest houses. The smaller properties often serve meals, which allows you to sample the variety of local dishes and the local spin on international favorites.

THE VOLCANOES AROUND SAN JOSE

Three mountains, each alive in its own way, punctuate the nearby countryside. These active volcanoes—Irazú, Poás, and Arenal—are worth exploring, and a journey to each can be combined with other attractions to make for an interesting day trip. Two of the volcanoes, Irazú and Poás, are about an hour from San José; Arenal is about three hours. All three seem content merely to let off steam—for the present—but they are capable of great destruction at any time. A fourth—but dormant—volcano, Barva, lies in the general vicinity of Poás.

The route to each volcano is different from the others, and each is interesting in its own right.

Irazú Volcano and the Route East

The road to Irazú, east of the capital, winds past a world of deep-green forests and coffee *fincas* (estates), which benefit from the mineral-rich earth, dusted by centuries of eruptions. The drive up to the volcano is spectacular, taking you more than 3,300 meters (11,000 feet) into the clouds that rim the misty peak, then to the edge of a bleak crater and the sulphurous lake in its pit. You can combine the trip with a visit to nearby **Cartago**, where the urban landscape of a 350-year-old city is a fascinating contrast to the natural beauty of the mountain. In Cartago you will find the basilica of La Virgen de los Angeles, the Black Madonna, patron saint of Costa Rica, whose legendary healing powers have attracted pilgrims for centuries.

If you want to make an all-day affair of your outing, you can circle the **Orosí Valley** and in the village of Orosí visit the oldest colonial church in continuous use in Costa Rica, or the Museo Franciscano, built in 1699 and today housing artwork and furnishings dating to the 18th century.

In this region, east of San José, you have an opportunity to explore Costa Rica in the wild, then visit a study center dedicated to better understanding and preserving such beautiful Edens. In the **Tapantí National Wildlife Reserve** in the Talamanca mountains you can wander more than 12,000 acres of evergreen forest, marvel at gigantic umbrella-leafed gunnera plants, stop by a stream for a picnic lunch, and take a dip at a pool near the base of a waterfall. On your way back to San José, you can stop in at the **Lankester Gardens**, where students and faculty from the University of Costa Rica tend to hundreds of species of indigenous plant life, and ask them about what you've seen at Tapantí.

If you would like to get a sense of pre-Columbian life in Costa Rica, plan to visit the country's principal archaeological site, farther out to the east, but still within only an hour-and-a-half's drive from San José: the **Guayabo National Monument**. Rangers here will guide you through digs that date to 500 B.C. The site can be an enlightening day trip, especially if you combine a visit here with a trip to nearby Turrialba, where you can experience the hustle and bustle of the open-air market in front of the railroad station, and perhaps pick up some of the country's rich coffee or samples of its woodcrafts.

The **Turrialba Valley** has also earned a distinction of a completely different sort. It is the river-rafting center of Costa Rica. Here you can select from a quartet of rivers that will provide a range of experiences—from a quiet drift that is perfect for bird-watching to a boiling, white-water tussle for those who are not happy until they are soaking wet.

If you'd like to find the Costa Rica most tourists never experience, drive the **Saints' Route**, southeast of San José, through the towns of Santa María, San Marcos, and San Pablo, where you can see farmers in the fields, vendors at work, and schoolchildren practicing their athletic skills.

Poás Volcano and the Route Northwest

Poás is the dominant feature of the landscape northwest of San José. Here you can stand on the rim of one of the few accessible volcanoes on the North American continent, gaze down into the huge crater with its turquoise-colored lake, and watch the mists of the cloud forest drift across the eerie moonscape before you. As with Irazú, the area surrounding Poás provides many additional experiences that can be combined with a trip to the volcano.

For example, if you want a closer, more controlled look at some of the country's incredible variety of bird life, you can see examples of the 850 bird species that have been recorded in Costa Rica at the **Zoológico de Aves** on the route up to, or back from, the volcano. Not far from the "Zoo-Ave," the **Butterfly Farm**, near Alajuela, has an incredibly colorful array of some of the more than 900 types of butterflies that live in or visit Costa Rica during the year.

Three of the capital district's more interesting cities are along the route to Poás. A visit to each of the trio works nicely in combination with a trip to the mountain, especially if your visit to Poás is shortened by the fog banks that frequently obscure the view, sometimes for hours at a time.

Alajuela, little more than a dozen miles northwest of San José, was home to Juan Santamaría, Costa Rica's national hero; here you can visit a museum that honors his memory. Just up the road is **Grecia**, where a hundred-year-old metal church dominates the town square. Another few miles farther on is **Sarchí**, where you can choose from the country's finest collection of handicrafts, including the decorative oxcarts that are the town's claim to fame.

For mile after mile your scenic drives here will take you through coffee *fincas,* and a visit to one of them can prove both interesting and enlightening. The **Café Britt**, a few miles northwest of San José, is the most popular and a lot of fun; you will be guided around a six-acre coffee plantation, where actors in costume act out the legends and history of coffee.

Barva Volcano and Braulio Carrillo

Less than an hour's drive north of San José is an extinct volcano, but one nonetheless interesting and certainly worth a trip. On the slopes of the Barva volcano you can take a walk in the cloud forest and let your imagination do the rest. The landscape, its soaring, vine-wrapped trees, rotting stumps, and meadows bathed in fog and mist, has a mysterious, overripe lushness.

Adjacent **Braulio Carrillo National Park** is one of the country's many delightful bird-watching experiences; toucans are the prize sighting here. While you might well not see them anywhere on your trip to Costa Rica, your chances are best at Braulio Carrillo.

The view from the highway as you motor through the mountains is of waterfalls cascading down slopes, deep twisting canyons, and panoramas of all-enveloping forests. Even when you are on the road you can't let up on the sightseeing.

Arenal Volcano and the North-Central Route

When you visit Arenal, farther out from San José to the northwest, past Poás, you will see a community where in 1968 molten lava and a rain of hot ash took their toll but at the same time replenished the soil with rich minerals.

On the way up to the mountain you travel past cattle ranches and coffee plantations, through the farming town of Naranjo and the charming village of Zarcero, with its winding streets, its Spanish-style, tile-roofed homes, and its famed topiary gardens with plant sculptures of just about any object that struck the artist's fancy. (We cover the Arenal volcano and surrounding region in the book's final chapter, North-Central Costa Rica.)

Like much of the rest of Costa Rica, Arenal seems determined to show that man's contraptions and concoctions can't hold a candle to nature's—literally. For if you can arrange to spend a night in the vicinity of the volcano, you will be treated to the natural version of a fireworks show: streams of bright-crimson magma cascading down the slopes, ash flashing like sparklers in the sky, and clouds of bright orange from the superheated lava puffing above the caldera.

But you are also in the area of beautiful crater lakes and the emerald-green water of **Los Lagos lagoon.** Hot springs spew forth from the volcano's natural plumbing and are channeled through the lovely, tile-roofed villa of the **Balneario Tabacón,** where you can soak in the hot, mineral-rich water. To round out your day's experience, view one of the country's most spectacular topographical attractions in La Fortuna falls, cascading 75 meters (250 feet) to the Río Fortuna through a narrow cut in the mountainside. Or spend some time on the other side of man-made Arenal Lake at the village of Tilarán with the Costa Rican version of cowboys from the nearby cattle ranches.

If you have additional time to spend in the area, head another hour north to the **Caño Negro National Wildlife Refuge** and spend at least a day. Here near the Nicaraguan border you will find the largest viewable selection of indigenous wildlife in this wildlife-laden country, from rare butterflies to jaguars and cougars.

THE CARIBBEAN COAST

In Costa Rica the land seems determined to force you to deal with contradictions. Here, every reward exacts its price. The route along the Caribbean coast, for example, is a sightseer's dream, a driver's nightmare. For long sections the road that hugs the coast is lined on one side by the purest of white-sand beaches, on the other by the glorious greens of the forest—and up the middle by ruts and potholes still unrepaired after a 1991 earthquake. If you can deal with the anomalies of the road, you will gain your reward, for along this coast you can turn down a sandy road and pull up to a stretch of beach that is all your own. Or cross the road into woodlands where tapirs, monkeys, sloths, and ocelots roam free. The swamps and flats are home to manatee, caiman, and tarpon; the canopy is filled with hundreds of species of birds.

The Southern Caribbean Coast

In this region of tropical lowland rain forests you will see a plentiful display of mammals, birds, and reptiles, but here you must watch out for some truly venomous vipers, and you will be battling biting insects most of the way.

Puerto Limón, the principal city on the Caribbean coast, is a colorful ethnic mix of Hispanic, black, and Asian peoples. You will get a sense of a bustling Caribbean port city, but you will probably want to move on to more interesting sights along the coastline.

Along the beach-hugging drive to the south you will pass bright white beaches set amid deep green forest. Down here you can swim, sunbathe, wind-surf, body-surf, or board-surf in the breakers, then spend some time at the **Aviary of the Caribbean** (Aviarios del Caribe), a privately owned wildlife sanctuary that includes a five-room bed and breakfast.

At **Cahuita National Park** you can combine some serious sunbathing with superb snorkeling over the nationally protected reef, then take a trek into the untouched rain forest nearby.

Just south of Cahuita is the small town of **Puerto Viejo**, a haven for beach types from simple sun-lovers to serious snorkelers. It is also a place to stop at a small café for a cold drink or a lobster sandwich. If you want to snorkel, surf, or hire a boat for some sportfishing, this is the place to do it on the southern Caribbean coast.

If you have decided upon an extended stay on the southeast coast, a combination of beach and Caribbean rain forest is nicely juxtaposed for you around **Punta Uva** near the Panamanian border. The beaches at Punta Uva are some of the nicest on the Caribbean coast, while the biological reserve at **Manzanillo-Gandoca** is a unique combination of freshwater marsh and sea turtle nesting area.

The Northern Caribbean Coast

This is one of the country's wildest and least explored regions, with forests so thick—and potentially dangerous—that even local guides use only the most commonly trodden trails. It is also a region of lowland rain forest and waterway systems of marshes, channels, and estuaries. A boat is a necessity here but, again, the rewards are worth the effort. The boat ride through the **Tortuguero Channels**, for example, snakes through jungles of leggy old-growth trees, where giant blue morpho butterflies dance above the wider lagoons, and parrots and toucans chatter constantly.

This area is one of the best places to observe the nesting ritual of the giant sea turtles. From May to September you can watch the huge females drag themselves up the beach, meticulously and tediously dig a nest in the sand with their flippers, lay dozens of eggs, cover the nest, and struggle back to the sea. If you are visiting an area about two months after nesting is known to have taken place (and if the nests have not been destroyed by high water, heavy rainfall, or predators), you can watch the tiny hatchlings race for their lives through a gauntlet of predators that line the land, air, and seaways. Permits are required for any part of the turtle-watching experience, care is essential, and guides are highly recommended, but the experience is once in a lifetime.

At the village of Barra del Colorado, visitors have been coming for more than 20 years to visit Archie Field's famed **Río Colorado Lodge**. Here serious anglers set out in search of tarpon and snook, two of the most popular game fish in the world.

THE PACIFIC COAST

With the city of **Puntarenas** as a hub, travellers can fan out up and down the west coast of Costa Rica and explore the great national parks that border the Pacific.

The Southern Pacific Coast

In and around the **Carara Biological Reserve**, for example, you will see crocodiles, iguanas, monkeys, and the beautiful scarlet macaws that nest in the area. Farther south, the town of Quepos is the doorway to **Manuel Antonio National Park**, a small but especially beautiful natural setting, where you may get a glimpse of the rare squirrel monkey.

Near the southern border with Panamá is the huge **Corcovado National Park.** This park will make a biological statistician's day, with its 500 varieties of trees, 400 species of birds, 140 mammals, and 120 reptiles. But behind the numbers is the beauty of the living plants and creatures, abundantly revealed. Getting to the park is a nightmare, the best approach being by water (the land approach is an hours-long hike), but the prize sighting can be a sinister-looking harpy eagle, one of the largest birds of prey in the world, and here you'll have another chance to spot the scarlet macaw.

After a trek into the humid, muddy, insect-filled world that reveals such wonders, you can lunch beneath a towering palm along a jungle-fringed beach of smooth, beige sand, while a momentary thought of where you come from passes through your mind. But then you hear about a trail on **Caño Island**, just offshore, beyond where the seabirds nest, where there are vestiges of the Indians who once lived here, so off you go on your next adventure.

The Northern Pacific Coast

In the **Monteverde Cloud Forest**, northwest of Puntarenas, it is the resplendent quetzal that will capture your imagination. The quetzal is one of the most remarkably colorful birds you will ever see. Its golden beak protrudes from a green-hooded head that tops a red breast, balanced by a V of split tail feathers that are gray-black on top, white underneath. Your quest for this and other elusive creatures will keep you slogging through the mud beneath towering trees hung with bromeliads.

In **Palo Verde**, where the Tempisque river empties into the Golfo de Nicoya, the treks are a bit easier and the sightings more numerous, particularly in the dry season in the dry forest. When the rains slacken the trees thin out, the smaller water holes disappear, and the animals congregate about those that remain, as if coming to pose.

Santa Rosa National Park, near the border with Nicaragua, is an appropriate symbol for what Costa Rica is and is not. For here in 1856, in what is now the national park, a band of Costa Ricans routed Walker's group of soldiers of fortune from up north, setting up the subsequent moment of glory for Juan Santamaría, whose selfless heroics made him a national hero. Given Costa Rica's nonmilitarist personality, it seems only fitting that the country's national hero would evolve from what in the history of most countries would be considered a minor skirmish. It is also fitting that the national park that surrounds the site is one of the most beautiful and biologically diverse anywhere.

Santa Rosa, at more than 120,000 acres, is one of the largest tracts of tropical dry forest in the Western Hemisphere. There is an abundance here of the guanacaste tree, namesake of the province and national tree of Costa Rica, as well as of the gumbo-limbo, or naked Indian tree, with its maroon-red trunk. Endangered cedars and giant ashes spread their crowns to the more abundant light in these thinner forests, while tree-dwelling vines hug the trunks and branches. The air above the trails and paths is home to the violaceous trogon, crested guan, long-tailed manakin, royal flycatcher, toucan (including the collared ara-kari), and many varieties of orioles, tanagers, and hawks. The canopy and the trail below are the stomping grounds for coatimundis, peccaries, tapirs, white-tailed spider monkeys, white-throated capuchins, and jet-black howlers.

Here, too, the sea turtles steal the show. Santa Rosa is one of the few remaining nesting places for the olive ridley turtle. Great *arribadas* (arrivals) feature a cast of thousands of the creatures, emerging from the Pacific Ocean to lay their eggs in September and October.

On the **Península de Nicoya**, near the town of Tamarindo, the stars of the show are the great green-black leatherbacks, weighing half a ton, waddling ashore and doing their own version of the turtle nesting ritual.

In the final analysis, Costa Rica is a kind of fantasy come to life. You've read about places like this, seen the colorful pictures, watched the documentaries . . . but nothing, absolutely nothing, has prepared you for the sight of those macaws, or the call for attention by that toucan, or the brief eye contact with the capuchin monkey, the drama of the turtles and their fight to survive. The roads will have been rough, the trails muddy and leg-wearying, the bugs make you want to scream, and your skin yearns for the feel of fresh cotton—*dry* cotton. But then one of the park rangers at Corcovado National Park is telling you about a hike in a stream up to a magnificent waterfall where you can take a natural shower, and the next thing you know you are reaching for your hiking sandals and wondering if you need a booster coat of bug repellent.

USEFUL FACTS

Climate and Seasons

For the most part, the temperature range across Costa Rica varies from mild (60s F, 15–20 C) to hot (90s F, 30s C). In the mountains and cloud forests the evenings and night-time hours can be cool, and the dampness may add to the sense of chill, but even in these areas the temperature can hardly be described as cold. Although on occasion it will get down around freezing, a fire in the hearth of a mountain lodge is more for effect than relief from the climate.

The two principal seasons are distinguished by differences in humidity and precipitation rather than temperature. The rainy season, *invierno,* runs from May through November. The dry season, *verano,* runs from December through April. As *invierno* is the Spanish word for winter and *verano* the word for summer, the traditional seasons of the Northern Hemisphere appear to have been reversed in Costa Rica. But even these designations are inexact. There is, for example, a brief period during July and early August when the rainy season may let up a bit; it is known locally as *el veranillo de San Juan* (the little summer of Saint John). And this "little summer" is right in the middle of what Northerners call summer.

Any generalities in Costa Rica, however, must be qualified with the specifics of the microclimates that prevail across the country. Rainy conditions are more prevalent on the Caribbean side of the continental divide and can push the envelope on either side of the May–November season. On the Pacific coast the north is drier, the south wetter.

Perhaps the best way to deal with the climate when travelling throughout Costa Rica is to expect warm weather (80s and 90s F, 25–35 C) and be prepared for rain.

What to Wear

As the climate in most of Costa Rica for most of the year is moderate to hot, light clothing generally suffices. However, it is wise to contact the Costa Rican Tourist Board for information about the area you will be visiting, in particular for an assessment of the prevailing weather conditions for the time of year you will be travelling.

During the rainy season and in the more humid sectors of the country, i.e., the southern Pacific coast and the Caribbean lowlands, prepare to get wet. How you prepare is pretty much your call. While such conditions would seem to suggest foul-weather gear (slickers, ponchos, raincoats), the rain is often accompanied by some of the hottest temperatures, and rain gear tends to hold in the heat. If you can deal with that, fine. A second option is simply to get wet. On jaunts through the steamier rain forests, for example, old clothing and all-weather sandals are a viable option. If you prepare mentally for the eventuality—if not the certainty—of being soaked, then getting there can be half the fun.

In the higher, damper environments, such as the cloud forests and mist-shrouded volcanoes, rain gear makes perfect sense. The ceaseless soaking and lower temperatures there may make you grateful for some rain protection and heat containment. In the less moist, more alpine climates of the mountains along the Central Valley, a sweater or light- to mid-weight jacket may come in handy, particularly in the evenings.

As in most beach areas around the world, and especially those close to the equator, stripping to as little clothing as is permissible is not a good idea. Protection from the sun is important on Costa Rica's beaches, where it can shine for long periods and grow very hot. Sunscreen preparations, wide-brimmed hats, beach wraps, and other protective garb should be a part of every beach-goer's arsenal. Many beaches are rimmed by lovely stands of trees, and the shade they afford should be taken full advantage of, but do not depend upon a brief respite under a tree as a substitute for sensible protection from the sun.

As for dress requirements, for most places and in most settings Costa Rica is informal. If you're in doubt about a restaurant, theater, or dinner party, it is always wise to call and inquire.

Entry Requirements

Entry into the country is permitted with a passport and a tourist card, which costs less than $5 and can be obtained at any Costa Rican consulate or usually from the airlines that serve the country. You must also present a round-trip airline ticket as evidence that you do not intend to make your stay a permanent one.

Citizens of the United States, Canada, and the United Kingdom may enter the country without a visa for a period of not more than 90 days. Citizens of Australia may enter the country without a visa for a period of not more than 30 days.

Flying to and within Costa Rica

There is direct air service to and from Juan Santamaría International Airport (18 km/11 miles northwest of San José) into and out of eight U.S. gateways: New York, Miami, New Orleans, Houston, Los Angeles, Orlando, San Francisco, and San Juan, Puerto Rico. Of the U.S. carriers, Continental and American have the most experienced personnel and offer the most extensive connecting patterns to go along with their direct and nonstop services from major U.S. airports.

The following airlines fly to and from Costa Rica: *LACSA,* the international airline of Costa Rica, operates between Juan Santamaría and Miami, New Orleans, New York, Los Angeles, San Francisco, and San Juan; Tel: (800) 225-2272. *American Airlines* has direct service to and from Miami International, and connecting service to its vast system throughout the U.S.; Tel: (800) 433-7300. *Continental Airlines* offers direct service to and from Houston; Tel: (800) 231-0856. *Delta Airlines* has direct service to and from Orlando; Tel: (800) 221-1212. *Mexicana* has direct service to and from Los Angeles International; it also has connecting service from several U.S. cities, via Mexico City; in the U.S., Tel: (800) 531-7921; in Canada, Tel: (800) 531-7923. *SAHSA,* the national airline of Honduras, has service to and from Miami, New Orleans, and Houston; Tel: (800) 327-1225. *TACA,* based in El Salvador, has direct service to and from Houston; it offers connecting service to and from New York's JFK, Washington Dulles Airport, Miami, and New Orleans; Tel: (800) 535-8780. *United* offers direct service to and from Miami; Tel: (800) 241-6522.

Visitors travelling from Canada, Australia, and the United Kingdom must connect to one of the above carriers. Travel agents and tour operators create packages that include air transportation, accommodations, tours, and assorted extras; consult your travel agent or the reservations desks of the above carriers for details. There are also charter flights available, particularly between Canada and Costa Rica; ask your travel agent.

Within Costa Rica, there are local airlines and charter air services that fly throughout the country. Their performance tends to be inconsistent, however. Travelair is the best choice among those with the most service. Most parts of the country are less than an hour by air from San José. For specific details, contact the Costa Rican Tourist Board or its U.S. information office (see "Further Information," below).

From the Airport

Although the destination listed for international air travel to Costa Rica is San José, Juan Santamaría International Airport is actually in Alajuela, about 20 km (12 miles) northwest of San José. Taxi drivers hawk their services right outside the terminal building. Cabs are metered, but make sure the driver turns the meter on before you depart. The ride into the capital should cost between $12 and $15; the trip takes about 20 minutes.

The Tuasa bus company offers service between the airport and San José. Buses depart every 15 minutes during the daytime peak-arrival periods from outside the terminal, just behind the car-rental counters. The trip to the Plaza de la Cultura takes about 30 minutes; the fare is about $3. Tel: 22-5325.

For renting a car at the airport, see "Renting a Car," below.

Driving to and in Costa Rica

The Inter-American Highway (formerly called the Pan-American Highway and in Costa Rica officially known as the Autopista Florencio del Castillo Norte) enters Costa Rica from Nicaragua in the north at Peñas Blancas and exits in the south at Paso Canoas on the Panamanian border. There are other border-crossing points for Nicaragua and Panamá, but they are reached effectively only in four-wheel-drive vehicles. You must clear customs and immigration at both points. (While it's possible to obtain and fill out tourist cards at the border, it is best to take care of that in advance in order to speed your passage and avoid the possibility of the post having run out of them; see "Entry Requirements," above.) The drive from Peñas Blancas to Paso Canoas is less than 15 hours, all on paved highway.

But you don't travel to Costa Rica to take the Inter-American Highway from Nicaragua to Panamá. Costa Rica is off-the-beaten-path driving, some of it *way* off the beaten path. Four-wheel-drive vehicles are highly recommended. Many of Costa Rica's forest, estuary, mountain, and lowland parks and preserves are accessible only by off-road vehicles, especially during the rainy season.

Liberia, the principal city of Guanacaste province in northwestern Costa Rica, is 77 km (48 miles) from Peñas Blancas. Puntarenas and Puerto Caldera, the principal Pacific coast ports, are 195 km (121 miles) and 205 km (127 miles), respectively. San José, the country's capital and principal city, is about 300 km (186 miles) from the Nicaraguan border.

A Costa Rican driver's license is not required unless you are planning to spend more than 3 months in the country; if not, you may use the license issued in your country or state. Driving is on the right-hand side of the road. Regulations concerning traffic lights, road signs, passing, yielding to pedestrians, etc., are similar to those in the United States and Canada.

The speed limit on major highways is 80 km/hour (50 mph). For primary and secondary roads it varies between 60 km/hour (37 mph) and 40 km/hour (25 mph). There are many service stations along major highways and principal secondary roads, most open only from 6:00 A.M. to 6:00 P.M. In the principal cities you will find some 24-hour stations.

Check with your insurance company about coverage outside your home country. Local roads can be treacherous, and so can the highways, because of the dramatic changes in terrain and frequent soakings during the rainy seasons. Fog is a common and dangerous threat in the higher elevations. In such conditions you don't want to find yourself without adequate insurance coverage.

In the cities, as even the locals will tell you, once behind the wheel it's every person for him- or herself; in that regard Costa Rica is no different from most other countries.

Renting a Car

The major worldwide car-rental companies—Avis, Hertz, and National—all have rental counters at Juan Santamaría International Airport, in the terminal building, just outside of customs clearance. They also have offices in downtown San José, as do quite a few smaller, local companies, including Adobe, Amigo, Discovery, Economy, Elegante, Holiday, Pilot, Poás, Toyota, and Tropical. Rental offices outside the San José area are few and far between, so you must make up your mind about how you will want to travel before you head out into the hinterlands.

The larger companies have reservations numbers in the United States, Canada, and many other countries. The Costa Rican Tourist Board will provide promotional materials that give names, addresses, and telephone numbers of local companies (see "Further Information," below).

Daily and weekly rates are available, as well as plans that feature unlimited mileage, but these can vary widely even among the three big international companies, so shop around. Some companies offer free pickup and delivery at hotels, 24-hour emergency road service, and size and type selections that range from subcompacts to sedans to four-wheel-drive vehicles. Rates range from about $200 per week for subcompact cars to $500 and more for the bigger four-wheel-drive vehicles (often a necessity if you're touring less-accessible areas). The better rates often require an advance booking, with penalties for cancellation, so inquire about all aspects of these plans as well.

To rent a car you must have a valid driver's license and be at least 21 years old. Some companies have a minimum age requirement of 23, others 25. Your license is adequate for 3 months. If you stay longer and intend to drive you must apply for a Costa Rican license. You will also need to present your passport and use a major credit card to rent a car. The major companies will not rent to you without a credit card; those that will usually insist that you leave a cash deposit, which could be $1,000 or more.

Take the insurance coverage, especially if you are not covered for foreign travel by your own insurance company. If you don't have coverage, you will be liable for the full extent of any damages. In anticipation of damages, some companies will hold a deposit against your credit card of as much as $1,500.

Since the deductibles on collision damage are often hundreds of dollars, check over the vehicle you have rented before you leave the rental company's grounds; otherwise you may find yourself paying for lost or broken components that were not the result of your negligence.

Getting Around by Bus or Train

Bus service is available throughout most of the major locations in Costa Rica, and to some of the more remote areas as well. There are no central terminals, not even in the capital. Some routes originate and end at the main office of the particular bus company. Often you must know the actual bus stop for the route you would like to take. General information is available from the Costa Rican Tourist Board, specific information from the individual bus company.

If you are on a tight budget, the bus is an alternative. The principal routes to and from both coasts will get you where you are going with dispatch. Both Puntarenas on the Pacific and Puerto Limón on the Caribbean are about 4 hours from San José. However, seating on board is cramped, and you will have to make your way from the bus stop to your ultimate destination once you arrive.

There is also train service between San José and Puntarenas and Puerto Limón, but the trips will kill most of the day and, as on the buses, seating is cramped and uncomfortable, and you'll have to arrange for local transportation to and from the train station.

Cruises

Major international oceangoing cruise ships call at both Puerto Limón on the Caribbean coast and Puerto Caldera on the Pacific coast, but seldom for longer than a day. Typically they provide packaged tours to sightseeing and shopping areas. Dockside, you can cut your own deal for a day trip into the national parks or preserves, but that will take some negotiating, probably with the drivers who remain after those going to the touristy areas have already left, and you'll have little frame of reference for what such a trip should cost or what it should include. As an example, a taxi rental for a half day at the wonderful Carara Biological Reserve, a short distance from the Pacific cruise-ship terminal at Puerto Caldera, can be had for about $70 plus tip, but the driver will probably open the bidding with a quote of $100 or more.

You can try to make arrangements in advance with local tour operators to meet you dockside, but this can be unreliable at best, as the operators or guides usually must travel from the Central Valley metropolitan area; they sometimes fail to make the trip if something better comes along, or are reluctant because they have shown up for such outings in the past only to find that the cruise-ship passengers have changed their minds and haven't shown up themselves.

A much more productive way to "cruise" Costa Rica is with one of the local cruise-ship operators who offer packages—from 4 days to a week and a half—exploring local waters and anchorages. This type of cruising can be the best way to see some of the national parks and nature reserves of Costa Rica, particularly on the Pacific coast, where they depart from the Pacific port city of Puntarenas. Given the difficulty of covering this expansive coastline by land, a cruise is a great way to see the flora and fauna of this biologically diverse country. Specifics about this method of touring the parks and preserves are given in the Caribbean Coast and Pacific Coast chapters.

Room Rates

Unless otherwise indicated, accommodations rates are for double rooms, double occupancy, European Plan (EP, without meals). Some rooms are sold with three meals (full American Plan, or AP) or with breakfast and dinner (Modified American Plan, or MAP), and those are indicated as such. The rates are those available at press time. Most room rates have not varied greatly over the past several years, but it is wise to double-check before you leave and certainly before you book. Hotels are required to add 14.4 percent in taxes to the room rate. Restaurants add an 11 percent sales tax and often a 10 percent service charge (*propina*) to the check. Extra gratuities, for exceptional service, are at your discretion.

Currency

The official monetary unit for Costa Rica is the *colón.* The exchange rate fluctuates against foreign currencies. Dollars are widely accepted, but using *colones* will save you from having to calculate and round off each transaction and, over the course of your visit, probably will save you money. All prices in this guide are listed in U.S. dollars.

You can exchange money at the airport, at banks, and in most major hotels. Traveller's checks in U.S. dollars are widely accepted.

Credit Cards

The big three international credit cards—American Express, Visa, and MasterCard—are accepted by an ever-increasing number of businesses throughout Costa Rica, including the major transportation, accommodations, food and beverage, and shopping establishments. However, it is never wise to assume this acceptance. If you're depending on using a credit card, check before booking or ordering.

Local Time

Costa Rica is on North America's central standard time (for example, Chicago), which is Greenwich mean time minus six hours. Because Costa Rica is close to the equator the number of daylight hours does not vary from season to season as greatly as in the more northern or southern regions of the hemisphere. For most of the year there are 12 hours of daylight, from about 6:00 A.M. to 6:00 P.M. Costa Rica does not observe daylight saving time.

Telephoning

The country code for Costa Rica is 506. Area codes are not used. Telephone numbers in Costa Rica are six digits. To reach an English-speaking international operator, dial 116.

Costa Rica was one of the last countries in Latin America to modernize its telephone system, but it now has one of the best in the region. Pay phones are common throughout the country and are generally in good working order.

Electric Current

Electric current is 110-volt, 60-cycle AC (the same as in North America). Travellers whose portable appliances do not run on that current should bring their own adapters. Most hotels and guest houses do not have the equipment needed to convert power. Sockets and plugs are of the type used in the United States and Canada.

Business Hours

Most government offices are open from 8:00 A.M. to 4:00 P.M., Monday through Friday.

Banks are open 9:00 A.M. to 3:00 P.M., Monday through Friday, but some branches stay open until 6:00 or 6:30 P.M., and some branches are open for a half day on Saturday. Merchants' hours can vary, but the shopping day in general runs from 8:00 A.M. to 7:00 P.M. As a rule of thumb, businesses are open from 8:00 A.M. to 6:00 P.M., with a lunch break from noon to 2:00 P.M.

National Holidays

National holidays include New Year's Day (January 1), San José Day (March 19), Holy Thursday, Good Friday, and Easter (variable, in March or April), Juan Santamaría Day (April 11), Labor Day (May 1), Saints Peter and Paul Day (June 29), Guanacaste Annexation Day (July 25), Virgin of Los Angeles Day (feast of the country's patron saint; August 2), Mother's Day (August 15), Independence Day (September 15), Columbus Day (October 12), feast of the Immaculate Conception (December 8), and Christmas Day (December 25).

Spanish-Language Programs

Spanish-language programs are popular with some visitors to Costa Rica. Holiday tours are combined with intensive language workshops, experiences of the arts and culture, visits to the Mercado Central, and one-day excursions to the volcanoes. Programs include homestays with daily 4-hour Spanish instruction; a 3-day crash "survival" course; a 4-week group course; and private tutoring.

San José companies offering Spanish-language programs include Centro Linguístico Conversa, Tel: 21-7649; Ilisa Instituto, in the U.S., Tel: (800) ESPANOL; Latina Instituto Universal de Idiomas, Tel: 57-0441; Instituto Británico, Tel: 25-2526; Intensa, Tel: 24-6353; and Southern Horizons Travel, in the U.S., Tel: (800) 333-9361.

Eco-talk

If you want to discuss or exchange ideas on Costa Rica's ecology and conservation standards, contact Bob Wells, a member of the Nature Conservancy, at CEDARENA, Centro de Derecho Ambiental y de los Recursos Naturales

(Environmental and Natural Resources Law Center), in San José. Tel: 53-7239 or 24-8239.

Cautions

Crime: Flaunting expensive jewelry, cameras, luggage, or rolls of cash may produce the same negative result in Costa Rica as it might on a street corner in Manhattan, Chicago, Los Angeles, or most major cities. Costa Rica is not considered a high-crime country, but a lack of common sense will bring out the criminals here, too. Be especially alert for pickpockets and purse-snatchers in the more crowded metropolitan areas, especially San José, Puntarenas, and Puerto Limón.

Car theft is a problem in some areas, particularly the theft of rental vehicles. Use sound judgment before you leave a vehicle on a secluded rural road, and when you are in an unfamiliar town or village ask at hotels and restaurants about sensible precautions.

If you are the victim of a theft, a mugging, or a burglary, contact the nearest police station. This will be important for insurance claims, even if it does not result in your regaining your lost property.

Medical Services: Costa Rica is considered one of the most medically advanced societies in Latin America. If you have a medical emergency you will probably be in better hands here than anywhere else in Central America. If you want to take extra precautions you can buy medical insurance before you leave your home country; some policies provide for evacuation by air if you get sick or have an accident.

Driving: Costa Rica has one of the highest auto accident rates in the world. Combine that with a system of roads that wind and climb through some challenging terrain and that—off the main highways—are often rutted and potholed, and you have a potential for problems. Along the Caribbean coast great stretches of road were crumpled in a recent earthquake and remain unrepaired. Costa Rican truck drivers have a dangerous habit of parking their rigs—large and small—in the middle of a road, even on blind curves, to take a siesta or have lunch. While local drivers tend to know where to expect this practice, unsuspecting motorists may discover it too late. Finally, as a pedestrian in and around the larger cities, do not assume that a red light necessarily means the oncoming traffic is going to stop for you. Make sure the coast is clear before stepping off the curb.

Drinking Water: In the major metropolitan areas of Costa Rica—San José, Alajuela, Heredia, Cartago—the drinking water is generally considered safe. In the countryside or in lightly populated beach areas, however, it can be suspect. If you want to decrease your chances of picking up something unfriendly, drink only bottled mineral water or soft drinks.

Insects: Insects constitute the greatest health problem in the country, particularly in the lowland rain forests and marshes. Swarms of mosquitoes are not uncommon during the rainy season, and they can make a feast of you if you don't wear repellent or long-sleeved garments. Disease from such bites is not common, although people contract malaria in various lowland areas from time to time, particularly on the Caribbean side of the country. Consult your physician before leaving home if you are concerned about malaria, because medication against it must begin before you leave and continue after you return.

Swimming Precautions: Drowning is perhaps the greatest threat to visitors. Some of the most popular beach areas in the country can be hazardous if you get carried away with the beauty of the place and suspend your common sense, especially by ignoring your limitations as a swimmer. Riptides are a factor in most of the 200 drowning deaths that occur each year. If you are caught in such a current do not fight it; many riptide drownings result from exhaustion. Instead, ride the current until it dissipates, then swim back at a 45-degree angle to the shore, to minimize being caught in the current again. It is a good rule of thumb always to swim with a buddy and never to swim while intoxicated.

On the Caribbean side of the country sharks can be a problem, sometimes following the lower orders of the food chain close to shore and even into the deeper channels of the estuaries and swamps.

Protection from the sun is important on Costa Rica's beaches; proximity to the equator results in more direct rays and a sun that can be very hot. Wide-brimmed hats and beach wraps are recommended, as is a high-numbered sunscreen.

Hiking Precautions: During hikes through the woods you should be aware of possible encounters with dangerous animals, especially venomous spiders and snakes. The barba amarilla is a particularly nasty snake that has accounted for the greatest percentage of the human deaths from snakebite. It can grow to a length of up to 2½ meters (8 feet) and is generally hard to spot because of its neutral colors: gray, olive-green, and brown. Snakes seek out the warmth of beaches and the packed earth of trails during the night; you should watch out for them in these areas, particularly during early-morning treks. Above all, do not reach into any place where you do not have a clear view of where your fingers will fall.

While trekking, be particularly cautious of dense trails that lead off the principal paths. Such routes could take you into animal lairs, to the edges of cliffs, or into swamps or other hazards. On the slopes of the Arenal volcano, for example, new vents are opening constantly and without warning, spewing poisonous gases into the air and spilling rivers of red-hot magma down the slopes. Several people are killed each year on Arenal, most of them tourists and all of them foolishly attempting to climb to the top. It is wise to enter such areas as these—if at all—only when accompanied by knowledgeable local guides.

Touring Costa Rica

A number of guide services and tour companies offer excellent tours throughout the country. A selection of the best includes: *Costa Rica Expeditions,* P.O. Box 6941-1000, San José; Tel: 57-0766; Fax: 57-1665. *Costa Rica's Temptations,* P.O. Box 1199-1200, San José; Tel: 20-4437 or 20-3169; Fax: 20-2792. *Geotur,* P.O. Box 469 y Griega 1011, San José; Tel: 34-1867; Fax: 53-6338. *Guindon Guided Tours,* Apartado 10165-1000, San José; Tel: 61-1008. *Jungle Trails,* Apartado 2413-1000, San José; Tel: 55-3486; Fax: 55-2782. *Southern Horizons Travel,* 6100 Simpson Avenue, North Hollywood, CA 91606; Tel: (800) 333-9361 or (818) 980-7011; Fax: (818) 980-6987. *Swiss Travel,* P.O. Box 7-1970-1000, San José; Tel: 31-4055; Fax: 31-3030. *Temptress Cruises,* P.O. Box 1198-1000, San José; Tel: 20-1679; Fax: 20-2103; in the U.S., 1600 N.W. Le Jeune Road, Suite 301, Miami, FL 33126; Tel: (800) 336-8423 or (305) 871-2663; Fax: (305) 871-2657.

Further Information

The Costa Rican Tourist Board—or, as it's known locally, the Instituto Costarricense de Turismo (ICT)—has offices in Costa Rica and the United States. Information and materials are available on a walk-in basis at the ICT office on the Plaza de la Cultura, on Calle 5 between Avenida Central and Avenida 2, in San José; Tel: 22-1090. There is also an information counter at Juan Santamaría International Airport.

For brochures and other advance information, contact the ICT at P.O. Box 777-1000, San José; Tel: 23-8423; Fax: 23-5452. Or you can contact the ICT's U.S. information office at P.O. Box 672712, Marietta, GA 30067-0046; Tel: (800) 327-7033.

—*Tony Tedeschi*

BIBLIOGRAPHY

SUZANNE ABEL-VIDOR, RONALD L. BISHOP, ET AL., *Between Continents/Between Seas: Precolumbian Art of Costa Rica.* Photographs by Dirk Bakker. Essays on the art of Costa Rica's early inhabitants.

CHARLES D. AMERINGER, *Democracy in Costa Rica* (1982). The political development of the country from World War II until the administration of Oscar Arias Sánchez.

CARLOS BALSER, *Jade Precolombino de Costa Rica* (1980). A bilingual study that focuses on items in the collection of the Instituto Nacional de Seguros, which operates San José's Jade Museum. Illustrated with color plates.

RICHARD BIESANZ, KAREN ZUBRIS BIESANZ, AND MAVIS HILTUNEN BIESANZ, *The Costa Ricans* (1982). A detail-packed overview of the land and the people, class and race, education, religion, history, politics, and more.

JOHN A. BOOTH AND THOMAS W. WALKER, *Understanding Central America* (1989). Essays on history, politics, government, the economy, and social conditions.

MARIO A. BOZA, *Costa Rica National Parks* (1988). Bilingual guide to the great national parks, refuges, and reserves.

THEODORE S. CREEDMAN, *Historical Dictionary of Costa Rica* (2nd ed., 1991). A reference book with entries on Costa Rican people, places, and events.

PHILIP J. DEVRIES, *The Butterflies of Costa Rica and Their Natural History* (1987). An entomologist's survey of nearly 550 species of butterflies recorded in Costa Rica.

ELIZABETH KENNEDY EASBY, *Pre-Columbian Jade from Costa Rica* (1968). A study, based on archaeological investigations, that offers insight into the stylistic and technical development of Costa Rican jade. Illustrated in color and black and white.

MARC EDELMAN AND JOANNE KENEN, *The Costa Rica Reader* (1989). An introduction to everything Costa Rican, from politics and government to the economy and foreign relations.

ADRIAN FORSYTH, *Portraits of the Rainforest* (1990). Dramatic and detailed color photographs by Michael and Patricia Fogden accompany an informative text on tropical flora, fauna, and overall ecology.

ADRIAN FORSYTH AND KENNETH MIYATA, *Tropical Nature* (1984). Essays based on several dozen trips the authors made to Central American forests, mainly in Costa Rica and Ecuador.

WILBERTH HERRERA S., *Mapa-Guía de la Naturaleza de Costa Rica/Nature Atlas-Guidebook* (1992). A bilingual atlas and nature guide.

DANIEL H. JANZEN, ED., *Costa Rican Natural History* (1983). Essays by distinguished scholars on the geography, climate, flora, and fauna.

LOIS KATZ, ED., *Art of Costa Rica: Pre-Columbian Painted and Sculpted Ceramics from the Arthur M. Sackler Collections* (1985). Hundreds of beautifully reproduced black-and-white and color photographs of Costa Rica's early ceramic art.

FREDERICK W. LANGE, ED., *Costa Rican Art and Archaeology* (1988). Detailed, academic essays on symbology, artistic traditions, ceramics, and works in jade and gold.

DONALD PERRY, *Life Above the Jungle Floor: A Biologist Explores a Strange and Hidden Treetop World* (1986).

Adventures in the jungle canopy of the Costa Rican rain forest, made possible by a network of ropes and platforms—a giant web—that the author constructed in order to study animals, plants, and insects at close range.

SETH ROLBEIN, *Nobel Costa Rica: A Timely Report on Our Peaceful, Pro-Yankee, Central American Neighbor* (1989). Essays on Costa Rican public and private life, prompted by the awarding of the Nobel Peace Prize to Oscar Arias Sánchez.

DORIS STONE, *Pre-Columbian Man in Costa Rica* (1977). A popular view of the archaeology of Costa Rica, with black-and-white illustrations.

F. GARY STYLES AND ALEXANDER F. SKUTCH, *A Guide to the Birds of Costa Rica* (1991). Plates by Dana Gardner. Definitive guide to the great ornithological feast that is bird-watching in Costa Rica.

DAVID RAINS WALLACE, *The Quetzal and the Macaw: The Story of Costa Rica's National Parks* (1992). A journalistic account of a system that intends not simply to preserve a remnant of wildlife and scenery but to perpetuate all of the country's biological resources.

ALLEN M. YOUNG, *Costa Rica: Nature, Prosperity, and Peace on the Rich Coast* (1984). A biologist's view of what Costa Rica is all about: peaceful living, reaching out to fellow human beings, and respecting nature. Black-and-white photographs.

———, *Sarapiqui Chronicle: A Naturalist in Costa Rica* (1991). An account of the author's 20-year study of the insect life in the rain forests of northeastern Costa Rica.

—*Tony Tedeschi*

SAN JOSE

By Richard Carroll

Richard Carroll, based in Shadow Hills, California, has travelled extensively in Mexico and Central America in his VW camper, and is the author of The Motor Camper's Guide to Mexico and Baja *and* A Photo Journey to Los Angeles, *and the coauthor of* Hidden Mexico *(3rd edition). He is also a regular contributor to the Copley News Service and to* Family Living *and* Motorhome *magazines, and has won four international writing awards.*

Costa Rica has come to be hailed as a superb Central American travel destination bursting with unexplored rain forests, mighty rivers, dramatic volcanoes, and beautiful beaches. Unfortunately, San José often shatters the travel-brochure images for first-time visitors. A gateway and natural hub to both coasts, San José, though it is surrounded by towering, cloud-draped mountains, often fails to inspire love immediately. The city's traffic is a mess—better than Rome, worse than Mexico City—and the architecture in general is far from impressive. However, initial impressions here are misleading. You have to give the city a chance.

San José deserves more than a one-night stand before you strike out for the sandy hideaways and natural wonders tucked away on the two coasts. *Josefinos* (citizens of San José) will urge visitors to set aside a few days to cut through the urban façade of North American fast-food joints and States-style marketing ploys and instead check out some intriguing city attractions. Sparkling clean and with a large middle class, San José is like an island unto itself, having rightfully acquired a reputation as the most democratic and peaceful capital city in Latin America. It has an ongoing tradition of supporting more teachers than policemen, and it has never suffered a major invasion or foreign occupation.

MAJOR INTEREST

Plaza de la Cultura
Teatro Nacional
Museo de Oro (Gold Museum)
Museo Nacional de Costa Rica
Museo de Jade (Jade Museum)
Museo de Arte Costarricense

Following the country's independence from Spain in 1821, San José emerged as the center of the coffee production that was the chief source of Costa Rican wealth throughout the 19th century. There was little mineral wealth—and no landed aristocracy—but the foreign demand for coffee, and later bananas and pineapples, brought steady income to Costa Rica and San José. British investment in particular was large, and the groundwork was laid for a society that demanded schools and roads from its government. In 1886 a law provided free and compulsory public education, and in 1889 a truly democratic election took place that is considered to be the first entirely free and honest election in Central America.

After some growing pains, San José developed into a prosperous city of formidable structures anchored by a national palace, national theater, and national library, with hotels, tree-lined boulevards, a streetcar system, and large estates. The city quickly grew out of its innocence. In the 20th century it razed many of its elegant buildings under the giddy influence of modernization and accepted immigrants like any good democracy, including thousands of genteel retirees from the United States. The capital spread out in all directions, but the successful, soft-spoken people here have never flaunted their wealth. Josefinos claim that they have learned much from the destruction of old San José buildings that should have been protected. Today preserving their historic architecture, as well as their forests and wildlife, is a national pastime.

About 90 percent of the people in San José are affiliated

with the Roman Catholic church, though in many cases only nominally. The San José churches are not flashy and grand, nor are their altars dripping with gold and silver, like those in Mexico and Spain. The church architecture in San José is an eclectic mix of ecclesiastical design modes, and the churches here are generally not considered visitor attractions.

Independent and proud, and a bridge to South America, San José heartily welcomes visitors. The friendly and outgoing people, who are primarily of Spanish descent, have no standing army, a low crime rate, a higher literacy rate than the United States, and some of the best health services in Central America.

Tourism, relatively new here, is now opening up the country to the mainstream traveller through the efforts of companies such as California-based Southern Horizons Travel and the Costa Rican companies Costa Rica's Temptations and Swiss Travel, which have organized travel packages and tours that appeal to a wider audience than the first wave of Costa Rican visitors, who were primarily backpackers, hikers, river rafters, nature lovers, and biologists chasing rare butterflies. (See Useful Facts for a list of tour companies and guide services.)

San José, at an altitude of 1,200 meters (3,900 feet), with year-round temperatures averaging 70 degrees Fahrenheit (21 degrees Celsius), is tucked away on the Meseta Central—which translates as "Central Plateau" but is most often referred to as the Central Valley. The city is framed on the north and east by the Cordillera Central mountain range, home to the Poás and Irazú volcanoes, and on the south by the profiles of the Cordillera de Talamanca and Fila de Bustamente ranges. San José and the surrounding areas of Escazú, Alajuela, Heredia, and Cartago embrace a whopping two-thirds of the nation's population. These folks seem to be moving about all at the same time, like busy worker ants on a mission.

For all the benefits of the city and the general high quality of Central American life, it's not a completely risk-free destination. Pickpockets and purse snatchers prowl about (it's said they are illegal immigrants from nearby countries who learned their craft in Miami), so beware of nimble fingers in search of wallets and jewelry, especially at bus stations. While it is rare for San José visitors to be held up and robbed at gunpoint, you'd be wise to leave

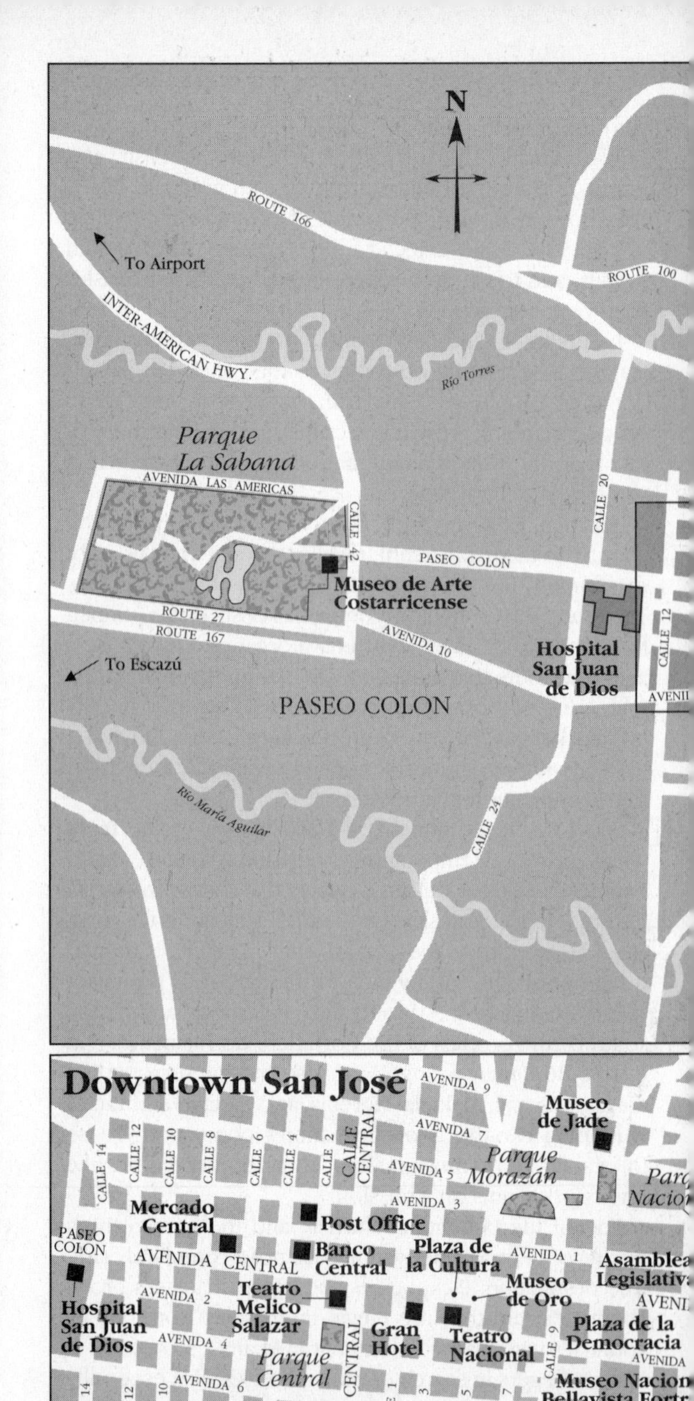
N
ROUTE 166
To Airport
ROUTE 100
INTER-AMERICAN HWY.
Río Torres
Parque
La Sabana
AVENIDA LAS AMERICAS
CALLE 42
CALLE 20
PASEO COLON
Museo de Arte
Costarricense
ROUTE 27
ROUTE 167
AVENIDA 10
CALLE 12
To Escazú
Hospital
San Juan
de Dios
PASEO COLON
Río María Aguilar
CALLE 24
Downtown San José
AVENIDA 9
AVENIDA 7
AVENIDA 5
AVENIDA 3
Museo
de Jade
Parque
Morazán
CALLE 14
CALLE 12
CALLE 10
CALLE 8
CALLE 6
CALLE 4
CALLE 2
CALLE CENTRAL
Mercado
Central
Post Office
PASEO
COLON
AVENIDA CENTRAL
Banco
Central
Plaza de
la Cultura
AVENIDA 1
Hospital
San Juan
de Dios
AVENIDA 2
Teatro
Melico
Salazar
Museo
de Oro
Gran
Hotel
Teatro
Nacional
Plaza de la
Democracia
AVENIDA 4
Parque
Central
AVENIDA 6
CALLE 9
CALLE 1
CALLE 3
CALLE 5
CALLE 7
AVENIDA 8
yards
412
meters
375
0
0
AVENIDA 10
CALLE 11
CALLE 13

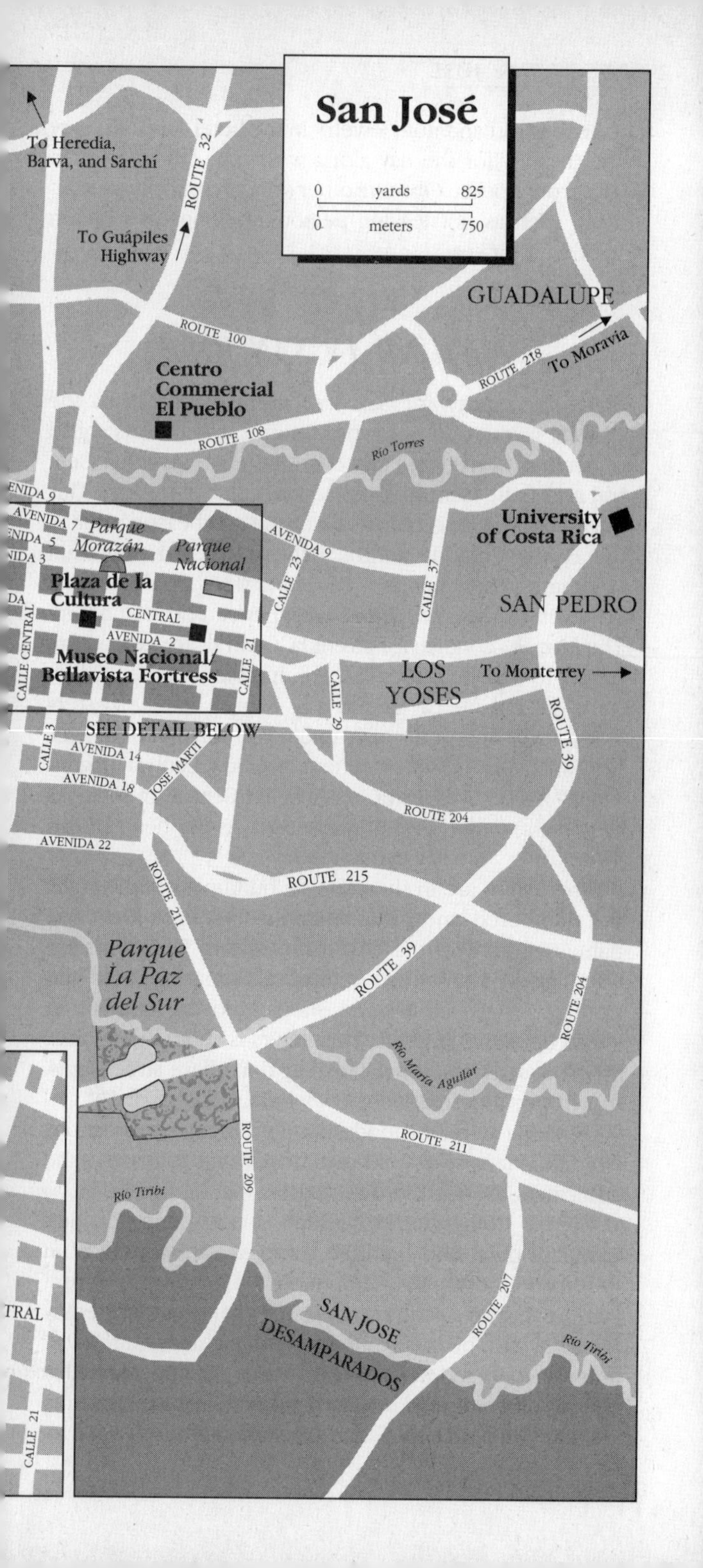

San José
0 yards 825
0 meters 750
To Heredia, Barva, and Sarchí
ROUTE 32
To Guápiles Highway
GUADALUPE
ROUTE 100
ROUTE 218
To Moravia
Centro Commercial El Pueblo
ROUTE 108
Río Torres
AVENIDA 9
AVENIDA 7
AVENIDA 5
AVENIDA 3
Parque Morazán
Parque Nacional
University of Costa Rica
Plaza de la Cultura
CALLE 23
CALLE 37
SAN PEDRO
CENTRAL
AVENIDA 2
Museo Nacional/ Bellavista Fortress
CALLE CENTRAL
CALLE 21
CALLE 29
LOS YOSES
To Monterrey
SEE DETAIL BELOW
CALLE 3
AVENIDA 14
AVENIDA 18
JOSE MARTI
ROUTE 39
ROUTE 204
AVENIDA 22
ROUTE 215
ROUTE 211
Parque La Paz del Sur
ROUTE 39
ROUTE 204
Río María Aguilar
ROUTE 211
ROUTE 209
Río Tiribí
SAN JOSE
DESAMPARADOS
ROUTE 207
Río Tiribí
TRAL
CALLE 21

your passport and gold jewelry in the hotel safe and carry your money for the day along with your credit cards in your front pocket. Observe other standard big-city precautions, such as not leaving personal belongings in plain sight on a car seat.

AROUND IN SAN JOSE

The first priority for San José visitors is to learn the general layout of the downtown area, designed as a grid of *avenidas* (avenues) and *calles* (streets). **Avenida Central** and **Calle Central** cross at the center of the city. This intersection is one block east of the southeast corner of the Banco Central (Central Bank) block, an important landmark to bear in mind. The *calles* west of Calle Central are even numbered; to the east they're odd numbered. The *avenidas* north of Avenida Central are odd numbered; to the south they're even numbered. **Paseo Colón** starts at Parque La Sabana (La Sabana Park), west of downtown, and runs east, ending at San Juan de Dios hospital, near Calle 14, where Avenida Central begins. The **Plaza de la Cultura**, on Avenida Central two blocks east of the Calle Central intersection, is the heart of San José.

Street signs are in short supply, buildings are generally not numbered, and most residents don't even know the names of many of the downtown streets. Directions are often given using such reference points as buildings, cantinas, trees, parks, and shops, and are sometimes stated in *metros* (meters; 100 meters is about one block). When you ask Josefinos why they don't have street signs, they reply, "Because we know where we're going."

Barrios (neighborhoods) sweep out in all directions from the **Plaza de la Cultura** and are home to many of the attractions included in this chapter.

Centro Comercial El Pueblo—a classy one-stop dining, shopping, and nightlife complex catercorner from the Hotel Bougainvillea, about eight blocks north of central downtown—is a great place to hang out and enjoy life after dark because of the variety of clubs and restaurants concentrated here in a small area. The Bougainvillea is a bit down at heel and in need of refurbishing; while we don't recommend it as an accommodation, it's a convenient place to stop in for a drink and an important landmark in the northern downtown area.

The University of Costa Rica is in **San Pedro**, on the eastern side of town just over 3 km (2 miles) from El Pueblo, along with a gaggle of restaurants and nightclubs catering to the university crowd. The campus is a top choice for a jog. Here you can meet students and teachers, sit in on a class, and catch the feel of Central America's best university. The campus and the restaurants, clubs, and student hangouts here are lively, and ideal for making contact with interesting folks from all parts of the world.

Los Yoses is also east of downtown, on the way to San Pedro, via Avenida Central, 200 meters west of the landmark fountain called Fuente de la Hispanidad, near the campus. It has changed in only a decade from a sleepy outskirts area of exclusive homes to a bustling commercial center. Spoon and Mazorca (see Dining, below) and Galerías Casa Alameda, an upscale shopping mall, are in Los Yoses.

A five-minute ride farther east, past Los Yoses on Avenida Central, is the **Monterrey** barrio, a quiet residential neighborhood where Vernon and Marcela Bell's guest home is located (see Accommodations). **Moravia**, 7 km (4 miles) northeast of downtown (past Guadalupe, a large suburb), is a shopping-center community, touristy yet an interesting place for a quick shopping spree.

West of downtown in the **San Bosco** barrio between Calles 28 and 36, **Paseo Colón**, the western continuation of Avenida Central, forms the spine of a neighborhood of the same name, anchored by the five-star Hotel Grano de Oro on Calle 30, two blocks south of Paseo Colón. Within a few blocks of the hotel are the Laurence Olivier Theater and the restaurants Mordisco, Da Pino Pizzeria, and Macchu Picchu (see Dining).

Historic **Escazú**, 8 km (5 miles) southwest of San José in the hilly suburbs, is reached via the new *autopista* (highway) that skirts the southern edge of La Sabana Park. Among the country's oldest towns, Escazú dates to 1561, when the Spaniards moved in and began to work the land. It has long been noted as the *bruja* (witch) capital of Costa Rica and the place where spirits from another world float about; here for a few *colones* you can have your fortune told or your palm read. Escazú features tingling clean air, nice restaurants, and a view of San José. It's a popular retirement center for North Americans.

Downtown

PLAZA DE LA CULTURA

Pura vida (literally "the good life") is also the affectionate local expression for "terrific" or "great." An excellent place to get a feeling for Costa Rican *pura vida* is the Plaza de la Cultura, the heart of the city (between Avenida Central and Avenida 2, and Calles 3 and 5). Sitting at a patio table under a white umbrella at the Café Parisienne, in front of the 62-year-old, colonial-style ▸ **Gran Hotel** overlooking the plaza and the open-air crafts market, you may feel as if you have taken a page out of Hemingway's *The Sun Also Rises.* The pulse is passionate and heady, as at the sidewalk cafés of Pamplona and the Left Bank of Paris before mass tourism. Papa and Picasso would love the international crowd that hangs out here, discussing books to be written and debating the state of Central American politics.

The plaza around the hotel is laid out in a maze of tiny, roofless stalls, where passive vendors sell trays of silver jewelry, hand-carved clay masks, colorful Guatemalan belts, area rugs, tee-shirts, and hammocks. Musicians may be playing old wooden marimbas over the buzz of the crowd, while steaming plates of *gallo pinto* (rice and black beans) and heaping bowls of fresh fruit are served to travellers, chatting Josefinos, and a congregation of other entertaining characters. Scanning the plaza and its tables, you will wonder who is on the lam—running from a bank deal gone sour, a phony stock setup, or a marriage on the rocks. Costa Rica has always been easy on shadowy, mysterious characters, looking the other way when political exiles arrive.

TEATRO NACIONAL

Using the Gran Hotel and the Plaza de la Cultura as the central landmarks, you will find that the San José puzzle falls neatly into place, piece by piece. A few feet to the east of the hotel, facing the plaza, is the spectacular and richly ornamented Teatro Nacional, the pride of San José. Designed in the style of the old Paris opera house, the theater is where President Kennedy met with the Conference of Central American Presidents in March 1963, a few months before his assassination. Presidents Bush and Reagan have also been in attendance here.

The 19th-century coffee barons, starved for culture, asked the government to tax their exported coffee in order to build a theater that would attract well-known performers. The tax was a cultural boon, and the theater is proudly called a jewel floating in a cup of coffee. Completed in 1897, the building has elegant floors and staircases of Italian Carrara marble, detailed murals, crystal from Venice, and paneling of precious Costa Rican hardwoods.

On the second level of the vestibule is a ceiling painting by Italian artist Aleardo Villa, entitled *Alegoría* (Allegory), that depicts, in vibrant color and detail, bananas and coffee being harvested and loaded onto cargo boats in the Caribbean port city of Limón. Tour guides, with great panache, like to point out Villa's obvious errors, such as the coffee pickers stooping to gather beans from bushes (coffee beans grow on trees). "Next time around," they say, "we'll use a Costa Rican painter."

Strangely, the building does not have an orchestra pit, though it is home to the internationally acclaimed Orquesta Sinfonía Nacional (National Symphony Orchestra). Currently, the theater is undergoing extensive earthquake repairs but is open to the public during the week for tours only.

After visiting the theater, step into the Old World–style **Café del Teatro** for a refreshment. Used during performance intermissions, the café is an extension of the theater and just as elaborate, with marble floors, large ceiling murals, and draped windows opening onto the plaza. You could be sitting in Florence, Madrid, or Paris as you listen to recorded classical music and sip a steaming hot chocolate, served in a tall glass at a small, marble-topped table.

MUSEO DE ORO

A couple of hundred yards to the north of the Gran Hotel, across the plaza past hammock vendors and begging pigeons near Calle 5, is the walk-down entrance for the Museo de Oro (Gold Museum), located underneath the Plaza de la Cultura. A sweeping marble stairway leads to a bottom floor and a dark room with foot-thick vault doors and armed guards at the ready. This phenomenal collection, owned by the Banco Central de Costa Rica, is a dazzling permanent exhibit of more than 20,000 troy ounces of pre-Columbian art pieces and a one-stop education on the history of gold and its relationship to the native Costa Ricans and everyday life in pre-Columbian Central America.

You can pick up an English-language recording near the main entrance and stroll through an exhibit of 1200–800 B.C. vases, battle ornaments, large gold plaques used as clothing ornaments, miniature animals, strings of gold beads, cases of gold bells that were hung in trees to keep spirits at bay, delicate frogs and toads (traditional charms of grave diggers), and small birds, symbols of intelligence. The exhibit ends with European glass-bead necklaces, circa 1502, that were exchanged for gold by Spanish *conquistadores*.

Adjoining the Museo de Oro is the **Museo Numismático** (Money Museum), which provides a survey of the money and coins of Costa Rica, and an explanation of how the money developed in conjunction with the country's history. The long, narrow room, also with thick vault doors, has large, well-lit Spanish-language information panels and rare photos to complement displays of coins dating to 1469 and examples of the country's colorful paper money, first issued in 1864. Open Fridays, Saturdays, and Sundays.

Walk back up the stairs, turn left to Avenida Central, and walk right (east) six blocks to the Museo Nacional and Bellavista fortress, just east of Plaza de la Democracia between Calles 15 and 17.

MUSEO NACIONAL AND BELLAVISTA FORTRESS

The Bellavista fortress, built around 1870 as the headquarters and barracks for the Costa Rican army, was converted in 1948 (the year the army was banned) into the Museo Nacional (National Museum). Bellavista, which means "pretty view," is an apt name. Located on a hill overlooking the city, the grounds and interior courtyard are beautifully landscaped with flowering bushes and shade trees. The museum displays pre-Columbian treasures from the Americas such as ceremonial pots, *metates* (stones for grinding grain) carved from volcanic rock, colonial furniture, exhibits on the history of the Costa Rican people, and vivid oil portraits of *conquistadores* Juan de Cavallón and Juan Vásquez de Coronado. In the dimly lit watch tower, objects of jade and delicately wrought gold figurines are displayed.

The meticulously groomed patio area contains ancient stone balls (some are four feet in diameter) from an unknown culture, almost perfectly shaped and carved without metal tools. A spectacular Costa Rican archaeological find, the stone spheres might have served as landmarks on the old trade routes that crisscrossed the country, or as religious symbols or burial-ground markers. The museum is closed Mondays.

From the back of the museum there is a splendid view of the city, framed on the left horizon by the Cordillera de Talamanca and on the right by the Cordillera Central, both often shaded by billowing clouds that play hide and seek with the towering peaks. Below is the Plaza de la Democracia, where visiting presidents were greeted during the prestigious Hemispheric Summit in 1989. The plaza was dedicated that same year as a national landmark representing 100 years of Costa Rican democracy.

MUSEO DE JADE

Hail a cab at the Museo Nacional and pop over to the Museo de Jade (Jade Museum), northeast of Parque Morazán. The museum is on the eleventh floor of the bustling National Insurance Institute building (Instituto Nacional de Seguros, INS), on Calle 9 at Avenida 7. The tall landmark building is easy to spot.

From the eleventh floor gaze down on the peaceful muddle of tin and tile roofs, then look outward to see most of the city and the surrounding volcanoes. Billed as the only institution in the world devoted to the jade of the Americas, the Jade Museum includes such treasures as jade pieces traded by the Olmecs from Mexico, and Mayan carvings of owls, winged bats, and other motifs.

As in many San José museums, the rooms are dark in order to display the wall and table exhibits in dramatic fashion. The Jade Museum integrates informative relief wall maps, color photo panels, ceramic vases displayed openly on a table, and hundreds of jade pieces that illustrate the history of the early Costa Rican native people.

Some scientists believe that certain blue jade pieces

here were designed by Costa Rican aborigines and carved from the ritual chisels of an even earlier people. Numerous old jade pieces have been found in Costa Rica, but jade quarries within the country remain elusive; Guatemala's Motagua river valley is the only known Central American source of jade. Much of the museum's jade collection came from looted ancient grave sites and was purchased by the museum from private collectors. Today it is illegal to sell jade in Costa Rica, though occasionally jade jewelry is offered for sale in the city's shops. In an adjoining room is the Sala de Arte (Art Gallery), which features large changing exhibits. There are some English-language signs in the Jade Museum; closed weekends.

MUSEO DE ARTE COSTARRICENSE

At the west end of Paseo Colón, where Calle 42 forms the eastern edge of La Sabana Park, is the splendid Museo de Arte Costarricense (Museum of Costa Rican Art), easily reached by city bus or cab. The building, a gorgeous colonial-style structure that until 1955 was the old international airport's terminal—complete with a control tower, tile roof, stone floor, wrought-iron work, an atrium, and large, dark ceiling beams—was proudly converted into what amounts to a national treasure and opened in 1978 as a showcase for Costa Rican artists.

Standing behind the building on fragments of the old runway, with the park at your back, use a little imagination and you'll be pulled back to a delightful time when elegant horse-drawn carriages and a few Model As and Model Ts rolled up the boulevard past stately mansions on their way to the airport to greet arrivals. Charles Lindbergh touched down here in 1932 on one of his barnstorming goodwill tours. (He had to buzz the tiny airport a couple of times in a frantic effort to get the waving citizens off the runway so he could land before running out of fuel. When he finally touched down he was not in a good mood.)

Inside the museum, the main art salon features works of 20th-century artists, including large murals by the great Francisco Amighetti, the works of Fernando Carballo and Rudy Espinoza, and humorous drawings by Max Jiménez, who depicted his fellow Ticos with a sharp pen.

Don't miss the second-floor Salón Dorado, encircled

by Louis Feron's 1940 wall relief mural depicting Costa Rica's beginnings, the native people, the introduction of the pineapple (now a minor crop), the birth of San José, law and justice, and the role of the ever-important coffee bean.

From the Museo de Arte you can see **Parque La Sabana** (La Sabana Park), a maze of trees and open grassy areas where Tico families lay out picnics and let the kids romp. La Sabana, an important reference and directional landmark—similar to Mexico City's Chapultepec Park and New York City's Central Park—is filled on weekends with joggers, bicyclists, tennis players, and with spirited volleyball and basketball games. La Sabana also has an Olympic-size swimming pool, soccer and baseball fields, handball courts, walking trails, and a small lake. On the southeast corner the city has built a national gymnasium over the old landing strips, and on the northwest corner a national stadium.

Elsewhere in San José

The **Museo de Entomología** (Entomology Museum), at the University of Costa Rica in the eastern suburb of San Pedro, has a large collection of butterflies and other exotic insects. But unless you are a biologist, why not see the butterflies alive and on the wing in one of the national parks or at the Butterfly Farm (see Around San José)? Call the museum (Tel: 25-5555) for visiting hours. Forget the zoo in Simón Bolívar park. The Parque Zoológico Simón Bolívar is not on a par with the open spaces of new international zoos that simulate a natural environment and allow the animals space to move about.

GETTING AROUND

Pick up a city map at the ICT tourist office (Instituto Costarricense de Turismo) located on Calle 5 at the entrance to the Museo de Oro, located underneath the Plaza de la Cultura. You will quickly learn your way around.

While moving about the city, beware when crossing streets—even at corners. The downtown streets were designed for carriages and carts; when the first major influx of cars rolled in during the 1950s it was love at first sight, and the horses galloped for cover. Today red lights don't mean a coffee bean; the cabbies and buses own the road, so forget about pedestrians having the right of way. Ticos are ordinarily the nicest people this side of Disneyland, but when they climb into a vehicle their eyes glaze over and they focus on getting from point A to point B with a lead foot and a prayer. Ticos themselves will tell you they turn into salivating monsters upon sight of a steering wheel. (But if you were brushed back by a careening car, the driver would probably stop, fuss over your clothing, and offer to buy you a cup of coffee.)

Flagging a taxi from 3:30 to 6:00 P.M. is a bit difficult, and when it rains you need some luck. A great place to find a cab is curb-side in front of the Gran Hotel on the Plaza de le Cultura. If you are near a hotel have the front desk or concierge call one for you.

San José taxis are efficient and clean, but most cabbies drive like the wind and don't use their meters, so establish the fare in advance. They readily accept dollars, and if you become confused with the Spanish numbers write the fare down on paper for verification, a solid safeguard that removes the stress of dealing with street-wise cabbies. In 1993 cab fares around the city averaged about $3 for visitors. The taxi fare from Juan Santamaría International Airport to San José (20 km/12 miles) is between $12 and $15.

The inexpensive San José buses are the best buy in the city. All have a central city stop from which they travel to an outlying area, then circle back. You can easily see a portion of the city, then get off the bus where you first boarded. There are lots of stops along the way where you might want to get off for a while, then get on a later bus. The buses can be crowded, however, and are not designed for comfort. If you explore the city and surrounding areas by bus, always check the time schedule for the last bus.

Driving a car in the city is not recommended, as it can be quite stressful. It's much easier to get around via taxis, buses, and on foot. If you are heading to a coast in a rental car, pick up the vehicle or have it delivered the night before. Get as much advice as you can from local people about the best routes to take, then depart early in the morning with map in hand. Car rentals can be arranged in advance of your trip or through one of the many local tour agencies (see "Touring Costa Rica" in Useful Facts).

ACCOMMODATIONS

On a ranked list of Central American accommodations, those of San José and the Central Valley would stand near the top, with a diverse selection of comfortable lodging choices and friendly, attentive hoteliers. Inquire about money-saving travel packages and airport pickup when booking. Rates quoted below are for a double room, double occupancy. Rate ranges span the lowest rate in the low season to the highest rate in the high season; taxes totaling 14.4 percent are added to the hotel tab. High season is November 1 to April 31, low season May 1 to October 31. Most accommodations can be booked through Southern Horizons Travel (see Useful Facts).

Hotels near the Airport

The ▸ **Hotel Herradura Resort and Conference Center**, on the road between Juan Santamaría International Airport and San José, about 6½ km (4 miles) from the airport and 20 minutes northwest of downtown, is a mid-size operation offering all the usual resort amenities, with an accent on efficiency: three restaurants, a lively, hard-drinking lobby bar, a European-style casino, an office of Swiss Travel, and shiatsu massage room service. Businesspeople book the Herradura, as do groups. It is fine for a one-night stay but is not for the romantic—and you can hear your neighbor's alarm-clock buzzer.

P.O. Box 7-1880-1000, San José; Tel: 39-0033; Fax: 39-2292; in the U.S. and Canada, Tel: (800) 245-8420. $125.

Next door, as you head toward town, is the ▸ **Cariari Hotel and Country Club**, opened in 1973, the place for the active, high-energy, sports-minded traveller who wants to golf 18 holes on a course designed by George Fazio, play tennis on one of ten Laykold courts, work out in a health club, stretch the legs with a jog, or do some laps in an Olympic-size pool where Sylvia Poll trains. (Poll, a Costa Rican, won a silver medal in the 1988 summer Olympics and is a national hero.)

Presidents Carter, Reagan, and Bush have checked in at the Cariari, as have Warren Beatty and other celebrities. Reminiscent of the Mexican Camino Real hotel's rooms, and with a garden setting, the spacious units here have king-size or double beds, a marble sink area, minibar, lock-up safe, and an excellent housekeeping service. Room 1061 near the pool is ideal for early risers.

Autopista General Canas, Ciudad Cariari, Apartado 737-1007 Centro Colón, San José; Tel: 39-0022; Fax: 39-2803; in the U.S. and Canada, Tel: (800) 227-4274, Fax: (305) 476-6150. $130.

Downtown

Downtown, the ▶ **Gran Hotel**, on Calle 3 at the corner of Avenida 2, overlooking the Plaza de la Cultura and the Teatro Nacional, is smack in the middle of the action. Opened in 1930, now a bit faded and bohemian and as international as Paul Theroux's sneakers, the Gran is popular with travellers who want to dig their teeth into the town and waste not a heartbeat of vacation time.

Book only on the fourth floor, which has recently been remodeled and partially refurnished and has cable television and air-conditioning. Try to get number 420, an inside room, for a better night's sleep, unless you want to look out on the plaza and people-watch from room 440. The Gran is nothing fancy, but the 24-hour room service, location, and rates are appealing.

P.O. Box 527-1000, San José; Tel: 21-4000 or 21-0796; Fax: 21-3501. $78.

Romantics will be pleased with the ▶ **Hotel L'Ambiance**, behind the Museo de Jade on Calle 13 at Avenida 9, a beautifully restored colonial mansion with a staff that looks after its clients like family. The six high-ceilinged rooms and one presidential suite, all different in design and tastefully decorated with antiques from Europe and North America, face onto an intimate central courtyard with a bubbling fountain.

If finances allow, spring for the serene presidential suite, a homey London-style sitting room with draped windows, overstuffed chairs, area rugs, a stately four-poster bed, and bath with elegant freestanding bathtub and bidet. The lovely garden dining room is another bonus. The hotel does not accept credit cards; personal checks in American dollars may be accepted with owner William Parker's approval, which should be arranged prior to your visit.

The hotel will also recommend Carlos, a guide with his own private car who speaks English and is honest and dependable. Carlos will pick you up at the hotel; you negotiate the rate and the sights to see with him. (Parker and receptionist/assistant manager Alexander Pizarro don't like their guests to drive in the city or on one-day country excursions, claiming that the road signs are so bad that the guests could end up on a dead-end road in Panamá with dented fenders and an empty tank.)

Costa Rican mailing address: P.O. Box 1040-2050, San José; Tel: 22-6702; Fax: 23-0481; international mailing address: c/o Interlink 179, P.O. Box 526-770, Miami, FL 33152. $70–$95; presidential suite $140.

Similar to L'Ambiance, the ▸ **Hotel Grano de Oro** is a former private residence recently converted into one of the country's best boutique hotels. The festive Peruvian and classical music, warm pastel colors, hanging plants, twirling ceiling fans, wicker chairs, hardwood floors, and garden setting will soften your spirit as you enter the property. Owner David Wroughton, an American who has spent most of his life in Peru, caters to North Americans, avoids booking groups, and offers casserole cooking (see Dining). And—horrors!—if a guest is caught smoking in his room he could be banished forever.

The comfortable public rooms are conducive to lounging with a glass of Chilean wine, a good book, and a dish of ice cream with fresh berries on the side. Room 11 has two double beds and is nicely located. The hotel has recently completed an addition of 15 rooms and a sun deck with three hot tubs; the sun deck affords views of Poás, Barva, and Irazú volcanoes. A chat about the city with Wroughton or co-owner Elden Cooke will be rewarding. Request the self-guided walking tour and city-bus information from the property to nearby restaurants and to downtown.

The Grano de Oro is 150 meters south of Paseo Colón on Calle 30, between Avenidas 2 and 4; it's a seven-block walk west to the Museo de Arte Costarricense. The hotel is 15 blocks directly west of the Teatro Nacional and the Plaza de la Cultura.

Costa Rican mailing address: Apartado 1157-1007 Centro Colón, San José; Tel: 55-3322; Fax: 21-2782; international mailing address: P.O. Box 025216-36, Miami, FL 33102-5216. $89–$97; garden suite $115.

The ▸ **Hotel Ambassador**, in the same general area as the Grano de Oro, between Calles 28 and 30 on Paseo Colón, could garner some good will from nonsmokers by refurbishing its odorous rooms and requesting smokers to puff outdoors. Businesspeople like the location and amenities, such as secretarial and translation service and conference rooms. The service is congenial, and the bar is a popular after-work stop for Ticos.

P.O. Box 10186, San José; Tel: 21-8155; Fax: 55-3396; in the U.S. and Canada, Tel: (800) 344-1212. $74–$95.

The high-rise ▸ **Corobicí Hotel and Spa**, also to the west of the central downtown district, near La Sabana Park, is booked by businesspeople who use the corporate suite and enjoy the nightclub, dancing, and casino—a one-stop nightlife location rare among San José hotels. The main office of Swiss Travel and San Jose's best spa and aerobics workout room are at the Corobicí. Request one of the top-floor rooms at the opposite end of the hotel from the nightclub. The Corobicí and the Cariari (see "Hotels near the Airport," above) are owned by the same Japanese corporation.

P.O. Box 2443-1000, San José; Tel: 32-8122; Fax: 31-5834; in the U.S. and Canada, Tel: (800) 227-4274, Fax: (305) 476-6150. $110.

Homestays

An innovation that has swept the travel industry and is spreading around the world is the homestay, affording the visitor—who stays in a private home with people of the country—an opportunity to have an "inside" encounter with the culture. People who come to San José for cosmetic surgery also find homestays a great way to recuperate stress free for a few days within a safe family environment.

▸ **Costa Rica Home & Host**, based in Minneapolis, Minnesota, offers a bed-and-breakfast package or a flexible meal plan, airport pickup, customized tours, personalized attention with either English- or Spanish-speaking hosts, smoking and nonsmoking rooms, homes that accept children and ones that don't, rooms with or without private bath, and helpful travel tips on getting around the city, complete with maps, orientation, and marked routes. You can be escorted to some attractions by your host or you can go on your own. Guests have stayed more than a month, and students for a year. Guests' special interests, such as art, language study, nature and wildlife, are encouraged.

The 60 or so participating homes and family hosts, all in and around San José, have been carefully selected by Costa Rican director Vernon Bell, originally from Lawrence, Kansas, who has lived in Costa Rica for more than 20 years, and his wife, Marcela, a marvelous cook and hostess. The Bells' nicely landscaped four-bedroom home, built in 1946 in the middle-class Monterrey suburb on the east side of town, is a typical home in the program. A block from bus service and a ten-block walk to the university and numerous restaurants, the unpretentious house has a comfortable living room, adjoining dining room, some dark wooden furniture pieces from Sarchí, and red tile floors.

Marcela's dinner could be a steaming paella, a hearts-of-palm salad featuring Vernon's commercially produced salad dressing, homemade strawberry shortcake, and fresh lemonade—with lemons from the Bells' lemon tree. Breakfast is often a variation of *gallo pinto,* with black beans, rice, chiles, and onions. Marcela makes pizza from scratch.

Costa Rica Home & Host, 2445 Park Avenue, Minneapolis, MN 55404; Tel: (612) 871-0596; Fax: (612) 871-8853. *Bed and breakfast category:* daily rates, $45 double; longer than 14 consecutive nights with the same host family, $33 double; for a private bath, add $5 per night; optional airport pickup, $10 per person; add 16 percent tax to above rates and $25 booking fee per person per week. *Bed and meals category:* daily rates, $95 double; breakfast, lunch, and dinner included; private bath, airport pickup, taxes, and booking fee additional, as above. No minimum stay required. *Deluxe homestay category:* daily rates, $125 double; breakfast, lunch, and dinner included; private bath, airport pickup, taxes, and booking fee additional, as above; your host acts as your personal guide in San José; costs of public transportation and entry to attractions are included in the price.

Hotel with a View

▸ **Tara**, a former estate converted in 1990 into a gorgeous, three-floor, 12-room hotel whose architecture was influenced by *Gone with the Wind,* is on three acres 15 minutes southwest of town in the suburb of Escazú, a mile high on Pico Blanco mountain overlooking the Central Valley. Tara's attractions are its unobstructed view, the homey elegance of the public rooms, service with a flair, and the remote mountain setting. Julio Iglesias has dropped in for a night or two, as have production companies that have used Tara as a location for television commercials.

The roomy suites, some with fireplaces, have names such as Scarlett, Rhett Butler, Charlotte, Charleston, Savannah, and Robert E. Lee. Each uniquely designed suite has shiny hardwood floors, overstuffed chairs, handcrafted furniture, and draped windows that open onto a large shared balcony that seems to float in the clouds on a misty day. The property is surrounded by trails that lead into nature areas ideal for bird-watching and photographing wildflowers. Other amenities include tennis, swimming, and a Jacuzzi.

Tara is a big hit with honeymooners, couples in a romantic phase, and those who love the personal touch of fresh-cut flowers, good room service, and a fine dining room with flickering candles and a dress code (no sneakers or jeans at dinner), for which—and for more on Tara—see "Dining with a View," below. Rates include transportation to and from the airport and downtown San José, and a Continental breakfast. Escazú, a mountain town with fresh breezes, was once a witchcraft center where *brujas* (witches) could put a jinx on you or relieve a nagging back pain. The tales of Escazú's roaming spirits live on in Costa Rica. (See also Shops and Shopping, for Biesanz Woodworks in Escazú.)

P.O. Box 1459-1250, Escazú; Tel: 28-6992; Fax: 28-9651. $120–$150.

DINING

Costa Rica has a slim cookbook and few national dishes, but some chefs display a Continental/French flair, influenced by North America; they create dishes that are savory and economical, utilizing an abundance of fresh seafood, fruits, rice, and chicken. Many of the finer restaurants and dining rooms that are making culinary statements are located in boutique hotels and inns, and they often cater to a sophisticated, demanding international crowd.

San José chefs prepare tasty soups, many fashioned after those of Mexico, which is ranked among the best soup countries in the world. Much better than Mexico's is the city's purified tap water, unique to this part of the world and a feature that adds immensely to the San José dining experience.

A Costa Rican staple is the famed *gallo pinto,* a traditional, unpretentious recipe of rice and black beans prepared a hundred different ways, with or without spices and chunks of chicken, pork, or beef. It's served throughout the city around the clock, and especially at breakfast. *Gallo pinto* lifts the spirit, fights the blahs, and is a shot of quick energy—very Costa Rican.

Black bean soup is another national specialty. It can be as thick as stew, or a thin consommé with a boiled egg floating in the broth and beans settling at the bottom of the bowl. The ubiquitous hearts-of-palm salad and appetizer (*cocktail de palmito*) are seen on most menus, as are bananas and plantains prepared in a variety of ways and often presented as hors d'oeuvres or used in desserts.

The immigrant influence on San José's restaurants and cafés is a tasty bonus. Tamales and tacos have been integrated into the city's cuisine, often listed as *platos Mexicanos* or *Tico-Mex* fare. Spanish, Argentine, and Chinese restaurants, States-style barbecue and steak houses, and Italian dining rooms also dot the culinary map.

Regardless of their ethnic composition, meals usually end with a cup of fine Costa Rican coffee. Lunch and dinner are not rushed in San José. Diners can remain at table as long as they wish, and smokers still reign, though a few rooms have established no-smoking sections.

An 11 percent sales tax will be included on your tab—and often a 10 percent tip (*propina*) as well. Watch for the *propina,* in order not to duplicate it.

Dining at Hotels near the Airport

In Costa Rica dining out is a big part of the nighttime scene. Some of the larger hotel restaurants feature live music on weekends, thus offering a one-stop dining/nightlife destination. The Cariari Hotel and Country Club, on the road to the airport, 20 minutes northwest of downtown, is proud of its upscale, formal, French-influenced restaurant **Los Vitrales**, adjacent to the casino. Overstuffed chairs, fine china and linens, fresh-cut flowers, background piano music, a large wine list, a marvelous shrimp dish in a light basil sauce, and a creamy spinach soup draw repeat business. Open 6:00 P.M. to midnight. Reservations advised; Tel: 39-0022.

Bon Vivant, in the Hotel Herradura, next to the Cariari, 6½ km (4 miles) southeast of the airport, is a formal room with linen, silver, and fine china, and an eager, black-suited maître d'hôtel at the door. The hotel has a small dance floor and live background music, and brings in a *folklórico* show on Thursdays. The kitchen is French-influenced, with excellent meat, salads, and service. Tel: 39-0033.

Downtown

Downtown, the maze of restaurants, cafés, and fast-food outlets can be confusing, each with an arresting sign.

Quick lunch stops when you're browsing about town are the informal and inexpensive **Super Taco Antojos**, with four city locations. The downstairs Antojos on Paseo Colón across from the Hotel Ambassador, noisy and energetic, is filled with businesspeople and secretaries who sit on crude red-and-white chairs amid greenery and rough, thick walls. The *tacos Mexicanos* are the way to go here. The open kitchen is usually sizzling with open-faced chicken tacos heaped with lettuce, avocado, and sour cream, with black beans on the side. For dessert try *flan de coco,* made daily. Hear live mariachi music on Thursday evenings.

Don't overlook **Spoon**, a splendid pastry/coffee shop chain with four or five locations, including an outlet adjoining the Plaza de la Cultura. Spoon is ideal for breakfast and lunch, and a favorite Josefino drop-in haunt for a quick bite or a cappuccino and a slice of freshly baked strawberry pie.

Mordisco Restaurant, the sister establishment to San Pedro's Mazorca (see below), is on Paseo Colón, west of Avenida Central. If your taxi driver is not familiar with Mordisco, have him take you to the Mercedes-Benz agency; the restaurant is 40 meters to the east. A meal at Mordisco could begin with a coconut *ceviche* appetizer made with chunks of *corvina* (white sea bass), coconut cream, and sweet potato or a *pozole* soup created with yellow corn, cheese, tomato, and creole seasonings, followed by a main-course breast of chicken topped with dried cashew fruit, rice, and vegetables. Wine can be ordered by the glass, and you'll dine to jazz sounds on some weekends. Tel: 55-2448.

A stone's throw from Mordisco (south of the Mercedes-Benz agency, on Avenida 2 and Calle 24) is **Da Pino Pizzeria Restaurante**. With authentic and traditional Italian cookery, down to the *minestrone, fettucine Alfredo, ensalada de camarones* (shrimp salad), and wine, this dining room could just as well exist in Chicago or on New York's Mulberry Street. The ambience is enhanced by a lattice ceiling, dark wooden chairs, draped windows, potted palms, and a red tile floor. The best table is mid-room near the window. Closed Tuesdays; Tel: 23-4895.

A clever way to check out a lodging choice, either for an immediate change or a future booking, is to drop in for lunch at the **Hotel Grano de Oro**. Converted from a private residence, this gem of a small hotel is 15 blocks directly west of the Teatro Nacional, on Calle 30; it's 150 meters south of Paseo Colón and a four-minute walk from Da Pino.

Opened in late 1991, Grano de Oro is a gorgeous property with a cozy dining room in the rear, and garden patio dining under two leafy mango trees. The casserole-style cooking features a corn chowder with bacon, a spicy enchilada pie, and chicken and mushroom lasagna served with a salad and fruit. Fried foods are not served here. You'll enjoy talking with owner David Wroughton, an American raised in Peru and the Amazon. No smoking. Dining reservations not necessary.

Like a good neighbor, Wroughton urges his guests to walk over to **Macchu Picchu Restaurant** on Calle 32 at Avenida 1 (turn off Paseo Colón at the Kentucky Coronel and walk 125 meters north), for their Peruvian seafood platter, a house specialty prepared for two. The spicy combo platter (less than $10) includes corvina, shrimp, and lobster.

Eight years old, Macchu Picchu is a 17-table, two-room hole in the wall with dark wooden tables, whiskey bottles perched on glass shelves, a fish net over the bar, and tiny napkins that dissolve in your hands. The canned background music is from the Andes, and between servings the two waiters usually go head to head in an intense chess game at a bark-covered bar that would make Tarzan feel at home.

Another outstanding dish here is *sopa aguadito de mariscos,* a fish soup with squid, shrimp, bass, a slice of lime, garlic, onions, rice, and cilantro. The clientele is a crazy mix, from French backpackers to well-dressed Josefino businessmen and gorgeous Josefina women stopping for an early dinner before the opera. Macchu Picchu is open for lunch from noon to 3:00 P.M.; dinner hours are 6:00 P.M. to 10:00 P.M. Reservations are not necessary.

(You may see and hear a lot about the restaurant at the Holiday Inn downtown, but the choices we offer here are all much better.)

Los Yoses and San Pedro

There is another branch of **Spoon** near the University of Costa Rica, a short drive east of town via Avenida Central in the Los Yoses neighborhood. In business 14 years at this location, this branch has a bakery display case jammed with macadamia and fudge brownies, caramel eclairs, and cheesecakes. The ambience here is a mix of coffee house and pastry shop, complete with rattan chairs and newspapers. Lunch favorites are crepes, lasagna, and chicken salad (*ensalada de pollo*). An excellent choice for assembling a countryside picnic, Spoon also will deliver to your hotel.

Across the street from the university in the San Pedro district, a short block from the church of San Pedro, **Mazorca** has taken a page out of California healthy. The gleaming yellow building, decorated with funky old wooden benches, is patronized by bright-faced college students in their bohemian stage who come here to consume what may be the healthiest food in Central America.

The owners visited the United States with pad and pencil in hand and came back with "feelin' good" 1990s lifestyle ideas. The restaurant, which does not allow smoking, has one of the city's top bakeries, with loaves of thick whole-wheat breads piled high on the counter. The vegetarian, 100 percent natural menu features such delightful creations as vegetable tamales; smashed beans; a tofu and soy cheese sandwich; salads with garden-fresh fruit and yogurt; thick vegetable soups; freshly squeezed carrot- and orange-juice drinks; and, on Fridays, a nonfat vegetarian pizza. Check the *plato del día* (plate of the day) and the dessert counter. Lunch for two is less than $10. Closed on Sundays.

Japanese Cuisine

Japanese investors have purchased the Corobicí Hotel near La Sabana Park. There they opened the **Fuji** restaurant, shipped in Costa Rica's only Japanese chefs, and installed a sushi bar and traditional *teppanyaki* tables with the standard Japanese decor of wall panels and subtle lighting—and white-hatted chefs with quick hands who put on a culinary show featuring the chopping knife and twirling fish. Dishes are authentic and typical. Open noon to 3:00 P.M. and 7:00 P.M. to 11:00 P.M. Closed Sundays. Reservations advised; Tel: 32-8122.

Costa Rican Cuisine

If you want to stick with authentic Costa Rican cuisine, try **La Cocina de Leña** in Centro Comercial El Pueblo, across the street and to the right of the landmark Hotel Bougainvillea. A Costarricense night here begins with dinner followed by dancing in one of the adjoining clubs (see Nightlife, below). The family-owned business is decorated like a colonial farmhouse, with wall candles, tile floors, red tablecloths, an open kitchen with a wood stove, and hustling waiters dressed in white. The menu, printed on a large brown paper bag, proclaims La Cocina "the best restaurant in town." It just might be right.

Favored choices at La Cocina are the green banana appetizer, a platter of *gallo pinto* with fried plantains and hot salsa, a tenderloin "Irazú" that you can cut with a fork, and *olla de carne,* an oversize bowl of steamed corn, potatoes, and roots in a beef broth—a one-dish meal. The thick corn tortillas served on the side are the size of an eye patch and go down like popcorn. Ask for proprietor Carlos Campos Fumero, who loves to offer suggestions and discuss dishes. Tel: 23-3704.

Another dining choice in El Pueblo is **Lukas**, a restaurant on the parking-lot side of the complex, with patio dining, an open kitchen, and typical San José white walls and red tile floor. Lukas serves a nice baked sea bass Costa Rican style, grilled shrimp with tomato sauce, mushrooms, and onions, and a loaded garlic bread that will keep the demons away.

Romantic Dining

East of downtown, next to the theater district, 100 meters north of the Magaly Theater and across from the senate building, **Bromelias Café y Grill** offers an upscale evening of French/Continental cuisine, formally dressed waiters, live guitar music during the week, and an Argentine tango pianist on weekends. Coat and tie are in order for dinner—along with a couple of hours to enjoy the culinary creations of owners Luis Fernando Yglesiás and Robert Lichtveld.

Bromelias moved into its present location, the 1928

customs building, a national historic monument, in 1990, and retained the flavor of the era with original floor tiles, pastel walls, huge potted plants, private wall booths with candlelit tables, and paintings by local artists, nicely lit and for sale. The proprietors recommend a fondue for two, a rich tangy house pâté, their Bavarian cream pie with passion fruit, and the hot French upside-down apple pie. A chef's specialty is a white corvina (sea bass) covered with slices of avocado and a light cream sauce. The extensive wine list has selections from France, Chile, and Spain. For lunch or dinner reservations, Tel: 22-3535.

For dinner on a smaller, more intimate scale, plan for an evening at the superior, colonial-style, seven-room **Hotel L'Ambiance**, located behind the Museo de Jade on Calle 13 near Bromelias, 125 meters north of a local landmark, a Neo-Baroque government ministry building called Casa Amarilla (Yellow House). The garden-style restaurant at the rear of the hotel, reached through an attractive interior patio, is furnished with white iron chairs, lattice wood, tall palms, and large modern art pieces, and has 12 cozy, candlelit tables, with piped-in classical background music to set the mood.

Two entrées of note are the mahimahi with saffron and a marvelous fettuccine mixed with fresh vegetables, garlic, and olive oil and sprinkled with parmesan cheese. All entrées are served with vegetables and freshly baked bread. Hotel L'Ambiance does not accept personal checks or credit cards. U.S. dollars and traveller's checks are okay. Restaurant hours are noon to 2:00 P.M. and 6:30 to 10:00 P.M. Reservations are made with the hotel's receptionist/assistant manager Alexander Pizarro; Tel: 22-6702.

Dining with a View: Escazú

Hire a cab for the 15-minute ride to the **Atlanta Dining Gallery**, located at **Tara**, a small resort hotel in Escazú, southwest of town overlooking the valley. (Have the driver call ahead for directions.) You enter a Southern-style mansion of columns, marble, and tile, to be met by a formally dressed doorman who ushers you into Richard and Barbara Shambley's grand re-creation of Tara, the famed *Gone with the Wind* mansion.

The Shambleys—former North Carolinians—purchased Tara in 1990 from a European baron who was using the property as a summer estate, and converted it into a hotel and restaurant. Tara is the ideal "rich-and-famous" hangout, though it hasn't yet been discovered by the rich and famous. You can picture Clark Gable and Vivien Leigh embracing on the deck, which overlooks thousands of twinkling lights in the valley. The formal dining room has a wood-burning fireplace, shiny wood flooring, Costa Rican art, large windows looking out at the valley, and tables set with Oneida silver, sparkling crystal, candles, and fresh-cut flowers. Guests usually fall quickly into a romantic mood, fired by the sound of two or three European languages, the panorama, and Tara itself.

French and Costa Rican chefs prepare a chicken dish in a curry sauce with raisins and coconuts, and do a nice job with fish bathed in a garlic and mushroom sauce. A crusty square of apple pie, served hot with raisins and a scoop of vanilla ice cream, is a specialty. The best table is in the far right corner.

Call for reservations; Tel: 28-6992. (Don't attempt to drive to Tara unless you are familiar with the city and surrounding area. You'll end up two hours late for your dinner reservations, or you might not *ever* find the place.)

Another look at the Central Valley from Escazú is available through the **Tiquicia Traditional Dining Night** package offered on Friday nights by local tour operators, most of whom provide pickups at major hotels. The 25-minute sunset bus ride is great fun if you are travelling with friends or if you want to rub elbows with travellers from other countries. The tour narrative is informative and often humorous.

The excursion ends up on a rural dirt road, high on an overlook bordering the Pico Blanco national park. At a restored adobe farmhouse here guests are greeted by a marimba player and a spectacular panorama of the Central Valley encompassing four provinces, towering mountain ranges, and valley lights that seem to be stacked on one another. The farmhouse, with rough-hewn logs, white walls, and large picture windows, is dimly lit by long, thin candles in order to provide a better view of the valley. The food, served buffet-style in the original kitchen, is hearty Costa Rican fare, with the shredded beef chayote tamales a standout.

After dinner, students from Escazú, dressed in red-and-white costumes, perform folkloric songs and dances backed by a rhythm quintet. Tiquicia Night is a five-hour outing, with departure at 7:00 P.M., Fridays only. Closed for the Christmas and New Year holiday period.

NIGHTLIFE

When the sun drops and the city's lights slowly begin to glimmer, San José softens: The traffic slows as folks take a deep breath and fall into the world of cozy candlelit cafés, lingering dinners, five-minute kisses, and hot dance clubs where the sweet bouquet of the latest designer fragrance drifts through the night on a salsa rift.

El Pueblo

First choice for a night out is Centro Comercial El Pueblo, catercorner from the landmark Hotel Bougainvillea on the north side of downtown. Often overlooked by North American travellers, El Pueblo is a slick, one-stop boutique, dining, and nightclub complex that could hold its own in any major city. El Pueblo resembles a Spanish village, with tile roofs, attractive patios, and fountains in a garden-like setting. Walkways lead to six discos, five restaurant/bars (see "Costa Rican Cuisine" in Dining, above), and smart, one-of-a-kind shops.

El Pueblo's nightclubs fire up in early evening, beginning with a zesty happy hour. Dress is casual, though the Josefinas are always smartly attired. The nightclub scene is reminiscent of that in the United States in the 1940s before the arrival of television, when a night out would include dancing, conversation, and enjoying a favorite band. Costarricenses are avid music buffs, familiar with the musicians and singers, and ready to reward them with hearty applause.

After dinner the place jumps with Latin sounds. **Los Balcones**, a small, narrow room, features a trio from Bolivia playing music from the Andes on native instruments; they lift the walls off their foundations when they swing into gear (their schedule of appearances is variable). Other nights, live music from other Latin American countries is featured. For snackers an open-stove grill on the small rear patio serves up plates of shish kebab, *chorizo* (sausage) goodies, and strips of grilled chicken. The best seats are at one of four tables on the patio overlooking the city lights, where you can breathe the fresh night air and still hear the music.

Nearby, **Infinito** has the feel of the classic movie nightclubs where Valentino strutted about and slinky ladies seductively fluttered their eyelashes. The dark room has large wall panels of colorful parrots, a small waterfall, and overstuffed chairs to settle into for enjoying salsa and bolero music. **Chavetas**, also dark and smoochy, where Ticos are often seen in coat and tie, is high energy, always busy, and filled with laughter and chatter. Black-leather booths, ceiling beams, white walls, a small dance floor, and a 60-drink list accent the entertainment, which ranges from a quartet with two lead singers to a violinist and a comedian.

Babaloo could be a back room in an old, high-ceilinged hacienda, laid out as it is with a red-brick floor, twirling fans, small black tables, and a tiny bar at the rear—an ideal place to meet Costarricenses. The music draws from bossa nova and Brazil, Costa Rica, Latin jazz-fusion, even batucada (a Brazilian percussion rhythm), depending upon the night.

The **Tango Bar del Che**, another cozy and dark international room, presents authentic music from Argentina. Singing takes the place of dancing, and, in case you forget the words, the lyrics to popular tangos are pasted in the front window. In contrast, **La Placita**, upstairs and across the street from the entrance to El Pueblo, has a small dance floor where young office workers practice safe sex on the dance floor with exotic Madonna-style moves in tandem.

Downtown

La Esmeralda, Avenida 2 between Calles 5 and 7, a short walk from Plaza de la Cultura, hits you smack in the heart with sounds from Mexico, the most popular music this side of the States, lovingly adopted by San José. La Esmeralda is not Los Portales in Veracruz, the Plazuela de los Mariachis in Guadalajara, or Plaza Garibaldi in Mexico City, but it is the home base for Central American mariachis.

The cavernous room has worn, red tables, wooden chairs, and large oil paintings depicting the original (1915) club location, and as a people-watching spot ranks right alongside the Gran Hotel's sidewalk Café Parisienne. Esmeralda is a great late-night stop where you will find guitar cases lined up at the ready and musicians milling about the entrance in full mariachi costume waiting for a last-minute gig. Three vans with signs that advertise Mariachi America, Mariachi Monterrey, and Mariachi Costa Rica wait at the curb to haul their bands to private party bookings.

The house trio plays sharply tuned quality guitars and sings tight harmony. Waiters scamper about, dressed in classic black-and-white garb, serving free platters of *bocas* (beans, chips, and sausage hunks in a spicy sauce); anything fancier just wouldn't fit. The drinks are strong, the menu typically Costa Rican, and the place is open till the owls stop hooting at 4:00 A.M. You can hire a band to surround your table and play "Borracho El Borracho," or sit back and watch scenarios unfold.

Key Largo, between Avenidas 1 and 3 on Calle 7, across from the Holiday Inn Aurora, is a legendary hangout that is bigger than life—a restaurant, a popular nightclub with dancing to a live band, and a second home for women of the night. As one Josefino described it: "It's a whore house, a nightclub, and a restaurant with simple Costa Rican food. Take your choice."

A brick walkway leads through a garden to the front door of a once-elegant mansion whose interior reveals a dusty crystal chandelier that illuminates an inlaid ceiling, a lamp on the right with the traditional flaming red light bulb, and marvelous old floor tile that is aging beautifully. On the left, easy-listening Mexican music is playing in a horseshoe-shaped bar where well-dressed ladies sit. Most of the women could pass as college students.

Adjoining is a room with a bandstand and a small polished dance floor where smoking is not allowed while you dance. On the walls are eight large black-and-white photographs of Bogart and Bacall and stills from the film *Key Largo,* including a six-foot-high classic photo of Bogie in his raincoat. Locals bring out-of-town guests here, and travellers drop in to dance and enjoy a plate of rice and chicken topped with red peppers and onions, with a fresh salad on the side. After 9:00 P.M. there is a small admission fee. (No checks accepted.)

Prostitution is legal in Costa Rica, and the women are generally nonaggressive. There is some cross-dressing, too. The health department supposedly checks and certifies the prostitutes on a regular basis. (The city has addressed AIDS and has a program in place to combat the disease, including one for school-age children, as well as large billboards urging people to use condoms.)

If you strike out for **Bar Mexico** on Calle 16 at Avenida 13, a hot live mariachi music room with tasty and generous *bocas,* it is best to hail a cab; the area around Bar Mexico could use a few missionaries and social workers.

Theater and Cinema

The gorgeous **Teatro Melico Salazar**, on Avenida 2 across from Parque Central, is hosting the Orquesta Sinfonía Nacional (National Symphony Orchestra) while the Teatro Nacional is undergoing earthquake repairs. Melico Salazar also offers operas during the summer months, concerts, musicals, and the colorful Folkloric Fantastic show; Tel: 22-3071. **La Perla**, a busy corner café adjoining the theater, is open around the clock serving Costa Rican dishes and excellent coffee—a good place for after the theater.

The city's lively theater scene is another way to immerse yourself in the culture and tune in to the Spanish language. Nine or so downtown theaters, such as the Carpa, Angel, Comedia, Aduana, Chaplin, Arlequin, and Máscara, present live productions. San Jose's Little Theater Group, formed more than 40 years ago and loaded with excellent actors, also mounts top productions in English. A big hit from the company was *The Mousetrap,* performed in 1992 at the Teatro Sala Garbo. Check *Costa Rica Today* and the *Tico Times* newspapers (both English language) for play listings and curtain times.

Movies from the United States, many of them first-run, are a big hit in San José; they are shown in the original English with Spanish subtitles. These Hollywood exports (along with excellent schooling) are a major reason why many Josefinos speak English or understand enough to be helpful. For cinema buffs who are planning an extended stay, the San José theaters won't let you down. A popular diversion for Ticos, the movie houses are clean and comfortable.

Hotel Casinos

The casinos scattered about San José in the larger hotels (see Accommodations, above) are not as high powered and mechanical as those in Las Vegas, as snobby as the ones on the French Riviera, or as down home as those in Reno and South Lake Tahoe. The dealers, after a game of roulette or craps, actually smile when they take your money. The casinos serve courtesy drinks and are open late.

The **Hotel Herradura**, on the road to the airport 20 minutes from downtown, has a popular European-style casino, as does the adjacent **Cariari Hotel and Country Club**. The Cariari is wrapped around Costa Rica's only championship golf course, an 18-hole beauty. Duffers work on their strokes during the day and hit the casino at night. Both hotels offer live music and dancing. The Cariari's **Los Mariscos Bar** soothes the high rollers with *bocas* and live music Thursday through Saturday. The casino at the downtown **Holiday Inn Aurora**, Avenida 5 at Calle 5, among the clouds on the 17th floor, is advertised as the highest casino in the world, with the best view.

The **Gran Hotel** has a small but busy casino, as does the **Corobicí Hotel** near La Sabana Park. Adjoining the Corobicí casino is their nightclub, which on weekends is crowded by 10:00 P.M. while a live, up-volume band plays for dancers and listeners. The bar at the left of the entrance is a good place to survey the scene and meet people. A doorman, who collects a small cover charge, pretends to screen the patrons while letting everyone in.

SHOPS AND SHOPPING

Costa Rica does not have an arts and crafts heritage like Guatemala or Mexico but in recent years has been working hard to establish a tradition of craftsmanship in wood, folkloric pieces, and leather. Quality leather shops, many with their own factories, have a stock of exclusive designs using fine Costa Rican leather and with prices far below those in the United States and Canada.

Downtown

Among the booths at the **Plaza de la Cultura**, outstanding work sometimes can be discovered, such as that of Poás-based Javier Aguero, who creates small, hand-painted clay wall masks using natural earth colors and feathers. They soon will be highly collectible, and prices will skyrocket.

Hammocks, a Costa Rican tradition, are of good quality (generally better than Mexican hammocks). Often made in Cartago, they are bartered and sold in the plaza; the vendors, usually relatives or friends of the hammock makers, are sharp dealers. They quote high and end low, and patience is a necessity. A hammock for two should cost about $25, though prices can drop a bit at the end of the day.

Two other good buys on the plaza are a variety of colorful, dangling earrings that you won't find north of the border, and simple women's sandals with a Guatemalan-style strap and leather soles, great for tramping about the country.

Keeping within the outdoor mode of shopping, walk to the **Mercado Central** (Central Market), carrying nothing that a pickpocket can get at, and explore the narrow walkways, crowded with shoppers purchasing fresh fish or bags of pungent oranges, onions, or garlic. Mounds of fruits and vegetables are neatly displayed, alongside taco and sandwich stalls, a small section of cut flowers, leather goods, and clothing for the family. The market is between Avenida Central and Avenida 1, west of the Central Bank, between Calles 6 and 8.

The **Mercado Nacional de Artesanía**, a large brown stucco building behind the 1909 La Soledád church, on Calle 11 and Avenida 2, was one of the first movements to organize and develop quality Costa Rican handicrafts under one roof. Don't be deterred by the mercado's shelves of tacky tourist teasers; look for featured crafts from various parts of the country, such as splendid baskets, butterflies, and flowers made from tightly woven fiber or rope by Grupo Palmital, an association of talented women from Cartago. Inlaid table bowls and silver earrings are also notable here.

There can be an understated exclusivity to shopping in San José. **Raba**, on Calle 11, not far from the Museo Nacional de Costa Rica, a half block south of Avenida Central, is a high-brow leather store dealing in finely crafted briefcases that range in price from $133 to $259, women's purses lined with soft pigskin ($52 to $185), and elaborate desk sets. Custom orders are a specialty. The family-owned business opened its doors in 1966, has been at this location for 15 years, and operates a busy workshop in the rear with living quarters upstairs. Tel: 57-2525.

The boutique **Annemarie**, another find, in the Hotel Don Carlos, between Avenidas 7 and 9 on Calle 9, is recognized city-wide as a shopping mecca. The store is crammed with more than 4,000 items, including works from 600 craftspeople who sell direct to the boutique. Veteran shoppers say the key to Annemarie is to take your time and sort through the shelf clutter. A highly polished, museum-quality toucan, carved from Costa Rican precious wood, is a good buy at $54, as are a jade necklace at $26 and hand-painted pottery at various prices. On display is a large collection of fine art by Costa Rican artists, a wall of colorful and unusual masks, and more jewelry and belts than you might ever want to see. If you don't spot an item you are looking for, an employee may be able to locate it. Tel: 21-6063.

The **Hotel Grano de Oro** gift shop (see Accommodations) has a large bin filled with the works of Peruvian watercolorists Wuayta and Luis Mendez, who use bright primary colors illustrating flower markets, street people, and vendors.

El Pueblo

Alba Art Gallery in Centro Comercial El Pueblo is bulging with Costa Rican, Central American, and some South American fine art. A major art dealer, director Mustehsan Farooqi has collected the local favorites, including works by Francisco Amighetti (oils, drawings, and woodblocks, from $400 to $4,000) and Rafael Fernandez (oils, pastels, and serigraphs ranging from $500 to $10,000). Farooqi, who is open evenings, also has a selection of pieces by Marina Silva and Fernando Carballo; Tel: 39-4324. (A second gallery is located on Calle 13 and Avenida 2, near the Museo Nacional; Tel: 21-4308.)

On the upper level of El Pueblo is **Del Río**, another upmarket leather shop, similar to Raba, which sells top-grain Costa Rican handmade purses and men's luggage. They have a local factory and eight stores in the area.

Los Yoses

In the Los Yoses neighborhood (east of downtown via Avenida Central, 200 meters west of the landmark fountain Fuente de la Hispanidad, near Spoon and the university) **Galerías Casa Alameda** will satisfy shoppers close to the cutting edge of art and fashion. Casa Alameda is a small elegant enclave of fashion, fine art, and import boutiques in a Beverly Hills mall-like setting. Take a cab to Galerías Casa Alameda; when you are ready to depart, one of the stores will call another for you. The landmark direction is "*este del automercado Los Yoses.*"

Stefanel sells Italian-chic designer clothing. **Villa del Este** displays high-quality Mexican silver serving platters and bowls, decorative Peruvian silver, fine Mexican glassware, pewter pieces, Turkish rugs, and some Italian antique furniture. The folks here are friendly and helpful. Tel: 24-1261, ext. 18.

A few steps across the interior patio, the **Galería Real** art gallery features the works of the best Costa Rican artists, sold with or without a frame; for collectors' convenience the gallery ships DHL. As an example, for Francisco Amighetti, a revered local artist who is featured in the Museo de Arte Costarricense, prices begin at $104 for a small rendering up to $1,000 and more. Speak with director María de los Angeles de Redondo. At the rear of the complex is the flashy **Vogue Boutique**, offering women's European designer fashions.

Café Ruiseñor, a sidewalk pastry shop at the entrance of Galerías Casa Alameda, is the perfect shopping-spree finisher. The owners, a young German-Dutch couple, have eight tables and a small salad bar, and serve pastries from original German-Dutch recipes for quiche, honey-nut, apple, and caramel-nut pies, chocolate truffles, and German-style cheesecake.

Moravia

North of downtown in Moravia, a suburb of San José located past the Guadalupe district on the road to San Jerónimo, 20 or so stores line **Calle Las Artesanías**, a one-way main street offering crafts of Central America. Diehard shoppers enjoy Moravia. The street has the full range of tourist trinkets, but focused browsers who dig through all that may find unusual ceramic wind chimes, gorgeous Peruvian hand-painted wall mirrors and wood carvings, and Guatemalan pot holders and decorative plates. But it's best to head straight to **Bri Bri**, an arts and crafts store centered around the work of a Costa Rican Indian tribe, to check out the dolls, the showy, one-of-a-kind, handmade jewelry, and the excellent pre-Columbian reproduction figurines, masks, and candleholders.

Two doors down, **Malety** sells genuine Costa Rican leather at competitive prices. Small wallets for women, smart men's cowhide belts, attaché cases from $59 to

$104, sports bags, and a hundred other original items are available. Custom orders are encouraged. Tel: 40-2273. (There are three other Maletys in San José. The main store is one block north and 75 meters west of the Plaza de la Cultura, adjoining Broisam parking. Tel: 21-1670; Fax: 22-7178.)

The best way to see Moravia is after 10:00 A.M. when city traffic subsides. If you must forgo Moravia, however, the same types of merchandise can be found elsewhere in San José, starting downtown with Annemarie (see above).

Escazú

Another studio working in museum-quality woodcrafts is **Artesanías Biesanz** (Biesanz Woodworks) in Escazú. Legendary Barry Biesanz, one of Central America's finest woodworkers, follows a reforestation program and is careful not to work with fresh-cut trees. In his studio/showroom, Biesanz and his hand-picked staff create small, high-quality pieces such as jewelry boxes, trays, bowls, and other colorful items whose designs depict Costa Rican folklore. Call for an appointment and directions; Tel: 28-1811, Fax: 28-6184. If you will be travelling the 20-minute trip by taxi from San José, Biesanz will give your cab driver directions.

Sarchí Oxcarts

Not in San José but nearby in the Central Valley village of Sarchí in Alajuela province is the home factory and showcase for the beloved Costa Rican *carreta* (oxcart), a symbol of the country that reflects its heritage, work ethic, and the ingenuity of its people. See the Sarchí section of the Around San José chapter for a description of the carts and information on seeing and purchasing small replicas or full-size models.

AROUND SAN JOSE

DAY TRIPS IN THE CENTRAL VALLEY

By Richard Carroll and Buddy Mays

Beyond the congested world of San José lies the larger, more beautiful world of nature. Located in the center of the country, San José is like a mother hen overlooking her brood. The city, in the aptly named Central Valley, is virtually surrounded by destinations that make for rewarding excursions—to see volcanoes, small coffee towns, and back-road farms, and to experience a life that is serene and relatively undisturbed by modern life. After a few days exploring San José, you'll find one-day trips out of the city a splendid change of pace.

It is best to be on the road early and, as suggested throughout this book and by the government, it is recommended that you do not drive yourself within the city or to the attractions surrounding San José. Blinding ground fog can sweep in at any time, the roads are narrow and poorly marked, and car accidents are numerous. Hire a car and an English-speaking driver/guide through one of the tour companies (see "Touring Costa Rica" in Useful Facts) and establish a price based on the destination or on hours out.

Experiencing nature and wildlife is the focus of the following one-day excursions from San José, which feature as centerpieces the Irazú volcano east of San José and the Poás volcano northwest of the city. South of Irazú

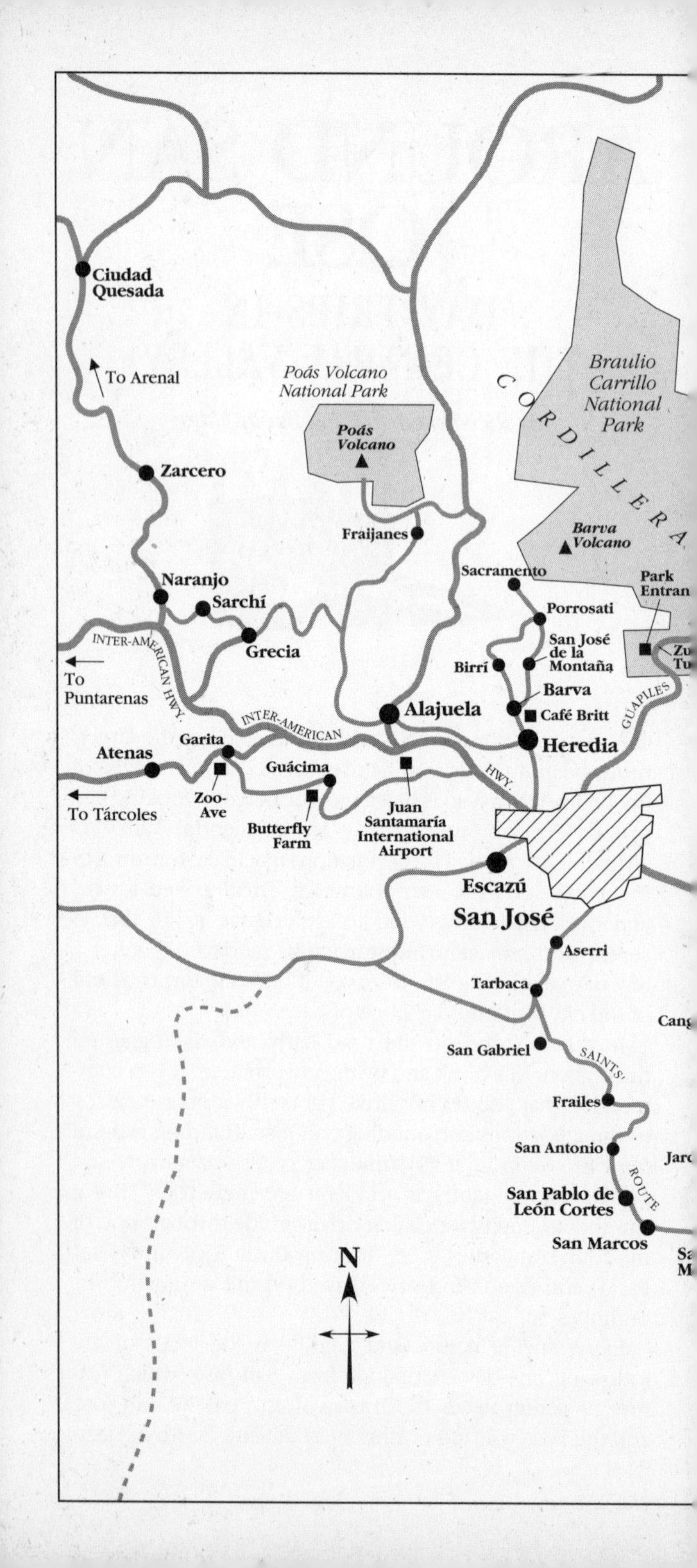

Ciudad Quesada
To Arenal
Poás Volcano National Park
Poás Volcano
Braulio Carrillo National Park
CORDILLERA
Zarcero
Fraijanes
Barva Volcano
Sacramento
Park
Naranjo
Sarchí
Porrosati
Grecia
San José de la Montaña
INTER-AMERICAN HWY.
To Puntarenas
Birrí
Barva
GUAPILES
Alajuela
Café Britt
INTER-AMERICAN
Heredia
Garita
Atenas
Guácima
HWY.
To Tárcoles
Zoo-Ave
Butterfly Farm
Juan Santamaría International Airport
Escazú
San José
Aserri
Tarbaca
San Gabriel
SAINTS'
Frailes
San Antonio
ROUTE
San Pablo de León Cortes
San Marcos
N

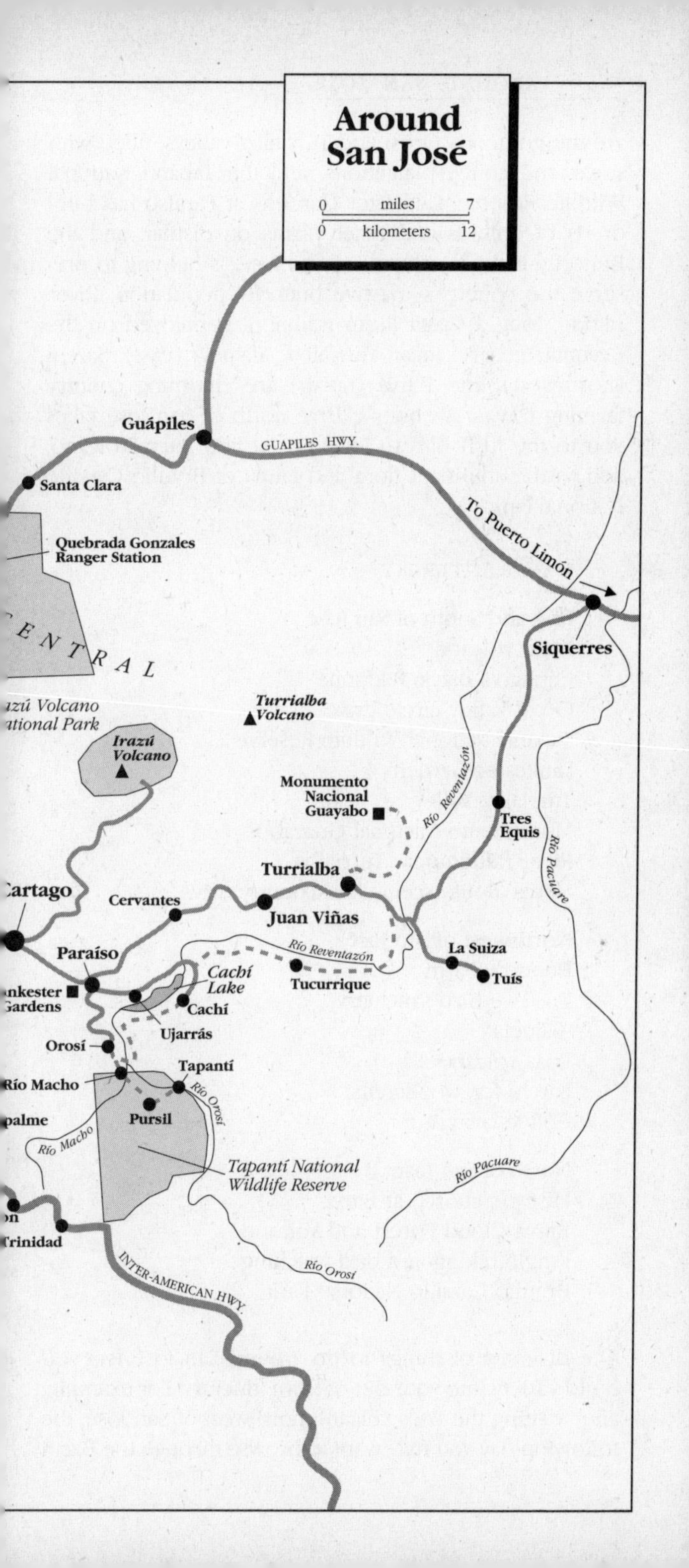

Around San José
0 miles 7
0 kilometers 12
Guápiles
GUAPILES HWY.
Santa Clara
To Puerto Limón
Quebrada Gonzales Ranger Station
ENTRAL
Siquerres
azú Volcano
ational Park
Turrialba Volcano
Irazú Volcano
Monumento Nacional Guayabo
Río Reventazón
Tres Equis
Río Pacuare
Turrialba
Cartago
Cervantes
Juan Viñas
Paraíso
Río Reventazón
La Suiza
Tuís
Cachí Lake
Tucurrique
nkester Gardens
Cachí
Ujarrás
Orosí
Tapantí
Río Macho
Río Orosí
Pursil
palme
Río Macho
Tapantí National Wildlife Reserve
Río Pacuare
on
Trinidad
Río Orosí
INTER-AMERICAN HWY.

are the gorgeous Orosí and Turrialba valleys, filled with sugar and coffee plantations, and the Tapantí National Wildlife Reserve. Lankester Gardens at Paraíso has hundreds of orchids and other plants on display, and the Butterfly Farm, northwest of San José, is helping to preserve the country's massive butterfly population. River rafting, long a Costa Rican tradition, is enjoyed on the Reventazón river near Turrialba. Alajuela (east), Sarchí (northwest), and Barva (north) are charming country farming towns. An hour's drive north of San José takes you to the lush Barva Cloud Forest and Barva volcano, and to the abundant flora and fauna of Braulio Carrillo National Park.

MAJOR INTEREST

East and South of San José
Irazú volcano
Cartago's Black Madonna
Orosí Valley circle drive
Tapantí National Wildlife Reserve
Lankester Gardens
Turrialba Valley
Monumento Nacional Guayabo
River rafting near Turrialba
Saints' Route scenic backcountry drive

Northwest of San José
Butterfly Farm
Zoo-Ave bird sanctuary
Alajuela
Poás volcano
Sarchí for woodcrafts
Coffee-farm tours

North of San José
Historic church at Barva
Barva Cloud Forest and Volcano
Jungle hiking and bird-watching
Braulio Carrillo National Park

The diversity of things to do around San José lets you build variety into your out-of-town itinerary. For example, after visiting the Poás volcano northwest of San José, the following day you may want to browse through the Barva area north of the city before setting off on another day for the Irazú volcano to the east.

The countryside surrounding San José is rugged and wild, laced with steep-sided mountain ranges covered with coffee and other crops. The roads are slow going—ideal for leisurely touring, but time-consuming. Visitors often don't allow enough time for both the city and its environs. They book a volcano tour and then cram in as many attractions as they can along the way—a quick stop at Lankester Gardens, a ten-minute look at the town of Cartago, and a glance at the Orosí Valley, vowing to return some day and "do it right."

You'll need eight hours for a visit to Irazú and the scenic Orosí Valley, plus a look at the Río Reventazón and a stop in Cartago with a walk through the basilica. Likewise, a wander through the Lankester Gardens, which features 800 species of native and hybrid orchids, and a drive in the Orosí Valley requires eight hours. So does a drive northwest to the Poás volcano and the Sarchí oxcart factory. Priorities may guide nature lovers to plan an even longer day for the journey to Braulio Carrillo National Park, with a walk in the cloud forest and the chance to spot some of the 450 species of birds found there. River rafters must dedicate an entire day to riding the rapids. A tour of the Café Britt coffee plantation takes half a day.

EAST AND SOUTH OF SAN JOSE

Begin the eight-hour excursion to Irazú Volcano National Park and the Orosí Valley by heading southeast from San José on the road to Cartago. Plan an hour and a half for the 53 km (33 miles) from the capital to the summit of Irazú volcano.

Driving into the Central Valley, you quickly find yourself in another world of greenery and coffee *fincas* (farms), in the Costa Rica of deep valleys and towering mountains. Visitors are always stunned by Costa Rica's landscape, which travel brochures do not manage to depict truly. There are vivid vistas of clouds and mountain ranges, the occasional rainbow, and a mighty sky where exotic birds can catch a thermal current and glide from the Pacific to the Caribbean within a few hours.

From Cartago the volcano is a 30-km (19-mile) drive on

a two-lane switchback road (route 8) up the side of the volcano, the only route to the summit.

Irazú Volcano

The tallest volcano in Costa Rica, Irazú towers 3,434 meters (11,260 feet), often disappearing into churning clouds, and is one in a chain of volcanoes that forms the spine of Central America. Ranked among the country's most spectacular drives, the road up to Irazú affords views in which the city of Cartago, the colonial capital until 1823, appears as a tiny checkerboard on the valley floor. The temperature drops as the car moves past grazing cattle on rolling terrain and fields of onions, potatoes, and corn growing in patches of black volcanic earth around tidy farmhouses without a blade of grass out of place.

About 5 km (3 miles) below the summit, stop at the **Linda Vista** roadside café for a cup of coffee and a view of the cloud-filled valley, where farmers carefully work the fertile soil. Thousands of business cards from all parts of the world are tacked on the café's walls—it's a temptation to add your own next to the Parisian lamp salesman's.

Photogenic scenes of tin-roofed houses, sure-footed goats, carpets of hilly green grass, and forests of fern unfold as your car or bus rolls along the road that leads directly to the park's entrance, through farming villages and over a one-lane bridge, affording vistas as dramatic as those in the Alps or the Rockies. You'll look down on drifting clouds and see men working on the side of the volcano where it would seem that only mountain sheep should tread.

The 5,705-acre **Irazú Volcano National Park**, open 8:00 A.M. to 4:00 P.M., is a stark moonscape of sheer-sided craters with a greenish-yellow lake of rainwater that gives off a pungent smell of sulphur. The active crater, an awesome giant measuring more than 488 meters (1,600 feet) across and 300 meters (980 feet) deep, is carefully monitored by scientists, who close the park and roads at a first warning of volcanic trouble. Over the years eruptions have ranged from large clouds of ash and steam to a shower of rocks and loose, cinder-like lava.

Visitors traverse a long path across the hardened lava bed—unlike at Poás volcano northwest of San José, eruptions here have been too recent for foliage to return—to viewing points overlooking the craters below. There's no hiking or bird-watching, just a dramatic, up-close look at evidence of nature's raw power.

In March 1963, the year the presidents of the Central American nations met with John F. Kennedy in San José, Mount Irazú erupted without lava flow, blanketing more than 650 square km (250 square miles) with a thick covering of ash, and causing farm losses in the millions of dollars, roofs to cave in, and the Reventazón river to flood. (The upside of the eruptions is that the ash reintroduces robust minerals to the soil, which helps plants and crops to thrive.)

On a bad day the temperature here can drop to freezing in a matter of minutes. Clouds rolling in, seemingly out of nowhere, can bring a rain squall with drops the size of a quarter. Pack a sweater or a windbreaker.

Cartago

After Irazú, your driver will probably head back down the volcano to Cartago, a religious center 23 km (14 miles) east of San José, home of the **Basílica de Nuestra Señora de los Angeles** and the famed statue of La Virgen de los Angeles, patron saint of Costa Rica, dating to 1635. On her feast day (August 2), thousands of pilgrims, some on foot, come from all parts of Central America to the revered basilica to pray in the small basement shrine to "La Negrita." The black Virgin Mary, holding the baby Jesus, is a symbol of the hope for salvation and helps devout pilgrims to cast away their ills. Hundreds of the faithful who have experienced miracle cures have left behind such testimonials as crutches, wheelchairs, and personal notes with attached photos. These relics fill an entire room.

The spacious and ornate gray-stone, white-trimmed basilica, built in 1926 to house the Black Madonna and upgraded after numerous earthquakes, has hand-painted walls and support columns, and is crowned with a clock that overlooks the town's central plaza. The basilica is the people's church, a meeting place where families linger after services and chat with one another while the children play.

Cartago, founded in 1563 by Juan Vásquez de Coronado, was the capital of Costa Rica during the Spanish colonial period. Although surrounded by a poor farming area, the city was believed to be rich by Spain's enemies, who, along with ragtag pirates, mounted frequent attacks in the 17th century. In 1823, two years after Costa Rica's independence from Spain, the capital was moved to San José. Today Cartago tends to its business of producing some of the world's richest coffee beans.

The buildings in Cartago—a small, compact city—line the streets cheek to jowl. Built around the church and plaza at an altitude of 1,462 meters (4,795 feet), Cartago has the feel of a small town where everyone definitely knows your business, right down to how you had your eggs for breakfast. Over the years, earthquakes have been humbling to the city. A massive tremor in 1910 destroyed most of the town, including the Central American Peace Palace, home of the Central American Court of Justice.

An ominous testimonial to nature's power is the **Ruinas de la Parroquia**, a sad reminder of the churches that have been built here, beginning in 1575, and knocked down by big shakes, such as those in 1841 and 1910. The block-long shard of a church, roofless and eerie, has been left to chirping birds, trees, and flowers, and an occasional skinny dog that slips through the gate and has the garden to himself.

After a stop in Cartago, follow the signs for the town of **Paraíso** for lunch at the **Continental Bar and Restaurant**. Near the city cemetery, the Continental is a clean roadside restaurant that serves a tangy ceviche cocktail, sea bass ten different ways, and homemade strawberry mousse. Paraíso, 9 km (5½ miles) southeast of Cartago and 32 km (20 miles) southeast of San José, is the gateway to the Orosí Valley.

The Orosí Valley

The **circle drive** that loops around the Orosí Valley, beginning and ending at Paraíso, runs roughly 22 km (14 miles) and is filled with photo opportunities. The valley is magical, a place to visit with paint brush and easel (or camera) and a good pair of hiking boots. The drive begins at Paraíso, where the road climbs over the Orosí mountains 2½ km (1½ miles) south to the lookout point called El Mirador de Orosí, with a spectacular view of the steep and narrow Orosí Valley, which appears more like a canyon. Fields of coffee plants cling to the mountains. The road leads south into the heart of the valley to the town of **Orosí**, a community so engulfed in greenery, lush plantations, and ancient, cloud-covered volcano peaks that it looks out of place, as if it were waiting to be gobbled up by vines.

In the center of town, the white adobe, brick-floored **Parroquia San José de Orosí**, the country's oldest (1735) church still in use, has beautifully carved benches and adjoins the **Museo Franciscano**, set in a monastery established in 1699 and overlooking a small garden courtyard. The thick-walled, fortress-like museum, remote and tranquil, displays religious statuary and holy garments, musty leather chairs, heavy furniture, and large oil portraits.

To continue the circle drive without a side trip to Tapantí National Wildelife Reserve, drive south from Orosí past the turnoff for the village of Río Macho. The main road then makes a sharp switchback as it heads north toward Cachí Lake.

TAPANTI NATIONAL WILDLIFE RESERVE

If you want to visit the Tapantí National Wildlife Reserve in the Talamanca mountain range you can take a side trip to the upper Orosí Valley, continuing from Orosí town 10 km (6 miles) southeast through the village of Río Macho and from there on an all-weather bumpy gravel road to Purisil, Tapantí, and the reserve's entrance. The 12,588-acre park is a dense evergreen forest dotted with orchids, mosses, bromeliads, vines, and large, umbrella-leafed gunnera plants that could easily shelter three people. There are marked trails, but hiking is limited. According to the rangers, much of the southern and eastern sections of the reserve are unexplored because of the thick evergreen coverage and the rough terrain. Because of the abundant rainfall, rivers, streams, and waterfalls are common. Birdwatching is popular here (211 species of birds), and regulars advise arriving early, around opening time. An exhibit room with displays of the park's flora and fauna is manned by a park ranger. Hours are 6:00 A.M. to 4:00 P.M.; closed Thursdays and Fridays. Bring rain gear or prepare to get drenched.

Driving back north toward Orosí from the Tapantí reserve, continue the Orosí Valley circle drive by crossing an old, one-lane swing bridge spanning the Macho river at Motel Río, alongside healthy-looking banana groves.

The circle-drive road travels northeast along the south side of Cachí Lake (sometimes called Charrara Lake), formed by the Cachí hydroelectric dam (Represa de Cachí) and a popular place to zip around on a windsurfer.

Less than 1 km (½ mile) northeast of the dam is the **House of the Dreamer**. Wood-carver Macedonio Quesada, in his mid-60s and known throughout the country for his "primitive" work, has created a sweet vision of life with a two-story wood-and-cane version of Robinson Crusoe's house, which overlooks a mini Grand Canyon. The workshop smells of freshly cut wood as Quesada and his assistant carve statues and designs from coffee plant roots, branches, and small logs. Quesada's work is collectible for those with a critical eye.

The road swings around the dam to the north side of the lake and heads west past the village of Ujarrás and its 17th-century church ruins, damaged by floods and earthquakes, back to the start of the circle drive at Paraíso. As you leave the region at Paraíso and drive northwest up a steep incline, the valley recedes below, and the mountains are so close that it looks as if you could pole-vault across the Orosí Valley from one peak to another.

LANKESTER GARDENS

Lankester Gardens, 1 km (½ mile) west of Paraíso, can be included in an Irazú–Cartago–Orosí Valley visit but is also offered by tour operators as an individual destination from San José (the gardens are a 15-minute drive southeast of Cartago, about 45 minutes from San José). Managed by enthusiastic folks from the University of Costa Rica, the large site is yet another Costa Rican nature preserve that appears, in this lush setting, to be a reserve within a reserve. More than 800 species of native orchids, ferns, arum plants, bromeliads, and other native forest plants line the paths. Many of the plants bloom year-round, but February through April is the peak flowering season. There are guided tours. Hours are 9:00 A.M. to 3:00 P.M.

The Turrialba Valley

The Turrialba Valley is east of Cartago and beyond Irazú, on the eastern, Caribbean side of the central mountain range. With remote hillside villages farming coffee, sugarcane, and healthy-looking crops you would love to gather up for a dinner feast, the Turrialba Valley offers untrammeled backcountry that is within easy reach of San José, as well as wild rivers that cut through the valley in ribbon-like swaths, allowing visitors to enjoy a little white water in a noncommercial, Alpine landscape.

The busy town of Turrialba, 64 km (40 miles) from San José, reached via Paraíso, then the towns of Cervantes and Juan Viñas, is dominated to the northwest by the 3,330-meter-high (10,919-foot-high) **Turrialba volcano.** (Finding your way unassisted to the volcano, a minor attraction compared to Irazú and Poás, is difficult; you'll be far better off having a tour company—see Useful Facts—arrange for a guide, who will take you on foot or on horseback, or in a four-wheel-drive vehicle.) The town's photogenic open-air market stalls, in front of the railroad station, reach a crescendo before noon.

GUAYABO NATIONAL MONUMENT

The nation's most important archaeological site is the Monumento Nacional Guayabo, a 536-acre site 19 km (11 miles) north of Turrialba on the Guayabo Settlement all-weather road. Guayabo is not Mexico's Palenque, Monte Albán, or Chichén Itzá, nor is it Guatemala's Tikal—all extensive Mayan ruins with pyramids and temples. It is more humble than those, though no less interesting. Guayabo park rangers assist in guided tours to the digs, which have uncovered petroglyphs, streets, retaining walls, and stone structures dating to 500 B.C.

Not much is known about the indigenous population of Costa Rica. When Columbus arrived, he found few people and little to exploit. Many cities had already been destroyed. It is known that there was an Olmec influence and that the people were skilled in the arts of stone carving, metal work, and, especially, pottery. For reasons that remain mysterious, the site at Guayabo was abandoned around A.D. 1400, not unlike those of the Mayas in Mexico and Guatemala.

Orchids and birds abound here, as does rain, which can exceed 300 cm (120 inches) annually. The monument is open weekends from 9:00 A.M. to 4:00 P.M. Bring rain gear and get an early start if you are driving from San José, in order to avoid the fog that sometimes rolls in.

After Guayabo, drop by the **Casa Turire** estate for a late lunch or a drink in their cozy plantation bar, and ask to see one of their rooms (see Staying in the Turrialba Valley, below). Casa Turire is 15 minutes southeast of Turrialba, past the road to La Suiza and before Tuís; for specific directions from Turrialba, Tel: 73-1111.

RIVER RAFTING IN TURRIALBA

The Turrialba Valley is also a center for river-rafting trips. Eighteen major rivers crisscross the country, pouring through tropical forests, along valley floors, and into numerous untouched nature areas best seen from a river.

The **Río Reventazón**, which rises on Irazú volcano and drains the eastern part of the Meseta Central before running down toward the Caribbean, is an excellent one-day white-water adventure for beginners (rated Class II–III, easy to moderate). Ranked among Costa Rica's most popular river-rafting trips, the float begins at Tucurrique, about 12 km (7½ miles) east of Cachí Lake and runs 19 km (12 miles) on the Reventazón to the Angostura bridge at Turrialba. In addition to white water, rafters experience the thrill of an adventure and a close-up look at tropical nature.

Experienced rafters can test their skills on the Class IV (difficult) section of the Reventazón, which has an age minimum of 14 years. The 24-km (15-mile) splasher begins at the Cachí hydroelectric powerhouse in the Orosí Valley with 5 km (3 miles) of constant rapids and a thrill a minute. The river snakes past steep mountains and a verdant landscape that can't be seen by car. The journey ends at Turrialba town.

There's also a Class IV one-day (29-km/18-mile) trip on the **Pacuare river**. The put-in is at Tres Equis, an hour's drive northeast of Turrialba on the old road to Puerto Limón on the Caribbean coast. The journey stretches northeast to Siquerres on the first protected wild and scenic river in Central and South America—another feather in Costa Rica's ecology hat. The rafts travel through a spectacular and remote tropical canyon, past numerous waterfalls and rapids. A two-day version of this trip includes hikes and a visit to an Indian village. The one-day rafting trip is $95 per person; the two-day/one-night rafting and camping trip is $260, all meals included. In the U.S., Tel: (800) 333-9361.

Costa Rica's river-rafting companies, based in San José, offer everything from one-day to multi-day trips for all skill levels. United States–based tour companies also offer seven-day/six-night white-water-rafting adventure packages that include rafting on the Reventazón and Pacuare rivers, and on the **Chirripó river**, south of Turrialba. One-day rafting trips include round-trip transportation from San José, breakfast and lunch, all equipment (including U.S. Coast Guard–approved life jackets and helmets), and experienced English-speaking white-water guides. (For names of companies and contact information, see Getting Around at the end of the chapter.)

STAYING IN THE TURRIALBA VALLEY

Cartago, a working town with an unpredictable climate and more butterflies than any other place in the world, does not offer quality lodging, mostly because of its proximity to San José. The joy of these eastern valley attractions is that after a day in nature you can return to your San José digs for a hot shower and a night out on the town. One alternative, however, is ▸ **Casa Turire**, 15 minutes southeast of Turrialba town, past the road to La Suiza and before Tuís.

Casa Turire should be thought of as a separate nature resort destination where you settle in for a few days and concentrate on the Turrialba Valley. One of the country's newest, most upscale full-destination hotel resorts, Casa Turire opened in December 1991. Your stay at the hotel—and the resort's setting—will forever be etched in your memories of Costa Rica.

The hour and a half drive from San José to Casa Turire (69 km/43 miles), past volcanoes and through valleys, ends at a plantation surrounded by thousands of acres of coffee plants, sugar cane, and macadamia nut trees. In a gorgeous backcountry setting of rain forests and the Caribbean watershed, the Reventazón river winds around Casa Turire in a lazy horseshoe, the river's murmur sweeping over the plantation house.

Owner Mario Rojas was born and raised here; his family

roots in this area reach back to his grandfather, who grew coffee and raised cattle. Mario and his wife, Michele, had been entertaining guests here for many years and knew what discriminating travellers liked, so they decided to build lodgings right on the plantation, similar to a big private home but managed as a hotel. The 27 hotel employees are like an extended family: Two of the chefs used to cook for the Rojas family, Carlos the bartender was formerly a gardener, and some of the female employees have been nursemaids for the four Rojas children.

The 16-room, Caribbean-style hotel has been created for demanding guests, with attractive public rooms designed around a cozy interior patio and accented with handmade floor tiles. Guest rooms are stylishly decorated with rare woods from the plantation and one-of-a-kind furniture pieces. Notable features are hair dryers, safety-deposit boxes, direct-dial telephones, and cable TV. Each room has a balcony that faces the river. Suite number 15, upstairs, offers grand views of distant mountains, fields of coffee plants, sugarcane, and the fast-moving river.

Guests can raft or kayak the Reventazón for a day, take a guided rain-forest and plantation tour, ride horseback, hop on a mountain bike and cycle 10 km (6 miles) to the end of the plantation, walk out the back entrance and play six holes of golf on a minicourse, take a dip in the spring fed swimming pool, relax in the game room, and bird-watch along quiet trails.

The dining room's chalkboard menu changes daily. Fresh fish, homemade ice cream, banana pie, and a Sunday buffet are specialties.

Arrangements can be made to fly into or out of Casa Turire's private airstrip. By plane, the Pacific beaches can be reached in 45 minutes, the Caribbean sand in 35 minutes. Drive to Casa Turire on your own only if you are a master navigator and have a high-tech road map; otherwise, transportation can be arranged from San José. If you insist on driving, call from Turrialba for directions; Tel: 73-1111.

The Saints' Route

Plan a full day to drive south from San José on a 108-km (67-mile) scenic circle tour known as the Saints' Route—so named because it passes through several villages named after saints, the most notable being Santa María, San Marcos, and San Pablo de León Cortés. On this romantic mountain journey you may feel as if you are lost on top of the world. You come to this sparsely populated region for the view and the serenity, and to see wonderfully appealing small mountain towns, each with a church and a soccer field. The backcountry Saints' Route winds south from Cartago on the Inter-American Highway 22 km (14 miles) upward through Empalme, turns off the Inter-American Highway to Jardín, and then continues on a 10-km (6-mile) stretch past three charming villages.

It looks as if the mountain on which it lies was scooped out and **Santa María** was dropped into place like a piece of a puzzle. Children play soccer on a dirt field, the people live in neat, yellow wooden houses trimmed in green, and there is a lush central park with flowering trees facing the Escuela República de Bolivia, a school of bashful students who don't see many foreign visitors. The road then leads west along the Panita river and over a one-lane bridge to **San Marcos**, where a cub scout meeting may be taking place in a park.

The road climbs 4 km (2½ miles) to the town of **San Pablo de León Cortés**, boxed in among steep mountains, pine trees, and coffee plantations. The temperature is lower up here. A blue, tin-roofed disco that hosts teenagers on Fridays and Saturdays exists in contrast to farmers on horseback and stores selling wood-burning cooking stoves.

Past San Pablo the route loops north through San Antonio to Frailes. A rusted road sign outside Frailes reads "San José 37 kilometers" (23 miles), but it will seem to you as if San José is on another planet. From Frailes the road takes you past San Gabriel north to Tarbaca, 18 km (11 miles) from San José, then through Aserrí to the capital. If you start out first thing in the morning, you can be back in San José by late afternoon, depending on the number of stops you make to photograph the scenery.

The landscape along the Saints' Route is the prime attraction, but be sure to pause at a village store or café for a refreshment and to meet the people. Peek inside the churches and stop along the roadway to say hello to the farmers, who like to be acknowledged.

—Richard Carroll

NORTHWEST OF SAN JOSE

On this side of the city it is wise to survey the attractions carefully and plan a route that encompasses your interests. The Poás volcano one-day excursion is the overwhelming star. With Poás as the primary destination you can easily include a visit to the Butterfly Farm, Zoo-Ave, and Grecia and Sarchí.

Poás, 58 km (36 miles) northwest of San José in Alajuela province, is a 2,707-meter-high (8,875-foot-high) basaltic volcano set in a 13,138-acre national park that wraps around the summit of the volcano like a green blanket. Poás, one of the few accessible active volcanoes on the continent, is highly regarded by naturalists throughout the world. As you head west from San José on the Inter-American Highway, the mountain suddenly pops into view in the far distance, dominant and grand. It is exciting to realize that soon you will be gazing into the crater, which at first consideration would seem accessible only to adventurous high-flying birds or helicopters.

Butterfly Farm

The Butterfly Farm, established by Joris Brinckerhoff and María Sabido, is the first of its kind in Central America. Depending upon your travel schedule, it can be included in the Poás volcano and Zoo-Ave excursions, for which see below. The farm breeds a hefty selection of the country's estimated 900 species of butterflies. Among the most colorful of all insects, butterflies and moths are also among the most numerous in species. Symbolizing beauty, freedom, inconstancy, and grace, they have appealed to the human imagination since the days of Greek mythology. The farm has a visitors' center, breeding area, and gardens where all four life cycles of the insects can be seen. Open hours are 7:00 A.M. to 4:00 P.M., and guided tours are available.

The Butterfly Farm is in a residential area some 25 km (16 miles) west of San José in La Guácima de Alajuela, near the airport and the entrance to the Campestre del Sol sports complex. The La Guácima bus departs San José from Avenida 1, between Calles 18 and 20, at about 11:00 A.M.; it will deliver you a few hundred yards from the farm. For bus information, Tel: 48-0115.

Zoo-Ave

From the Butterfly Farm it is a 9-km (5½-mile) drive west to Zoo-Ave (Zoológico de Aves), near the Inter-American Highway and La Garita de Alajuela. Costa Rican bird life has long been one of the country's major tourist attractions, with a reported 800-plus species inhabiting the country for at least part of the year. Zoo-Ave's open-air aviary, in a park setting, affords the opportunity for an up-close look at an array of the country's indigenous and sometimes elusive birds. The orange-fronted parakeet, the great curassow, the scarlet macaw, and the toucan, which when flying looks as if it has a banana in its mouth, add handsomely to a Costa Rican snapshot book.

Alajuela

Tidy Alajuela, the capital of Alajuela province, is 21 km (13 miles) northwest of San José (just off the Inter-American Highway—follow the signs) at an altitude of 958 meters (3,141 feet) in a prosperous growing region of mangoes, coffee beans, and bananas. In 1821 Alajuela was at the center of a strong movement for independence from Spain and was the capital for a brief period in the 1830s. It was the home of Juan Santamaría, a Costa Rican soldier and hero who in 1856 defended against the invasion by William Walker, an American adventurer who attempted to take over Nicaragua and who was executed in 1860. Santamaría's statue stands proudly in the city; there is also the modest Juan Santamaría Historical Museum here.

FROM ALAJUELA TO POAS

The 37-km (23-mile) road from Alajuela north to the Poás visitors' center snakes upward past small coffee *fincas,* neatly painted houses splashed with flaming bougainvillaea plants, yucca fences, and tranquil pastures filled with black-and-white holstein cows. In this area drivers will often stop to visit coffee plantations where beans are picked by hand on the steep terrain—not unlike grapes at a vineyard and with the same loving care. Farther up the road are greenhouses for ferns and flowers, an old bridge that local guides jokingly call the religious bridge (because everyone prays before crossing), and roadside stands selling giant, juicy strawberries neatly packaged in cellophane.

Poás Volcano

The smell of smoke from wood-burning stoves wafts through the air as the bus enters Poás Volcano National Park and travels past a stand of bamboo and a forest of ferns to arrive at the visitors' center. This mammoth volcano's caldera, 2 km (1 mile) in diameter, has active fumaroles up to 300 meters (984 feet) deep in the forbidding crater. Arrive early in the morning for best viewing. From a lookout point at 2,400-plus meters (over 8,000 feet) you'll peer down into the crater for (with luck) a clear view of the turquoise-tinted water before the misty clouds slide in. The eerie setting would make a splendid backdrop for a murder mystery. Nature trails have been constructed on a hard volcanic bed through the mini cloud forest; you'll make your way past mossy tree trunks and large ferns where chirping birds cut the silence and hummingbirds flirt with wildflowers.

Check with your driver to make sure he allows time for a leisurely walk along the **Escallonia Trail**. Signposted in Spanish, it runs from the crater to the visitors' center and is dotted with massive, ancient Escallonia trees. These large-leafed trees, with trunks that look like sculptures, are native to South America; their great shallow roots spread out around the base, similar to the aerial roots of banyan trees. Carry a handbook on Costa Rican birds here; it's great fun to try to identify the colorful creatures you'll see. Another hiking choice is a 40-minute uphill climb to **Laguna Botos**, an extinct crater lake at 2,750 meters (9,000 feet) elevation.

The visitors' center has photos of the last major eruption (in 1967), a busy seismograph recording activity, informative illustrations of the effects of the volcano on the environment, and nature displays. A small store sells souvenirs and books about the region. Park hours are 8:00 A.M. to 3:30 P.M. Camping is not allowed. Bring a fold-up umbrella and a windbreaker or light parka.

Twenty minutes down from the volcano, in the town of Fraijanes, is **Recreo**, a small village restaurant where you can order a hot sugarcane drink, a barley and papaya shake, or a bottle of Imperial beer (the local brew) to whet your appetite. Popular with Josefinos and truck drivers, Recreo is wildly funky but consistent and clean. The tin-roofed, screened-in room has plastic tablecloths, tree-stump stools, and a wall flowered with yellowed business cards. Stick your head in the kitchen to say hello to the cooks and see the old wood-burning red-brick stove. The country fare is *gallo pinto,* plantains, homemade coleslaw, and a healthy serving of flan.

GRECIA

A 30-minute drive southwest of Poás down a narrow, bumpy road will bring you to the small farming town of Grecia, the country's pineapple center. You may see trucks on their way to market, loaded high with fruit or with sugarcane. Grecia is very tidy and clean, and people here are relaxed and approachable; the locals like to practice their English-language skills on visitors. The **Parroquia Las Mercedes** church in Grecia, constructed in 1892 of iron and metal, is one of Costa Rica's prettiest and most photogenic houses of worship. The long, narrow, dark-red building, trimmed in white, overlooks the town park, where villagers pass the time in the evenings and chat after Mass on weekends.

Sarchí

From Grecia it is a quick hop northwest (about 8 km/5 miles) to Sarchí on a poorly marked road that oxcarts once used for the journey to Puntarenas. Shops here, along the one main road that leads into and out of town, are filled to the doorways with woodcrafts—furniture, chairs, desks, polished salad bowls, and every possible version of the brilliantly painted *carreta* (cart). Perfectly suited for the country's narrow paths and steep mountains, the colorfully painted *carretas* have been created by the Chaverri family in Sarchí since the beginning of the century. Pulled by a team of oxen, they are still sometimes used as a means of transportation and to haul coffee beans and other crops.

The Chaverri oxcarts are painted with vibrant enamel colors, using butterflies, flowers, fruits, and other traditional patterns over a bright yellow, green, or red background. The large wooden wheels carry painted geometric designs resembling a mariner's compass, and they turn with a resonant, almost musical knocking that makes each cart unique and identifiable to the farmer's family. Manuel Chaverri says, "The sound of a *carreta* echoing through the countryside at sunset was once the signal to warm up the soup, light the candles, and set the table for dinner."

Such trusty carts have travelled the roadways throughout the country since the 18th century. Painted wheels first made their appearance in the 1870s at the feast of Santiago, the patron saint of the region. For years the oxcarts, loaded down with coffee beans, made the long journeys from points in the Central Valley into San José and even the grueling nine-day trip between Cartago and the Pacific port of Puntarenas. You will occasionally see an oxcart on the road or in the fields. For the most part, however, the *carreta* has been replaced by four-wheel-drive vehicles and trucks. Today *carretas* are often displayed in all their splendor in hotel lobbies, sometimes overflowing with flowers, a proud handcarved piece of history that captures everyone's heart.

The **Chaverri family factory**, in the center of the shopping area of Sarchí's main street, has a showroom of oxcarts of various sizes that are now viewed as folkloric art and used as decorative pieces; some are even modified as home bars, serving tables, or settings for flowers. They range in price from $2.20 for a small replica to $700 for a real working oxcart, which takes a craftsperson eight days to complete. Models of all sizes can be made using nine gorgeous Costa Rican woods, among them danto, roble, corteza, chirraca, and cedar; they can be shipped worldwide (disassembled; they are easily reassembled). The Chaverris also sell small oxcarts for children, walking sticks, carved benches, end tables, and other furniture with the same bright designs. Tel. or Fax: 45-4411.

Twenty-five years ago the Chaverris had the oxcart business to themselves; now there are five additional factories in the Sarchí area.

Sarchí is about 45 minutes northwest of San José, via Alajuela. If you are on a day excursion to Alajuela by bus, you can continue to Sarchí from the Tuasa bus station, with departures from 5:00 A.M. to 7:30 P.M.

The Britt Coffee Tour

For a half-day outing at a coffee *finca* (farm) and an entertaining overview of the Costa Rican coffee industry, **Café Britt** has a nice offering. Guests are gathered up at their San José hotels by guides, and in a brightly colored Café Britt bus (which bumps along like the bus in the movie *Romancing the Stone*) are driven to the six-acre Britt Plantation 12 km (7½ miles) north of San José; the coffee plantation and factory are located between the cities of Heredia and Barva (see below). The program here usually includes lunch at the Palenque restaurant and a clever hour and a half tour of the *finca,* conducted by costumed actors who, as part of the tour, act out on a small stage the legend and history of coffee, along with a video presentation.

Coffee cultivation in Costa Rica began in 1779. It takes a new coffee plant around four years to produce; it then continues producing for 25 years or more. The finer coffee is grown at 1,220 meters (4,000 feet) or higher. Ideal growing conditions—which the Costa Rican mountains provide—require a warm and humid climate, preferably with sunlight on the plants for only part of the day. The white flowers of the coffee plant, produced in beautiful dense clusters that last only a few days, are called Costa Rican snow hereabouts. Coffee harvesting is labor-intensive. Students and anyone else available handpick the ripened red berries from October to January in the Central Valley, and from June to November in the Turrialba Valley. Coffee, which Costa Ricans proudly export to the United States, Germany, and England, is a mainstay of the country's economy.

Café Britt presents a short demonstration on how to properly taste and drink coffee—featuring a loud "boo" for anyone who reheats it. The coffees tasted are light and dark roasts, decaffeinated, and espresso. You can purchase coffee direct from Café Britt (they also have a shop at the airport) and have it shipped home if you wish. Tel: 60-2748.

Tours of other coffee *fincas* are available through many San José tour companies and most hotels.

—Richard Carroll

NORTH OF SAN JOSE

Rising to heights of more than 3,800 meters (12,500 feet) in some areas, and dominating the country's midsection from Ciudad Quesada northwest of San José to Chirripó National Park to the southeast, Costa Rica's Cordillera Central (Central Highlands) is spectacular. Rugged, pristine, and extraordinarily scenic, this symphony of towering peaks, impassable forests, jewel-like volcanic lakes, and glittering waterfalls is what tropical mountain ranges are all about.

Travelling north and east into the Cordillera from San José and the hot, congested Central Valley is like journeying to another world. Here, in the fragrant, smog-free mountain air, temperatures may be 30 degrees Fahrenheit (17 degrees Celsius) cooler than in the valley, and quite often drop to near freezing at night. Dense banks of clouds and mist often blanket the verdant landscape like smoke, reminding well-travelled visitors of a moor in Devon or Cornwall. Home to 6,000 species of plants, 200 kinds of mammals, 500 types of birds, and 200 species of reptiles, the highlands are literally a mountainous Eden.

Towns and villages here are usually compact and picturesque, but few have any attractions for visitors. The local inhabitants—most of them coffee, potato, or dairy farmers—are a friendly and amusing people whose humorous disposition is legendary (those living in more remote areas, for example, call themselves La Gente Brumoso—Foggy People—because they spend much of their day in clouds).

Barva Cloud Forest and Volcano and Braulio Carrillo National Park are both within an hour's drive north of San José, but roads into the Cordillera are twisty, steep, and unmarked, and it's easy to get turned around. You can certainly drive yourself into the mountains (car rentals are available at the San José airport and from city hotels), but it's cheaper, less troublesome, and far more fun to join an organized day tour from San José. Most hotels in the city offer a wide range of sightseeing and hiking excursions designed to fit any budget.

However you travel, allow yourself two or three days to explore this phenomenal region—particularly if you plan to hike the forest trails of Barva Cloud Forest or Braulio

Carrillo National Park. If you prefer to stay in or near the mountains instead of going back to San José to stay every night, there are several pleasant inns and inexpensive hotels in the Cordillera.

North into the Cordillera Central

For anyone unfamiliar with San José, leaving the city by private automobile is always a chore. Road signs are scarce, traffic is usually heavy, and Costa Rican drivers leave much to be desired where courtesy is concerned. If you're driving a rental car and get lost (and you probably will), ask for directions to route 9 north or the road to Heredia and Barva. Route 9 begins in downtown San José as Calle Central and leaves the city in a northeasterly direction.

The small colonial city of **Heredia** (population 30,000) lies 10 km (6 miles) due north of San José on route 9. Founded in 1706 by Spanish settlers and today the capital of a province of the same name, it is a bustling little community whose basic economy depends on coffee. The university here (Universidad Nacional Autónoma) is one of the country's best, but, like most Costa Rican agricultural towns, Heredia offers little in the way of attractions for visitors.

Four kilometers (2½ miles) north of Heredia on route 9 is the village of **Barva**, a picturesque community of about 5,100 inhabitants, the last town of any size on the road—and the gateway to Barva Cloud Forest and Volcano. If you're not in a hurry, visit the photogenic **San Bartolomé** church, built in the late 1800s. Most tours organized by San José hotels stop here for about 20 minutes.

Barva Cloud Forest and Volcano

About 1 km (½ mile) north of Barva the road splits; route 9 goes to the left, and a numberless road to San José de la Montaña bears off to the right. Both roads lead to Barva Cloud Forest and Volcano, but the left-hand fork is a bit shorter. Route 9 climbs steadily upward through coffee plantations, lightly forested pastureland, and the villages of Birrí and Porrosatí to Sacramento, a tiny mountain hamlet about 15 km (9 miles) up the mountain from

Barva. The final few kilometers of the road before reaching Sacramento are marred with potholes and studded with boulders, but the route is passable if you take it slow.

From Sacramento it's possible to drive the last 3 km (2 miles) to the official entrance of Barva Cloud Forest, but only if you have a four-wheel-drive vehicle. Most visitors, however, park on the road near the village and walk (your car won't be bothered). The elevation is about 2,100 meters (7,000 feet), so unacclimatized lowlanders should take it slow.

At the national park entrance station (Barva Cloud Forest and Volcano are part of Braulio Carrillo National Park), all visitors—whether alone or with a guided tour—must sign in with the ranger before proceeding into the park. Hikers are welcome to wander at will, but because the forest is so dense, rangers strongly recommend not leaving the main pathway to scenic Barva volcano. If you're part of an organized nature tour, however, the guide will probably take you deep into the jungle along overgrown trails that are not marked on any map.

Lush, green, and lovely, Barva Cloud Forest blankets the slopes of 2,906-meter-high (9,530-foot-high) Barva volcano like a thick, green shag carpet. The highest and coolest segment of 110,000-acre Braulio Carrillo National Park (the main part of which is covered separately, below), this magical landscape might have leaped from the pages of a Tolkien fantasy. Great banks of fog and mist roll across the corrugated landscape of moldering stumps, towering, vine-covered trees, and moor-like meadows; strangely shaped mushrooms and bright-pink volcano flowers sprout everywhere, adding blotches of color to an otherwise totally green and misty world. The volcano caldera itself, about 2 km (1¼ miles) up the main trail from the entrance station, has been dormant for thousands of years. The crater contains a small, exquisite, emerald-green lagoon, surrounded by jungle vegetation, that you can walk to. If elves, trolls, and hobbits were real, this is where they would live.

Numerous species of large and small animals reside in the dense forest, but even if you're with a guide you'll find them difficult to spot. Bird-watchers armed with binoculars or spotting scopes, however, will find themselves in heaven. Several hundred species of tropical avians reside here; among the most common are yellow-thigh finches, black-faced grosbeaks, flame-throated warblers, and golden-browed chlorophonias. Barva is also home to the legendary quetzal, or "resplendent trogan," a long-tailed, vividly colored, extremely timid fellow reputed to be one of Costa Rica's most beautiful birds.

Hiking and bird-watching in Barva can be a memorable experience. If you're without a guide and want to stay safe, however, stick to the park's maintained trails. When hiking you might also carry a raincoat, flashlight, compass, snacks, and a canteen of water, just in case.

STAYING IN THE BARVA AREA

Elegant appointments and magnificent views of the Central Valley are what guests find at ▶ **Finca Rosa Blanca** (White Rose Farm), located a few minutes from Barva village. To get there turn west onto the Santa Bárbara road at the San Bartolomé church in Barva (the road isn't marked—you'll have to ask), and drive 5 km (3 miles) to the farm's entrance driveway on the right. The turnoff is marked by a small sign.

Perched on the side of a hill overlooking a nearby coffee plantation, this eight-room, American-owned bed and breakfast is expensive but grand. Outside it resembles a petite white castle; inside, guests enjoy the ultimate in comfort. A circular, see-through glass roof over an orchid-filled, three-level living room is just the beginning of the elegance at Rosa Blanca. The master suite—complete with hand-carved circular stairways, giant shell-shaped tub, oversize shower, and private balcony with panoramic views of the Central Valley—encompasses four different chambers on two levels. Six double rooms, two in private *casitas* (small bungalows) a few yards from the main house, are huge and ultramodern. Full American breakfast is complimentary; dinner is available for an extra cost ($20 per person).

▶ **El Pórtico Hotel**, a low-slung, medium-priced mountain inn that offers visitors 13 comfortable but not fancy rooms, sits just off route 9 about halfway between Barva and the village of Sacramento. Common rooms and many guest chambers offer beautiful views of the surrounding mountains; the grounds and garden here are pleasantly landscaped with ponds, flowers, and local shrubs. Rooms contain twin beds and clean (but basic) bathrooms. El Pórtico's small indoor **restaurant** is famous throughout the Barva area for sirloin steaks cooked Costa Rican style (with rice, beans, and fried plantains).

▸ **Hotel El Cypresal**, about 5 km (3 miles) northeast of Barva on the road to San José de la Montaña, is a rustic but pleasant lodge with 24 *casitas*, sauna, volleyball court, and a large indoor restaurant. Some *casitas* have outdoor patios with lawn furniture; all have lots of room, television, fireplaces, and views of the highland landscape. Several acres of grounds are agreeably landscaped with subtropical plants and flowers, and a pair of talkative toucans hold court in an outdoor cage.

El Cypresal is owned by a Spaniard who likes to boast that his wine cellar is superb and that the restaurant's traditional Spanish paella is the best in Costa Rica. This moderately priced hotel caters to small conventions, and businesspeople and their families from San José and Alajuela are an important part of the clientele. To reach El Cypresal from Barva, take route 9 north toward Sacramento for 1 km (½ mile) to the obvious fork, bear right on the road to San José de la Montaña, then drive north 4 km (2½ miles).

Braulio Carrillo National Park

Officially established in 1978, Braulio Carrillo National Park encompasses more than 100,000 acres of mountainous, jungle-covered terrain north and east of San José. One of Central America's least explored regions, the park was created by the Costa Rican government (with assistance from several international conservation agencies) in a last-ditch effort to save the primary forest here from loggers. Except for the Barva Cloud Forest and Volcano entrance near the village of Sacramento, the only western access to this huge reserve lies 40 km (25 miles) northeast of downtown San José on the newly opened Guápiles Highway (also known as the San José–Puerto Limón highway). The highway bisects the park from southwest to northeast for about 20 km (12 miles).

Braulio Carrillo is a nature lover's utopia and one of the richest areas on earth in tropical flora and fauna. More than 450 species of birds and 135 kinds of mammals (including three species of New World monkeys), 100 different reptile species, and 6,000 kinds of plants reside in this huge, wet, dense forest. Because of the park's extraordinarily rugged terrain, however, only a few trails—none of them very long—breach its boundaries. The southernmost hiker's path, known as the **Zurquí Trail**, begins about 40 km (25 miles) northeast of San José near the entrance to the kilometer-long (half-mile-long) Zurquí highway tunnel and runs north from the Guápiles Highway. If you want to explore the trail, park at the Zurquí ranger station about 1 km (½ mile) southwest of the tunnel entrance, and pay a small entrance fee. The trail itself—steep, 2 km (1 mile) long, and usually very muddy—leaves the highway to climb into the forested hills about 100 meters (325 feet) southwest of the station.

Heading northeast from the Zurquí tunnel, the Guápiles Highway zigzags its way into the mountainous heart of Braulio Carrillo like a sun-crazed snake. On the higher ridges, waterfalls cascade from every slope; in the deep, twisting canyons below the highway, raging torrents rush downward toward the Caribbean coast. Panoramas of the all-enveloping forest and the network of deep, twisting gorges are stupendous from virtually everywhere along the highway.

The park's other principal hiking trail begins at the **Quebrada Gonzales ranger station,** 23 km (14 miles) northeast of the Zurquí tunnel. Following a cascading jungle stream through towering groves of *javillo, higueron,* and naked Indian trees (the latter are easily recognizable because of their reddish bark and sparse canopy), the path loops through the forest for about 3 km (2 miles) before returning to the ranger station.

This is snake country, so wear boots if you brought them and don't put your hands or feet in places you can't see. Costa Rica has an abundance of reptiles, both poisonous and nonpoisonous, but because of Braulio Carrillo's virtually undisturbed terrain the national park has more than its share.

One of the largest snakes you may run into here is the bushmaster, a deadly, brownish-colored pit viper that may grow as long as three meters (nine feet). Fortunately, it is a nocturnal feeder and seldom comes into contact with human beings. Another nasty fellow is the barba amarilla (mistakenly called the fer-de-lance), which grows up to 2.5 meters (eight feet) long and is usually colored gray, olive-green, or brown. Aggressive when disturbed and found throughout South and Central America, the barba amarilla is probably responsible for more deaths in the Americas than any other snake. A smaller but just as deadly jungle inhabitant is the eyelash viper, or palm viper, a green or yellow tree snake that reaches an average length of 60 cm (two feet). Finally, there is the black-ringed coral snake, a docile, two-foot-long reptile decorated with broad red and black bands. Extremely pretty and not at all aggressive, it will bite only if truly agitated.

The easiest creatures to observe in the dense forests of Braulio Carrillo, especially if you're carrying binoculars or a spotting scope, are the brightly colored tropical birds. Bird lists are sometimes available (and sometimes not) at the Zurquí and Quebrada Gonzales ranger stations; if you're interested, ask. About 450 species inhabit the rain and cloud forests here, many of them commonly spotted by hikers. Among the largest and most attractive of Braulio Carrillo's avians are wild toucans; if you haven't yet seen one, you probably will here. Distinguished by inordinately large, curved-tip bills and vivid coloration, these gorgeous 40-cm-long (16-inch-long) birds usually congregate in the tops of tall trees in groups of five or ten. Toucan flight is slow, cumbersome, and noisy because of their stubby wings (you can hear them coming long before they arrive), yet they spend much of the day flapping clumsily from tree to tree in search of food. Fruit and insect eaters, toucans flip a morsel into the air with the tip of their bills, catch it gracefully, then swallow it whole.

There are other hiking trails in Braulio Carrillo in addition to those near the Zurquí tunnel and at Quebrada Gonzales ranger station, but rangers don't broadcast their whereabouts for a very good reason. The forest here is so dense—and, to unaccompanied amateur jungle walkers at least, so dangerous—that longer, less well maintained trails should be explored only in the company of a guide. If you're interested in more difficult hikes into Braulio Carrillo, contact a local trekking company in San José (see "Touring Costa Rica" in Useful Facts); guided tours into the rain and cloud forests range from half a day to several days in length, and in cost from $45 to $300.

There are no accommodations of any kind in Braulio Carrillo National Park, so once you've completed your visit you must drive back to San José or, if your plans include the Caribbean coast, go on eastward to Puerto

Limón (107 km/66 miles from the park's eastern boundary). If you choose to head east, the Guápiles Highway leaves Braulio Carrillo near the village of Santa Clara, about 10 km (6 miles) east of the Quebrada Gonzales ranger station.

—Buddy Mays

GETTING AROUND

Though the skies are clear most mornings, San José and the Central Valley do experience a rainy season, with the heaviest rainfall from August through October. High season runs from November, the most beautiful month of the year, to June. Through the months of May, June, and July there are rain squalls and stunning cloud formations.

East of San José

The roads east of San José that lead to major attractions generally have two lanes and are well maintained but poorly marked. You will find it necessary to ask directions along the way if you are driving yourself. A car with a driver/guide is recommended for the scenic Saints' Route drive, the Tapantí National Wildlife Reserve, and the Turrialba Valley. A visit to the Irazú volcano via a tour van offers a splendid overview of the countryside.

San José's efficient ground operators pick up at the hotels in early morning in 16-seat minivans that move quickly through traffic and are manned by friendly, well-informed guides. Excursions, which adhere to a strict time schedule, range from a tour of the city, river rafting, the Irazú and Poás volcanoes, the highlands of the Cordillera Central, the Orosí and Turrialba valleys, Cartago, and combinations of the above. Individual one-day tours from San José generally range from $22 for a four-hour city tour to $85 for an 11-hour white-water-rafting trip on the Reventazón with breakfast and lunch. Southern Horizons Travel, in conjunction with Swiss Travel, sells more than 20 one-day tours.

The public buses, which are slow and often crowded, also serve the major towns and attractions. A bus schedule is available at the ICT tourism office in downtown San José, on the Plaza de la Cultura adjacent to the entrance to the Museo de Oro.

Costa Rican **river-rafting** trips can be booked directly with companies in San José or with your travel agent.

One- to seven-day trips are offered, ranging from easy family floats to raging white-water adventures. Rafters get wet, assist in paddling, enjoy lots of laughs, and see Central American nature from a dramatic perspective. The rafts usually hold six people and a guide. The equipment is excellent and the guides are knowledgeable. Pack a swimsuit or shorts, sunglasses with a strap, an old pair of sneakers, a light rain jacket, and a hat, but forget about awkward flip-flop sandals and jeans, which quickly become water-logged and unwieldy. White-water rafting on the Reventazón and Pacuare rivers is often at its best from August through the second week in November.

River-rafting companies include *Ríos Tropicales,* P.O. Box 472-1000, San José; Tel: 33-6455; Fax: 55-4354. *Costa Rica Expeditions,* P.O. Box 6941-1000, San José; Tel: 57-0766; Fax: 57-1665. *Aventuras Naturales,* P.O. Box 812-2050, San Pedro; Tel: 25-3939; Fax: 53-6934. *Southern Horizons Travel,* 6100 Simpson Avenue, North Hollywood, CA 91606; in the U.S., Tel: (800) 333-9361 or (818) 980-7011; Fax: (818) 980-6987.

Northwest of San José

The roads northwest of San José are similar to those to the east of the city—well maintained but with few road signs. A guide and car are ideal for visits to the Butterfly Farm, Zoo-Ave, and Sarchí; you can browse through the first two of these attractions at your leisure and have plenty of time for shopping in Sarchí. Poás volcano, like Irazú, is a one-day excursion, with no accommodations or camping allowed within the park. With San José so close, the lack of tourism infrastructure in many of the towns is not a problem. Alajuela is less than 3 km (2 miles) from the Juan Santamaría International Airport, and Sarchí is about an hour northwest of San José.

North of San José

For those who aren't interested in taking organized hotel tours to the Cordillera Central attractions, rental cars are available at Juan Santamaría International Airport outside San José and from most of the city's larger hotels. There is frequent bus service from San José to Heredia and to Barva, but because of the rough road buses do not run to Sacramento or to the Barva entrance to Braulio Carrillo National Park. Buses also make the run from San José to

Puerto Limón on the Guápiles Highway through Braulio Carrillo several times each day; bus drivers would probably let sightseers off in the park, but getting picked up again later in the day might be a problem.

The beginning of route 9, the road from San José to Barva Cloud Forest and Volcano, is hard to locate if you don't know your way around the city. It starts in downtown San José as Calle Central and exits the city in a northeasterly direction. If you're driving a rental car and get lost, ask anyone for directions to Heredia, Barva, or Sacramento. The Guápiles Highway from San José through the heart of Braulio Carrillo National Park to Puerto Limón starts in downtown San José as Calle 3 and also runs northeast out of the city.

If you're interested in making a guided backcountry foray—from a half-day walk to a week-long backpacking trip—into either Barva Cloud Forest or the main part of Braulio Carrillo National Park, contact a local trekking company such as Jungle Trails in San José (see "Touring Costa Rica" in Useful Facts). Accompanied by a guide/naturalist, you'll visit areas that you could never find by yourself and see far more wildlife than you thought possible. If you plan to drive yourself to the segment of Braulio Carrillo lying along the Guápiles Highway, park your vehicle at one of the ranger stations instead of leaving it along the highway. Unfortunately, the park has recently been plagued by thieves who break into unattended rental cars belonging to tourists.

For the best views of the mountains, try to get an early start. Clouds and fog usually roll into the Cordillera around 11:00 A.M., and panoramas are of course much better when the skies are clear.

The best time of year to visit Barva Cloud Forest and Volcano and the main part of Braulio Carrillo National Park is during the dry season, December through April. Rain can fall any day of the year, however, so take a raincoat no matter when you go. Hikers should also carry a compass, food, water, and a flashlight in case of an emergency.

ACCOMMODATIONS REFERENCE

Unless otherwise indicated, the rate given is the projected rate for a double room, double occupancy, and does not include tax. Price ranges span the lowest rate in the low season to the highest rate in the high season. As prices are subject to change, always double-check before booking.

East of San José

▸ **Casa Turire**. P.O. Box 303-7150, **Turrialba**. Tel: 73-1111; Fax: 73-1075. Children under 12 not accepted; no facilities for the handicapped. $85.

North of San José

▸ **Finca Rosa Blanca**. P.O. Box 41-3009, **Santa Bárbara de Heredia**. Tel: 39-9392; Fax: 39-9555. $115 for a double to $195 for the master suite.

▸ **Hotel El Cypresal. Barva.** Contact P.O. Box 7891-1000, San José. Tel: 37-4466; Fax: 21-6244. $55.

▸ **El Pórtico Hotel. Barva.** Contact P.O. Box 289-3000, Heredia. Tel: 37-6022 or 38-2930; Fax: 38-0629. $55.

THE CARIBBEAN COAST

By Buddy Mays

Buddy Mays, a freelance writer and photographer who specializes in travel and natural history, has travelled extensively in the rain forests of Central and South America. He is the author of several books, and his work has appeared in such publications as Travel & Leisure, The National Geographic, Audubon, Sunset, Forbes, *and* Travel Holiday *magazines. He is a contributor to* The Berlitz Travellers Guide to the American Southwest *and lives in Hot Springs, Arkansas. He has been a special consultant for this guidebook.*

When Christopher Columbus dropped anchor near present-day Puerto Limón on Costa Rica's Caribbean coast in 1502, he was searching for an easy trade route to the Far East. What he found instead was an unwelcoming landscape of dense tropical rain forest, a hostile Indian population, rampant disease, unpalatable water, and more biting insects and deadly snakes than a respectable European could imagine—or endure. The busy explorer and his small flotilla of ships didn't stick around for more than a few weeks.

Things have changed in 500 years, of course, and today Costa Rica's spectacular eastern coast—some 160 km (100 miles) of uninhabited, palm-lined beaches, wildlife-

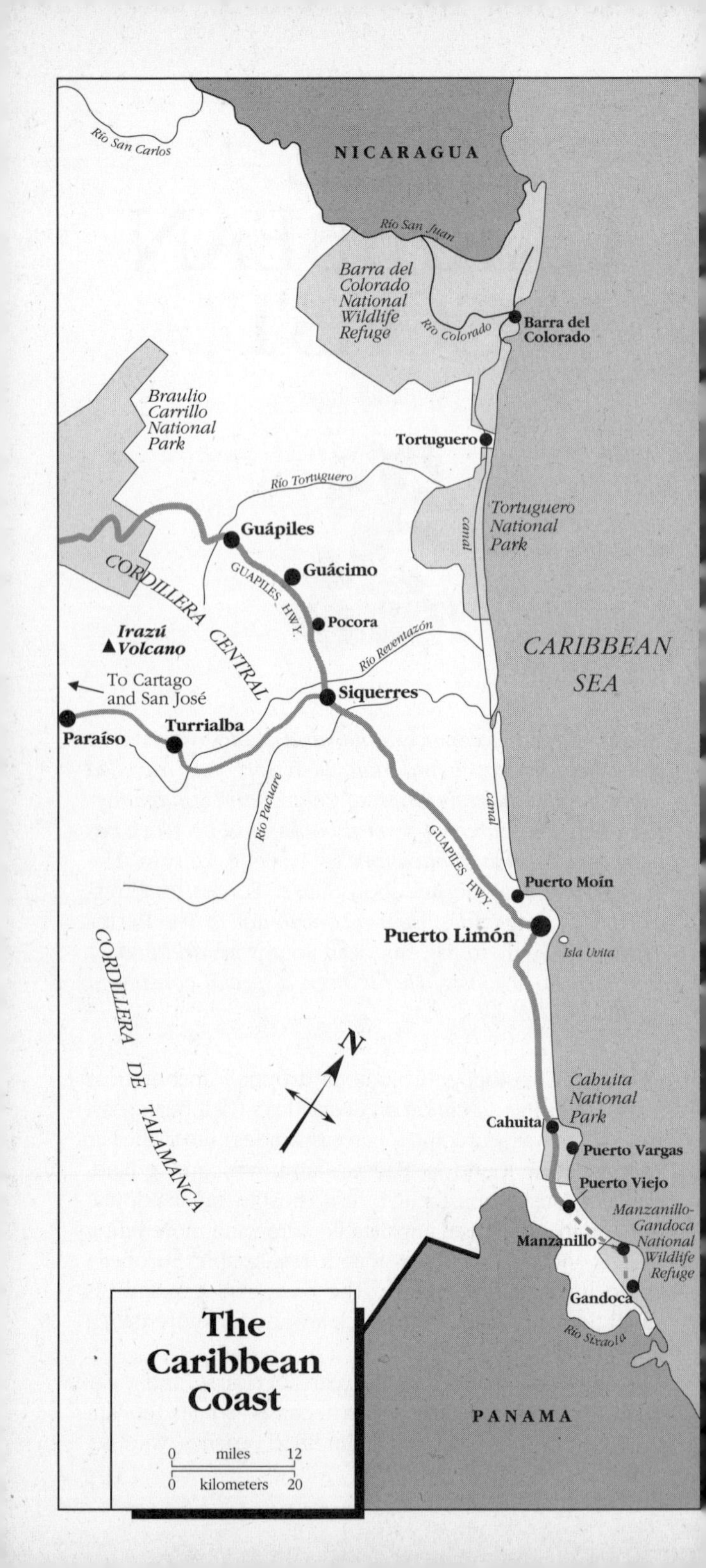

Río San Carlos
NICARAGUA
Río San Juan
Barra del Colorado National Wildlife Refuge
Río Colorado
Barra del Colorado
Braulio Carrillo National Park
Tortuguero
Río Tortuguero
Tortuguero National Park
canal
Guápiles
Guácimo
GUAPILES HWY.
CORDILLERA CENTRAL
Pocora
Irazú Volcano
Río Reventazón
CARIBBEAN SEA
To Cartago and San José
Siquerres
Turrialba
Paraíso
Río Pacuare
canal
GUAPILES HWY.
Puerto Moín
Puerto Limón
Isla Uvita
CORDILLERA DE TALAMANCA
N
Cahuita National Park
Cahuita
Puerto Vargas
Puerto Viejo
Manzanillo-Gandoca National Wildlife Refuge
Manzanillo
Gandoca
Río Sixaola
PANAMA
The Caribbean Coast
0 miles 12
0 kilometers 20

rich wetlands, and dense unexplored rain forests lying between the Nicaraguan and Panamanian borders—is one of the country's most popular resort areas. Mainly because of the remote location and a 1991 earthquake that destroyed property and roads, life here is less sophisticated than in other parts of Costa Rica and some areas are hard to reach, but the region is still gorgeous and certainly worth a visit.

You'll need several days each to explore the northern and southern segments of this verdant, low-lying coastal area, particularly if your plans include a visit to the Manzanillo-Gandoca National Wildlife Refuge near the border with Panamá or a boat trip up the Tortuguero Channels to Tortuguero village and Barra del Colorado in the north. If you plan to do both (and both areas are well worth seeing), allow at least a week. Just the drive from San José to Puerto Limón on the Guápiles Highway, for example, takes the best part of four hours, longer if you hike the trails of Braulio Carrillo National Park (see the Around San José chapter) on the way.

Even if you spend the night in Puerto Limón and get an early start, you won't reach either Puerto Viejo in the south or Tortuguero in the north until mid-morning. The distance from Puerto Limón south to Puerto Viejo, the gateway to Manzanillo-Gandoca, is only about 60 km (37 miles), but the trip takes several hours because of the rough, earthquake-damaged road. And while it is just 117 km (73 miles) from Puerto Moín (Puerto Limón's port) north to Barra del Colorado by boat via Tortuguero village, the entire trip will take a full day. Most visitors spend at least one night in Tortuguero before travelling farther north.

The terrain along the northern and southern coastlines is basically similar—a contrasting combination of jungles, swamps, and long, empty beaches—but there are significant cultural and logistical distinctions between the two areas that you might wish to ponder when planning your Caribbean-side trip.

For example, the sparsely settled north is inhabited mostly by Hispanics and native Indians, while the vast majority of residents along the more populated southern coast are Creole-speaking Rastafarians of Jamaican descent. Most visitors will notice quickly that the Rastafarians are simply not as outgoing, friendly, or as hospitable as the Ticos and Indians in the north.

Another difference in the two areas is reachability. All travel to and along the northern coast is by boat or airplane; consequently, moving about here is fairly slow, and sometimes travel arrangements are difficult to make. The area south of Puerto Limón, on the other hand, is far more accessible to visitors because of the Puerto Limón–Cahuita–Puerto Viejo highway that hugs the shoreline all the way to Panamá.

And if you're a wildlife watcher, consider this: Wild animals are undoubtedly more numerous in the north's remote, uninhabited jungles than they are in the more densely populated south, but the critters are often harder to spot because of the thick vegetation and lack of roads and hiking trails. However, if you're interested in watching giant sea turtles nest, the beaches of Tortuguero National Park offer some of the best turtle-gawking opportunities in the world. And always remember that, whatever direction you choose, you'll have to deal with gnats, mosquitoes, snakes, spiders, and the potential for getting lost in the jungle. Carry plenty of insect repellent, watch where you put your hands and feet, and *never* go off into the rain forest by yourself.

MAJOR INTEREST

The Southern Coast
Banana plantations
Puerto Limón
Beaches
Cahuita National Park's coral reef
Snorkeling and surfing
Manzanillo-Gandoca National Wildlife Refuge

The Northern Coast
Tropical lowland rain forest
Tortuguero Channels
Wildlife-watching
Tortuguero National Park
Turtle nesting and hatching
Barra del Colorado National Wildlife Refuge
Tarpon fishing at Barra del Colorado

THE SOUTHERN COAST

Puerto Limón and the southern coastal area are populated mainly by Rastafarians, most of them descendants of Jamaican banana-plantation workers who arrived in the late 1800s. The principal language spoken here is not Spanish but Creole, a rapid and virtually indecipherable (to nonspeakers, at least) mixture of Spanish and English; the music you'll hear most often in bars, restaurants, and private homes is reggae and calypso.

Tropical lowland rain forests along the Caribbean are fun to explore, but there are things here—biting and stinging insects, poisonous reptiles, venomous spiders, and prickly plants—that can hurt you. Probably the least aggravating of these are *purrujas,* tiny, almost invisible gnats that inhabit the wetlands adjacent to the coast. The most dangerous jungle resident is the barba amarillo, or *terciopelo,* a large, aggressive snake whose bite can kill an average-size human being in minutes. Wherever you meander in the rain forest, wear boots if you have them (lodges often have rubber boots they will loan to guests), and step carefully. Avoid putting your fingers, hands, or feet in places you can't see, and if you leave your hotel room at night, even when you plan to walk just a few yards to the dining room or lounge, carry a flashlight. Above all, don't harass or attempt to pick up a creature with which you are unfamiliar.

Insect repellent is another necessity here, at least on hiking trips into the wetlands and rain forest. According to government statistics, several thousand cases of malaria were reported along the Caribbean coast in 1992; although 99 percent of the victims were banana-plantation workers, sooner or later, say government officials, the disease will find its way into the tourist regions (you might consider starting a malaria prophylactic program before you go into the area).

EAST TO PUERTO LIMON ON THE GUAPILES HIGHWAY

The Guápiles Highway from San José to Puerto Limón exits Braulio Carrillo National Park a few kilometers northeast of the Quebrada Gonzales ranger station and runs east. Near the town of Guácimo it turns southeast and leaves the mountains to enter the lower, warmer climes of the Caribbean tropical lowlands. Here, large segments of rain forest adjacent to the highway have been chopped and burned back to make room for macadamia nut farms, ornamental plant nurseries, cattle ranches, and banana plantations. Because of this forest destruction, the area is far less scenic than the mountainous terrain of Braulio Carrillo to the west, but where farmers and ranchers are concerned it is certainly more livable.

For travellers, little of interest lies along this stretch of lowland road. If it's near lunchtime when you drop out of the mountains, stop at the **Restaurant Las Palmas**, about 9 km (5½ miles) southeast of Guácimo near the village of Pocora. Located on the Río Dos Novillos (Two Calves River) and shaded by a grove of huge rain-forest trees, this pleasant roadside café serves passable hamburgers and magnificent chicken sandwiches. A shallow pool on the adjacent Río Dos Novillos has been stocked by Las Palmas's owner with pan-size *tilapias* (a tasty species of African bass), and for about $3.50 luncheon guests can catch their own entrée and have it cooked to order by the chef. Part of the operation here is ▶ **Cabinas Las Palmas**, which consists of a few clean but small cabins in the back that are rented to travellers on a daily or weekly basis.

You may notice large clouds of smoke in the air as you head southeast from Las Palmas toward Puerto Limón and the Caribbean; they are caused by local farmers burning back segments of rain forest to make way for banana plantations. Bananas aren't indigenous to Costa Rica, of course (or, for that matter, to Central or South America—scientists say they originated in Asia), but were probably brought to the New World by Spaniards in the late 15th century.

Bananas are of great importance to most Costa Ricans, not only as food but also because they are the country's number-one export crop (most go to the United States and Europe). You'll see these tasty yellow fruits growing virtually everywhere in the tropical lowlands—from residential back yards to the 5,000-acre plantations bisected by the Guápiles Highway on its way to Puerto Limón. Banana plants aren't particularly difficult to cultivate, but they do require an enormous amount of time and patience. After producing only a single *racimo* (bunch), each banana shoot, or "branch," dies. It is immediately replaced by a new shoot from the same trunk, but a full nine months elapses from the start of the bud to harvest. And, like most fruits, bananas are highly susceptible to insects. To help keep fruit flies at a distance, *racimos* are often encased in blue, insecticide-impregnated plastic bags—a costly and time-consuming process on a large plantation.

The final 35 km (22 miles) of pavement on the Guápiles Highway northwest of Puerto Limón were badly damaged by the 1991 earthquake, which hit 7.6 on the Richter scale, killed 45 people, and destroyed numerous towns and villages throughout the area. The road itself is rough and hazardous in sections, and you'll notice that highway bridges seem to be raised seven or eight inches above the pavement. In reality, it was the road that dropped during the earthquake, while the bridges, supported by solid concrete abutments, stayed where they were.

Puerto Limón

The coastal city of Puerto Limón (population 70,000), capital of the province of Limón, is not what anyone would call picturesque. Many of the city's buildings were destroyed or badly damaged in the 1991 earthquake (most noticeably the Hotel Las Holas, now little more than a pile of steel rods and broken concrete), and, like most tropical ports, the place is run-down and a bit seedy. Puerto Limón's principal claim to fame is the fact that Christopher Columbus, on his fourth voyage to the New World in 1502, spent 17 days in the area repairing his tiny flotilla of storm-battered ships. The city celebrates the event with a five-day carnival called El Día de la Raza (The Day of the People), held in October. The event draws thousands of Ticos and tourists, and features parades, bullfights, art exhibits, food fairs, and lots of live music. If you plan to attend, take your earplugs and make hotel reservations as early as possible.

Puerto Limón's population is a colorful ethnic mixture of Hispanic, black, Chinese, and native Indian. Most residents here are friendly and helpful, but if your wallet is fat or you're wearing lots of jewelry it's not a good idea to wander around the city at night. Local police say the downtown area turns mean when the sun goes down, and more than one tourist out on the town has been unceremoniously relieved of his or her belongings by local hoodlums.

The downtown section of Puerto Limón lies adjacent to the harbor and is concentrated in a few square blocks. If you like to walk, take a stroll to palm-shaded **Parque Vargas** (the main city park) along the old seawall, which was constructed more than a hundred years ago to protect the town from winds and high waves. The island you'll see lying about a half mile offshore just opposite Parque Vargas is **Isla Uvita**, where Columbus landed in 1502 to repair his ships. (Tours to the island aren't offered by local guides because there's simply nothing to see.) Two blocks directly inland from Parque Vargas is **Market Square**, a noisy, colorful collection of stalls and vendors where you can buy anything from freshly caught fish to local arts and crafts.

About 5 km (3 miles) northwest of downtown Puerto Limón on Calle Portete (the Portete road, the main street skirting the harbor and the Caribbean), there's a good place for a picnic—**Parque Cariari**, a quiet, shaded city park encompassing several acres on a bluff overlooking the sea. Facilities here are rustic, but the park has some tables, rest rooms, and great views of the Caribbean. Several dozen varieties of tropical birds and a small family of three-toed sloths call the park home, so take a camera. A block southeast of Parque Cariari is **Playa Bonita**, Puerto Limón's main municipal beach. **Kimbamba**, a noisy but well-managed beach bar and café that sits just a few yards from the water, serves drinks and meals outdoors.

STAYING IN PUERTO LIMON

Seated atop a steep bluff overlooking the Caribbean, 3 km (2 miles) northwest of downtown Puerto Limón on Calle Portete, the ► **Maribu Caribe Hotel** is probably the city's most comfortable accommodation. Each of the 52 guest rooms here has a queen-size bed, a telephone, and air-conditioning, and the hotel also maintains a pool and a top-notch open-air **restaurant**. There's no direct access from the Maribu Caribe to the beach (hotel management suggests that guests use Playa Bonita, the municipal beach, a ten-minute walk to the northwest on Calle Portete), but the restaurant and most rooms have nice views of the Caribbean.

One km (½ mile) northwest of the Maribu Caribe on Calle Portete is the ▶ **Matama Hotel**, the only other fairly decent hostelry in Puerto Limón. Heavily shaded by large jungle trees, the grounds here are nicely manicured and pleasantly cool; the management operates a small zoo on the property, which houses a pair of jaguars and several species of jungle birds. Guest rooms, some with small private gardens, are clean, but tiny and somber; the restaurant is adequate, but you're better off dining at the Maribu Caribe. Matama has no direct beach access, although Playa Bonita, the main public beach, is just across Calle Portete.

South of Puerto Limón

Only one highway leads south out of Puerto Limón toward Cahuita, Puerto Viejo, and the border with Panamá, an unmarked, straight-as-an-arrow ribbon of narrow asphalt that begins downtown near the harbor and then sticks to the Caribbean coast like glue. The road has no official name or number, but if you get lost leaving Puerto Limón, just ask for directions to Cahuita.

The drive south along this beach-hugging highway is unforgettable. As with the Guápiles Highway west of Puerto Limón, the pavement here, damaged in the 1991 earthquake, is badly rutted in spots, but with the Caribbean and its pure-white beach on the left, and a dense tropical forest on the right, the landscape is gloriously scenic. You'll see a few signs of human habitation along the highway—mostly hut-filled clearings where laundry hangs from makeshift clotheslines and half-naked children frolic with dogs or goats in dirt yards—but mainly the terrain consists of beach and forest with little in between.

Travellers are welcome to stop and swim, sunbathe, and beachcomb anywhere they can reach the water along the 47-km (29-mile) stretch between Puerto Limón and the village of Cahuita. Overnight camping isn't recommended, however. Large waves—not of the tsunami variety, but powerful enough to wash away a tent—occasionally roll onto the beach from the open Caribbean to the east. The area is also remote and lonely; it rarely happens, but beach campers have been roughed up and robbed in the past.

Thirty-two kilometers (20 miles) south of Puerto Limón the highway bisects a large banana plantation that was the epicenter of the 1991 earthquake. From this point south, drive slowly and keep an eye out for drop-offs and deep potholes; this segment of road was totally destroyed by the quake and has been only temporarily repaired. Bridges along this route are one lane, so be prepared to yield the right-of-way when necessary.

STAYING ALONG THE CARIBBEAN SOUTH OF PUERTO LIMON

A small sign announces the turnoff to ▶ **Aviary of the Caribbean**, or Aviarios del Caribe, as it's called in Spanish, located 30 km (19 miles) south of Puerto Limón. Nestled between the highway and the sea in a privately owned and operated wildlife sanctuary, this charming five-room bed and breakfast will appeal to anyone who loves nature and the outdoors.

The two-story compound sits in a tree-dotted clearing overlooking a network of freshwater canals and lagoons. Ground-floor guest rooms are airy and spacious, with queen- or king-size beds, cooling fans, and private baths. Upstairs there's an open-air dining room and a large common area with a library, and a television and video room.

If you're a serious animal-watcher you'll be encouraged by the owners to spend at least a couple of hours on the nature trails that wander through a 220-acre swatch of primary rain forest adjacent to the lodge. Here you're likely to see lots of rain-forest birds, as well as monkeys, sloths, river otters, and Central American caiman. The Aviary itself keeps several pets, including a clan of toucans, a three-toed sloth, and several species of reptiles. If you want to explore the nearby lagoons and canals without getting your feet wet you can rent canoes, with or without guides, for a modest fee. A full breakfast is included in the room price; dinner is available upon request (there's no official restaurant).

Larger but more rustic is the ▶ **Hotel El Atlántida**, a 14-room lodge located a hundred meters from the Caribbean on the northern outskirts of Cahuita. The rutty, 3-km (2-mile) access road turns east toward the sea off the main highway about 40 km (25 miles) south of Puerto Limón.

Atlántida's guest rooms, all with verandahs, cooling fans, comfortable double beds, and private bathrooms, are small, clean, and basic. The staff doesn't speak much English, but they'll do their best to see you have everything you need. The lodge has no restaurant, but there are several small eateries within walking distance, all of which serve seafood and traditional Costa Rican meals.

Cahuita Village

Inhabited mainly by Rastafarians whose Jamaican ancestors worked on the banana plantations in the area, the beach village of Cahuita, 47 km (29 miles) south of Puerto Limón, depends heavily upon tourism for its livelihood. Among the town's touristic offerings are excellent surfing and snorkeling conditions, a glass-bottomed-boat concession, and a pleasant, if cluttered (with drift logs) beach. Cahuita is also within walking distance of the northern end of Cahuita National Park.

For several reasons, Cahuita isn't really a place in which most sophisticated travellers will want to spend much time. Except for the national park (access is much easier farther to the south), the beach, and a boat ride over a nearby coral reef, there is little to see or do. Restaurants and gift shops here are overpriced, and the town's streets and few hotels are noisy, filled with boisterous teenage surfers whose paramount aim in life is to find the largest wave and the nearest party. If you wish to spend an hour or two poking around, however, park your car (and lock it), then rent a bicycle from the small bike-rental shop at the south end of town. You can also rent snorkeling equipment here.

Cahuita National Park

The main entrance to Cahuita National Park (officially known as the Puerto Vargas entrance) is on the east side of the main highway about 4 km (2½ miles) south of Cahuita, at an easy-to-find junction marked by a large roadside sign. Follow this access road about 1 km (½ mile) to the park boundary. If there's a ranger on duty at the entrance station, you'll have to pay a small entrance fee; if not, drive on through and don't worry about it.

Cahuita National Park, encompassing about 2,700 acres, was established by the Costa Rican government to protect a 600-acre **coral reef** from pollution created by nearby banana plantations. It also safeguards a dense segment of primary seaside rain forest that was somehow overlooked by loggers earlier in this century. The park's wide, white beaches are far cleaner and prettier than those found near Cahuita village to the north, and the snorkeling over **Carrecife de Cahuita** (Cahuita Reef) is superb. Home to lobsters, green sea turtles, 35 varieties of coral, and more than 120 species of fish, the reef extends from the shoreline to about 450 meters (1,500 feet) offshore. A 7-km (4-mile) nature trail meanders between the beach and the forest edge, and can be joined at any of 40 access points from the main park road. Picnic sites, rest rooms, and a small camping area are also available.

The never-logged and seldom-disturbed Cahuita **rain forest** contains an abundance of wildlife, including anteaters, sloths, raccoons, small cats, snakes, and, of course, birds by the hundreds. The most obvious and obnoxious residents here, however, are howler monkeys. Swinging through the trees overhead, troops of these furry acrobats often follow motorists or hikers along the 6-km (3½-mile) road that winds through the park. The inharmonious jungle symphony they create (one scientist described it as a "roll of distant thunder preceded by the death-agonies of half a dozen tortured jaguars") can be terrifying to the uninitiated.

Howlers range throughout Central and South America, and are Costa Rica's most common variety of monkey. Varying in color from pure black to burnished gold and sporting a long, protruding dog-like face, they are nearly always found in forested areas, usually in the tallest trees. Two other species of monkeys—a small, shy breed called spider monkeys, and cute, mischievous, baby-faced primates known as white-throated capuchins (locally but mistakenly called white-faced monkeys)—also reside in Cahuita.

Puerto Viejo

Puerto Viejo lies 6 km (3½ miles) south of the Cahuita National Park turnoff on the main highway. If you're driving a rental car you'll have to stop at a small police post north of the village; just leave your car on the road, walk inside, and tell the on-duty officer that you're a tourist. The post is located here to help stop the smuggling of electronic goods, cigarettes, and liquor from nearby Panamá.

Strung out north to south along the main road, Puerto Viejo, like Cahuita village to the north, depends heavily upon sun-seekers and nature-lovers for its survival. Many of the town's permanent residents are Rastafarian farmers or fishermen who double as guides or tour leaders. Two Indian tribes—the Bribrí and the Cabecar—also reside in the area, but tribe members usually stay close to their official rain-forest reservations near the Panamá border.

Along Puerto Viejo's main street you'll find a few souvenir shops, several small cafés, and a gasoline station, but not much else. **Stanford's Caribe Restaurant**, specializing in fresh lobster and located on the left as you travel south, is probably the best restaurant in town. Their food is plentiful, the drinks are cold, and the second-floor, open-air dining room has a nice view of the nearby Caribbean coastline. If you're looking for a party, head for the **disco** on Stanford's ground floor, open Thursday, Friday, and Saturday nights.

The village is so small that you can easily walk to whatever destination you choose, but most area lodges rent bicycles if you'd rather ride than ramble. If you do rent a bike, be aware that the river bridges on either end of town are narrow and without protective guard rails. More than one cyclist has gone to the Puerto Limón hospital with broken limbs after losing his or her balance on the bridge and falling into the river below.

The Puerto Viejo area is known best for its snorkeling, surfing, and sportfishing. Snorkeling equipment may be rented from most hotels in the area, and surfboards can often be leased or purchased from locals (many surfers spend a few weeks at the beach here, then sell their boards to residents for money to get home). If you'd like to go ocean fishing, ask someone at Stanford's Caribe Restaurant to recommend a captain. The most popular sunbathing **beach** in town is a long, beautiful stretch of black sand a ten-minute stroll to the north. The black sand is from volcanic activity in the area several thousand years ago.

STAYING IN PUERTO VIEJO

▸ **Pizote Lodge**, offering individual bungalows and barracks-like motel rooms, sits in a large, shady glade 300 meters inland from the beach and about 1 km (½ mile) north of Puerto Viejo on the main road to Cahuita. If you have a choice, ask for a bungalow: Private baths, quiet verandahs with easy chairs, and lots of space make them far more peaceful and private (though more expensive) than the basic motel rooms.

The lodge has neither air-conditioning nor hot water, but fans keep the rooms fairly cool, and most guests don't mind cold showers after a day in the hot, humid climate. Pizote's congenial, open-air **restaurant** specializes in fresh fish and regional cuisine, and offers live entertainment in the form of a house-trained toucan that enjoys free run of the facilities and has been known to snitch a morsel or two from diners' plates. If you need a public telephone, the adjacent Pizote bar has one of only three in the Puerto Viejo area.

Five kilometers (3 miles) south of Puerto Viejo on the main road, the ▸ **Hotel Punta Cocles** is a low-slung jungle compound spread over several partially cleared acres of lightly sloping hillside. With its spacious, air-conditioned rooms, top-notch restaurant, pool, and manicured grounds, the hotel is like a port in a storm for travellers who have been driving, diving, or walking all day.

The 19 moderately priced cottages at the Punta Cocles are connected to each other (and to the restaurant-pool area) by thatch-covered walkways. Vividly colored tropical birds are everywhere, and other critters—snakes, huge spiders, and poisonous frogs—call the grounds home as well. The animals usually keep their distance and expect you to do the same, but carry a flashlight if you leave your room at night. The **restaurant** here, adjacent to the pool and common patio, serves fresh fish and traditional Costa Rican foods such as *gallo pinto* (black beans and rice) and *casados* (combination plates of rice, beans, vegetables, and meat). The Caribbean is within easy walking distance, about 1 km (½ mile) to the east along a gorgeous nature trail that begins near the reception area. You can also rent bicycles, horses, kayaks, snorkeling equipment, and binoculars on the property.

Punta Uva and Manzanillo-Gandoca National Wildlife Refuge

The rough, narrow dirt track that heads south from Puerto Viejo to the hamlets of Punta Uva and Manzanillo and the Manzanillo-Gandoca National Wildlife Refuge hugs the coast like a lover. The road is passable but in such bad shape from earthquake damage that motorists who drive at speeds in excess of 30 km/hour (19 mph) stand a good chance of blowing a tire or ruining a shock absorber.

The village of **Punta Uva**, 7 km (4 miles) south of Puerto Viejo, is little more than a scanty accumulation of huts and houses along the road. The long, clean, palm-lined **beaches** here, however, are probably the prettiest on the Costa Rican Caribbean. Beach access is via any of the sandy, unmarked roads that turn left off the main drag. At Punta Uva itself (a rocky point jutting into the sea near the village), the **snorkeling** over a small coral reef is superb.

The refuge sits at the very end of the road, 14 km (9 miles) directly south of Puerto Viejo and less than 10 km (6 miles) from the Panamá border. To reach the main entrance, keep going south along the beach through the fishing village of Manzanillo, until the road ends at a small parking area. The local fisherman who lives in the adjacent shack speaks English and will make sure no one bothers your car. The main beach trail into the reserve begins at the parking area and is easy to spot.

The 24,000-acre Manzanillo-Gandoca reserve protects about 10 km (6 miles) of sea turtle nesting beach, plus a substantial segment of primary rain forest and several thousand acres of freshwater swamp and marsh. Access is by trail only; about 15 km (9 miles) of unmaintained hiking paths meander along the beach and through the forest. It's probably a good idea to stick to the trails along the beach if you don't have rubber boots and aren't accompanied by a guide. The inland pathways that skirt the edge of Gandoca lagoon and spiderweb through the forest are often extremely muddy: Mosquitoes, crocodiles, and venomous snakes are sometimes a threat in the dense cover as well.

Except for the palm trees, this rugged coast—indented by rocky coves and dotted with tiny islands—often reminds visitors of the scenic shoreline of Maine. The rain forest here has sizable populations of tapirs, monkeys, crocodiles, sloths, and ocelots, while the marshes and mangrove swamps are home to tarpon, West Indian manatees, and caiman. And, like most wildlife reserves and national parks in Costa Rica, Manzanillo-Gandoca is a bird-watcher's paradise, home to more than 350 species. Especially common here are parrots, five different species of which reside in the refuge. Sociable and easy to observe, they often gather in larger trees along the forest trails, cackling like crazy to themselves or at anything that moves in the forest below.

There are no tourist facilities at Manzanillo-Gandoca yet, and good maps of the reserve simply don't exist. If you want to hire a guide, ask at Stanford's Caribe Restaurant in Puerto Viejo, or arrange a tour in advance through a San José travel agent or tour operator (see "Touring Costa Rica" in Useful Facts). Locals suggest that hikers carry fresh water, lunch, insect repellent, a compass, and a raincoat.

THE NORTHERN COAST

The northern half of Costa Rica's beautiful Caribbean coast—from Puerto Limón northwest to the Nicaraguan border—is undeniably one of the country's wildest and least explored regions. Covered by a virtually impenetrable carpet of verdant jungle known officially as "lowland tropical rain forest," the land here is flat, hot, humid, and, not surprisingly, abundant in wildlife. Sloths, tapirs, and jaguars are far more common than cattle, and the forest is so thick (and dangerous) that even local guides will enter only on well-maintained trails. Human habitation is rare; fewer than a dozen tiny villages exist along the entire 140-km (87-mile) stretch of coast from Puerto Limón to Nicaragua.

The few hotels and lodges in this isolated segment of Costa Rica are, for the most part, pleasant and well kept. Tourist accommodations here depend solely upon foreign visitors for their livelihood, and they do their best to make guests happy and content. Most are without hot water, telephones, or television sets, but their rooms are clean, their restaurant offerings are tasty and plentiful, and staff members are helpful and friendly.

Some roads have been cut through the forest, of course, but travel in this huge expanse of jungle wilderness is most often by boat, along a network of natural and man-made coastal waterways known as the Tortuguero Channels. Lying inland less than a mile, and running parallel to the sea, these liquid highways—comprising rivers, lagoons, and hand-dug canals that connect the natural waterways—offer the only viable access for visitors wishing to explore this undisturbed landscape.

At one time the Costa Rican government operated a twice-weekly boat service from Puerto Moín (Puerto Limón's deep-water port) to the Nicaraguan border via the Tortuguero Channels. That service was canceled in 1992, however, shortly after an earthquake changed the shape and depth of the channels, making it impossible for larger government boats to negotiate the waterways. Today travellers wishing to visit the northern Caribbean coast can hire—and pay for—a private boat and guide in Puerto Moín (or let a San José tour planner do it for them; see Useful Facts) to ferry them up the channels; or they can stay at a Caribbean coast lodge that provides its own free transportation.

If your time is limited, you can take a boat from Puerto Moín to the village of Tortuguero, spend as little as one night at a Tortuguero lodge (some lodges here require a two-night minimum stay), then return to Puerto Moín by boat the following day. If you have several days, consider spending two or three nights in Tortuguero, then going on north to the village of Barra del Colorado for a fabulous day or two of tarpon or snook fishing. From Barra del Colorado you can then fly back to San José via Travelair (the in-country Costa Rican airline) at a surprisingly low cost. It's possible to reverse this route by flying into Barra del Colorado first, but arranging boat transportation south back to Tortuguero and Puerto Moín might be difficult (all tourist boats are based in Puerto Moín).

Puerto Moín

If you're driving east from San José to Puerto Limón on the Guápiles Highway, you will find Puerto Moín on the left about 6 km (3½ miles) north of Puerto Limón. Watch for the concentration of cargo ships and huge loading cranes, visible from the highway; the access road, on the left, is marked by signs. If you've come from the southern Caribbean coast and driven through Puerto Limón itself, you will come to Puerto Moín at the north end of Calle Portete (the road along the beach).

Puerto Moín, the only deep-harbor port on Costa Rica's Caribbean side, ranks just below Puntarenas, on the Pacific, in export and import capacity. Among the most important goods arriving and leaving here are oil, coffee, bananas, beef, and sugar. The port holds little of interest for visitors, but it's the only place on the coast where you can catch a boat north through the Tortuguero Channels to Tortuguero National Park, Tortuguero village, and Barra del Colorado. The private dock from which all tourist boats leave is about ½ km (¼ mile) north of the commercial port itself. There aren't any signs, so if you get lost, look for a gate with uniformed guards in attendance, or just ask: "*Donde están los botes que van a Tortuguero?*" (Where are the boats that go to Tortuguero?).

Tortuguero Channels

The 77-km (48-mile) boat ride north via the Tortuguero Channels from Puerto Moín to Tortuguero village is undoubtedly one of the most memorable sojourns a visitor to Costa Rica can make. Indeed, if there is an *African Queen* experience to be had in Costa Rica, it is offered by the Tortuguero Channels.

Varying in width from 30 to 300 feet, in depth from 2 to 15 feet, and running parallel to the Caribbean less than a kilometer (½ mile) inland, this network of waterways slithers through the solid and solitary green bastion of jungle like a great brown serpent. In many places huge rafts of bright-green water hyacinths threaten to choke off the waterway completely; in others, the water is so shallow that boats often momentarily run aground. Giant blue morpho butterflies dance, dart, and hover over the lagoons like azure pie plates on elastic strings, while high above in the leggy, old-growth giants that line the banks parrots, toucans, and a hundred other species of brightly colored birds chatter constantly.

Most of the privately owned boats that make the long run north are of the "throw-it-together-and-hope-it-floats" variety. Fifteen to 20 feet in length, constructed of thin plywood or fiberglass and powered by noisy outboard motors (if the wind is wrong the smell of gasoline can be overpowering), they usually have homemade wooden seats and a canvas top. Be prepared for a long ride during which you can't move around in the boat. You might spend ten minutes here or there watching a three-toed sloth or a troop of howler monkeys, but most boat drivers make only one or two stops on the entire trip.

Perhaps the most utilized stopover is at **Bare y Cabinas Madre de Dios** (Mother of God Cabins and Bar), 37 km (23 miles) north of Puerto Moín in the tiny farming village of Pacuare. Many boat drivers will tie up at the small dock here for a half hour while passengers stretch, use the bathrooms, or drink strong coffee and eat a sandwich in the dockside open-air café. The owner of Bare y Cabinas Madre de Dios usually has something of interest from the animal world—a tame river otter or small caiman—for entertaining visitors.

Tortuguero National Park

A few kilometers north of Pacuare, the Tortuguero Channels breach the southern boundary of Tortuguero National Park. Officially founded in 1970, the park today encompasses nearly 50,000 acres of tropical lowland rain forest and wide, white beach. The latter, about 22 km (14 miles) in length, is the largest mating and nesting site in the entire Caribbean for green, hawksbill, and leatherback sea turtles.

Many other wild animals reside in Tortuguero. Howler and white-throated capuchin monkeys, three-toed sloths, and Central American tapirs are just some of the park's permanent, fairly-easy-to-spot (particularly along the channels) inhabitants. If you haven't yet seen a wild tapir, you might here. Shy, dark-brown, snouted animals about the size of small donkeys, they are basically forest dwellers but often feed along the shores of the waterways in early morning and late evening (tapir paths to and from the water are used by jungle Indians). Tortuguero area residents say that a healthy population of jaguars—known locally as *el tigre*—also reside in the park. Tree climbers, water lovers, and the largest wild feline in the New World, these retiring creatures generally stay as far from human habitation as possible, however, and are seldom seen by man.

In the waterways themselves there are crocodiles, caiman (a species of freshwater crocodile), river otters, West Indian manatees, and a two-meter-long (six-foot) living fossil known as the gaspar fish, which has inhabited the region for more than 90 million years. Swimming in the Tortuguero Channels, by the way, is not a good idea. Sharks often enter the lagoons and rivers from the nearby Caribbean, and in the muddy waters have been known to mistake bathers for something good to eat.

The Tortuguero rain forest is so dense and wet (the park averages about 500 cm, or 200 inches, of rain each year) that not even local guides go very far inland without good reason. If you wish to explore the park on your own, you can do so by renting a dugout canoe or by joining a guided nature walk, both of which are offered by most Tortuguero village lodges.

TURTLE WATCHING AT TORTUGUERO

Of all the attractions and adventures awaiting travellers in the Tortuguero National Park area, observing the giant sea turtles as they lay their eggs on the nearby beach is by far the most popular. The primary turtle nesting season here is from May through September, but these huge reptiles can usually be seen at any time of the year. Nearly all of the lodges in the Tortuguero region offer year-round guided turtle-watching expeditions as part of their menu of guest activities.

Three species of giant sea turtles nest on Tortuguero's beaches: the green turtle, about three feet in length and weighing up to 500 pounds; the hawksbill, usually weighing around 250 pounds; and the leatherback, sometimes growing to five feet in length and weighing up to 800 pounds. All three varieties make the long mating-nesting migration from various parts of the Caribbean every two or three years; female turtles usually dig and fill four different nests during each migration period.

Watching one of these huge marine reptiles slowly drag her ungainly body across the beach from the sea, tediously dig a nest in the sand with her flippers, lie motionless while depositing the eggs, then refill the hole and struggle back to the sea is an experience that is not soon forgotten. The process usually begins in the late evening, when a female leaves the water in search of a nesting site above the high-tide line. Buried boulders, roots, even hard sand, will often make her turn back, but once a suitable spot has been located she will begin to dig. When the nest is deep enough (usually about two feet) the turtle swaps ends, places her tail in the hole, and lays about 100 eggs. She then re-covers the nest carefully, after which she sluggishly drags herself back to the sea.

If a female is disturbed by lights or movement as she crawls up the beach in search of a nesting site, she will simply turn around and return to the sea. Once the egg-laying process has begun, however, she will stay on the nest until finished. It is during this time that human observers can quietly approach to watch and take photographs. From beginning to end the laying procedure can last more than two hours.

If the nest is not destroyed by high water, heavy rainfall, or predators such as crabs, seabirds, or humans, the eggs will hatch in about two months. Once free of their shells, the two-inch-long baby turtles claw their way to just below the surface and, when air temperatures have cooled, make a dash for the nearby sea. Even if they head in the right direction (sometimes they don't), this is a dangerous stage in a baby turtle's life. Many are taken by predators seconds after leaving the nest; those that do reach the water are at the mercy of fish, sea currents, and a hundred other dangers.

During the peak of the Tortuguero National Park nesting season it's against the law to be on the beach at night without a guide and an official permit, the latter available from the national park office in Tortuguero village for about $2 (this includes a modest park entrance fee).

Tortuguero Village

The village of Tortuguero lies at the northernmost spur of Tortuguero National Park, 77 km (48 miles) north of Puerto Moín. Straddling a narrow strip of palm-shaded sand between Tortuguero Lagoon and the Caribbean, this sleepy shantytown of 300 people is made up of perhaps three dozen wood-and-thatch houses, a park ranger station, two tiny hotels, a disco (open on Friday and Saturday nights), and a couple of small *tiendas* (shops). If you've forgotten something important, the largest and best-stocked store here is the Paraíso Tropical, which sells souvenirs, film, cold drinks, snacks, and locally made handicrafts.

The wide, green **Tortuguero Lagoon**, on the western side of the village, is one of the prettiest segments of water on the Tortuguero Channels. Boat docks, canoe rentals, and the national park ranger station are located on the lagoon shore near the center of town. A hundred meters to the east of the village lies the Caribbean. The long, unbroken white-sand beach here is a great place to sunbathe and look for seashells, but locals recommend that you not venture very far out in the water. Large numbers of sharks and barracudas inhabit the area, and even village residents seldom swim in water deeper than their waist.

STAYING IN TORTUGUERO

If you're desperate or broke, the price is right at Tortuguero's two small downtown hotels—about $4 per night—but the rooms are cramped, hot, totally airless (there are no fans), and you'll have to share a cold-water bathroom. Both establishments are also near the disco, and on Friday and Saturday nights guests literally can't hear themselves think. Camping on the beach is allowed in some areas (with permission from the local national park ranger), but it isn't a good idea. Venomous snakes (principally the large and deadly barba amarilla) come onto the beach from the forest at night in search of food.

▸ **Mawamba Lodge** is located on the Caribbean side of Tortuguero Lagoon about 100 meters from the sea and less than 1 km (½ mile) north of Tortuguero village. Nestled in an oasis of coconut palms, fruit trees, and ornamental plants, the lodge offers 28 fan-cooled guest rooms with private cold-water baths. While the rooms are clean and spacious, the walls are paper thin, so don't expect much privacy or quiet. Mawamba's large enclosed **restaurant** serves three meals a day. Guests are served family-style; entrées consist of huge platters of whatever the cook could buy or catch that morning, but the food is always delicious. The lodge offers nature walks, turtle-watching expeditions, fishing trips, and rental dugout canoes, all for an additional charge.

▶ **Jungle Lodge**, on the left (west) side of Tortuguero Lagoon about 1 km (½ mile) north of the village, is reachable only by boat. Each of the 30 small but nicely arranged guest rooms at this secluded hostelry has a cooling fan, a covered verandah, and a private bath with hot water. Dugout canoes, guided jungle walks in the surrounding rain forest, and turtle-watching expeditions to the beach are available at a small additional charge, and a free ferry is available for anyone wishing to visit the village or the beach. The lodge has its own **restaurant** that specializes in traditional Costa Rican dishes.

Rustic ▶ **Hotel Ilan Ilan**, 3 km (2 miles) north of Tortuguero, sits in a grassy, well-shaded eight-acre jungle clearing on the western, or rain-forest, side of the lagoon (guests must catch a lodge ferry to reach the village and beach). Twenty guest rooms, each with cold-water bath, cooling fan, and shaded verandah, are clean but small and slightly run-down. Escorted nature hikes, turtle-watching expeditions, and half- and full-day fishing trips are available at an additional fee. Ilan Ilan has its own **restaurant**, which features both American and Costa Rican food.

▶ **Tortuga Lodge**, with 25 rooms, lies 4 km (2½ miles) north of Tortuguero village, also on the western or jungle side of the Tortuguero Lagoon. It too is accessible only by boat, and guests must ride a lodge ferry (free) to the village or beach. Rooms here are large, fan-cooled, and have private cold-water baths. A huge shaded verandah with comfortable wood-and-leather furniture offers a nice view of the palm-shaded grounds and lagoon. Basically a fishing lodge, Tortuga features guided half- and full-day fishing excursions in addition to nature hikes and turtle-watching expeditions. The lodge has its own **restaurant**.

Mawamba Lodge, Jungle Lodge, Hotel Ilan Ilan, and Tortuga Lodge request that prospective guests make reservations in advance from San José. Except for Mawamba (at which one-night stays are welcome), all specialize in three-day, two-night packages (you can stay longer if you wish, of course) running from Sunday to Tuesday, Tuesday to Thursday, or Friday to Sunday. Package stays include bus and boat transportation from San José to the lodge and back, room, meals, and some local activities.

Barra del Colorado and the Río Colorado Lodge

From Tortuguero, you can return south by boat to Puerto Moín via the Tortuguero Channels, or continue north another 40 km (25 miles) through the **Barra del Colorado National Wildlife Refuge** to the Río Colorado and the tiny coastal village of Barra del Colorado. If you choose the latter, you'll have to travel by boat, and unless you can convince a local fisherman to make the trip, transport will have to be arranged in advance through a travel agent or tour operator in San José. The two-hour boat ride from Tortuguero to Barra del Colorado along the Tortuguero Channels is extraordinarily scenic. The lowland tropical rain forest encompassing the Barra del Colorado National Wildlife Refuge is dense and totally without signs of human habitation. Here, as in Tortuguero National Park, wild animals, especially birds, are abundant.

The village of **Barra del Colorado**, located about 1 km (½ mile) upstream from where the wide and murky Río Colorado empties into the Caribbean, is inhabited mostly by fishermen and their families. There are actually two parts to this tiny hamlet, Barra del Colorado Norte (North) on the river's north bank, and Barra del Colorado Sur (South), directly opposite on the south bank. Neither has anything for visitors (nor are they a safe place to wander about on a Saturday night), although a small store in Barra del Colorado Sur sells snacks, film, and a few souvenirs.

Outsiders come to Barra del Colorado for one reason only, to stay at Central America's most famous fishing resort, ▸ **Archie Field's Río Colorado Lodge**. The first two cabins at the lodge were constructed in 1973; today this cozy, bright-blue compound built on stilts near the center of Barra del Colorado Sur has 18 spacious rooms, a complex of open-air dining rooms and breezy verandahs, its own zoo, and one of the best-equipped fleets of sportfishing boats in the Caribbean.

Some of the best tarpon and snook fishing in the world is found along Costa Rica's northern Caribbean coast, and most guests at the lodge are serious anglers. A typical day here begins at 5:00 A.M., when a monumental breakfast is served on the open-air verandah. Precisely an hour later Archie's fleet of modern, 20-foot-long fishing boats—each carrying a professional guide and two anglers—leaves the dock and heads for the mouth of the Río Colorado, a five-minute boat ride to the east.

Of the two principal game fish found in the Barra del Colorado area, tarpon—bony, torpedo-shaped creatures weighing from 20 to more than 100 pounds—are by far the more popular. From December through May these voracious fish migrate into the Río Colorado delta by the thousands to feed on shrimp and other small crustaceans, and at the peak of the season a single angler may hook as many as 30 or 40 tarpon a day. The real fun, however, is not in landing the fish (all tarpon caught here are released unharmed), but in the battle itself. When hooked, tarpon fling themselves from the water in a display of aerial acrobatics that no other game fish on earth can come close to matching.

Like most of the other resorts and lodges along the northern Caribbean coast, Río Colorado Lodge offers package trips at reduced rates, and requests that arrangements be made in advance (walk-ins are welcome if space exists). If you book a package (see Accommodations Reference), the price includes everything except alcoholic drinks and fishing lures, both of which can be purchased at the lodge.

Returning to San José

From Barra del Colorado you can return to Puerto Moín by chartered boat via the Tortuguero Channels, but transportation south is difficult to arrange (a boat must come from Puerto Moín to pick you up). It's far quicker and cheaper to fly from the village to San José on Travelair, the domestic Costa Rican airline. The airstrip here, a two-minute walk from Río Colorado Lodge, is large enough for twin-engine aircraft; the one plane a day to San José departs at 7:00 A.M. and costs about $48 per person. If you do fly, keep your camera around your neck, not in your luggage. The flight passes over the Barra del Colorado rain forest and, nearer to San José, the steaming crater of Poás volcano; on a clear day views from the aircraft are spectacular.

GETTING AROUND

It's probably a good idea to make all arrangements for accommodations and tours on the Caribbean coast from San José prior to heading east. Drop-ins are welcome at hotels and lodges in Puerto Limón and south along the coast, but capacity is limited and advance reservations are always appreciated. Car rentals aren't available here (not even in Puerto Limón), so if you plan to drive yourself, arrange for a vehicle in San José. If you decide not to rent a car, you can arrange a complete custom-tour package, including transportation, accommodations, meals, and activities, from one of San José's tour companies (see "Touring Costa Rica" in Useful Facts).

Puerto Limón and the Southern Coast

Except for the earthquake damage beginning 35 km (22 miles) northwest of Puerto Limón, the Guápiles Highway from San José via Braulio Carrillo National Park is in good shape. South of Puerto Limón along the coast, however, it's another story. The closer you get to the earthquake's epicenter, the worse the road becomes, and south of Cahuita there is more gravel than asphalt. From Puerto Viejo to Manzanillo-Gandoca National Wildlife Refuge the road literally falls apart, and even local drivers do not often exceed 30 km (19 miles) per hour for fear of damaging their cars.

You'll need several days to explore the southern Caribbean coast properly. It's possible to make the entire 213-km (132-mile) trip from San José to Puerto Viejo in one day, for example, but because of the earthquake-damaged roads the drive will take eight or nine hours without stops. If time isn't a problem, a better idea might be to stop in Puerto Limón for the night, drive south to Puerto Viejo the next day, then spend two or three days sightseeing while based at Pizote Lodge or Hotel Punta Cocles. On your return you might spend at least one night along the coast at Aviary of the Caribbean or Hotel El Atlántida before driving back to San José the following morning.

The best time to visit the southern Caribbean coast is during the rainy season, May through November. Prices for accommodations are lower, the surfers have all gone home (surfing is best in the Cahuita–Puerto Viejo area from December through April), and the weather is several degrees cooler than during the dry season.

Fuel is sometimes hard to find along the coast, so if you're driving a rental, fill up with gasoline in Puerto Limón before heading south toward Puerto Viejo. If you suddenly find your tank empty, look for small, hand-printed signs along the road in Cahuita and Puerto Viejo saying, "*Se vende diesel y gasolina.*" When fuel is available, it will usually cost $3 to $4 per gallon and come unfiltered from gallon-size plastic bottles.

Unless you have a fuel tank for a stomach, don't trust the water or ice in this part of Costa Rica, even at lodges where the hotel staff claims everything is *muy purificado.* Most experienced travellers here (and even residents of Costa Rica) carry with them a small, portable water filter or a gallon or two of drinking water from San José.

The Northern Coast

Travel from Puerto Moín north to Tortuguero and Barra del Colorado via the Tortuguero Channels along the Caribbean coast is by boat only. If you stay in a Tortuguero lodge or resort and book the room in advance, boat transportation from Puerto Moín to Tortuguero and return is generally included in the price. If you make your own arrangements, however, the cost from Puerto Moín to Tortuguero (one way), is $175 to $200 per person, depending upon the size and luxuriousness of the boat. The Tortuguero Channels trip has become extremely popular in the past few years, so try to arrange for your boat through a travel agent or tour operator in San José as far in advance as possible (if you just show up at the dock in Puerto Moín hoping to find an empty boat for hire, you may be out of luck). And don't expect to have the craft to yourself; if the driver can fill an empty seat, he'll do it.

For those who wish to continue on north to Barra del Colorado from Tortuguero village, transportation should also be arranged in advance from San José; the cost is $75 to $100, depending upon what kind of boat is available. If you stay at Archie Field's Río Colorado Lodge, however, you'll be picked up in Tortuguero by one of Archie's boats and transported to the resort at no charge. A one-way ticket from Barra del Colorado to San José on Travelair, Costa Rica's domestic airline, is $48 per person. There's one plane a day, departing the village at 7:00 A.M. Although you can begin your tour of the northern Caribbean coast by flying from San José to Barra del Colorado, then heading south down the Tortuguero Channels by boat, arranging transportation will be more difficult and more costly.

Plan to spend three or four days in the northern Caribbean area, if possible. Because all travel here is by boat, getting from one place to another takes time. You'll also pay the lowest price for accommodations, at least in Tortuguero, if you book a three-day, two-night package (three of the four principal lodges in Tortuguero require a minimum stay of two nights anyway).

From the standpoint of price, the best time to visit the northern Caribbean coast is during the rainy season, May through November. You'll probably spend some of your time wearing a raincoat, but the cost of accommodations is considerably lower during this period. The peak of the turtle-watching season is May through September, but remember that turtles can usually be seen every month of the year. If you're an angler, the best tarpon fishing is from December through May; the peak of the snook season is August to December.

ACCOMMODATIONS REFERENCE

Unless otherwise indicated, the rate given is the projected rate for a double room, double occupancy, and does not include tax. Price ranges span the lowest rate in the low season to the highest rate in the high season. As prices are subject to change, always double-check before booking.

Limón and the Southern Coast

▸ **Aviary of the Caribbean.** Contact P.O. Box 569-7300, Puerto Limón. (No telephone). $50.

▸ **Cabinas Las Palmas. Pocora.** Tel: 76-5289; Fax: 76-5198. $20.

▸ **Hotel El Atlántida. Cahuita.** Tel: 58-1515, ext. 213; Fax: 28-9467. $35–$45.

▸ **Hotel Punta Cocles. Puerto Viejo.** Contact P.O. Box 11020-1000, San José. Tel 34-0306; Fax: 34-0014. $70.

▸ **Maribu Caribe Hotel.** Calle Portete, **Puerto Limón.** Tel: 58-4010 or 58-4543; Fax: 58-3541. $65.

▸ **Matama Hotel.** P.O. Box 686, **Puerto Limón.** Tel: 58-1123; Fax: 58-4499. $65–$125.

▸ **Pizote Lodge. Puerto Viejo.** Contact P.O. Box 230-2200, Coronado. Tel: 58-1938; Fax: 29-1428. $40 (room), $66 (bungalow).

The Northern Coast

▶ **Archie Field's Río Colorado Lodge. Barra del Colorado.** Contact P.O. Box 5094-1000, San José. Tel: 32-4063 or 32-8610; Fax: 31-5987; in the U.S., Tel: (800) 243-9777; Fax: (813) 933-3280. Six-day, five-night package, $1,310 per person, double occupancy, AP; seven-day, six-night package, $1,650 per person, double occupancy, AP.

▶ **Hotel Ilan Ilan. Tortuguero.** Contact P.O. Box 91-1150, San José. Tel: 55-2031; Fax: 55-1946. Three-day, two-night package, $198 per person, double occupancy, AP.

▶ **Jungle Lodge. Tortuguero.** Contact P.O. Box 1818-1002, Paseo de los Estudiantes, San José. Tel: 31-4808 or 31-5428; Fax: 32-7284. Three-day, two-night package, $198 per person (double occupancy).

▶ **Mawamba Lodge. Tortuguero.** Tel: 71-7282 or 23-2421; Fax: 55-4039. $45.

▶ **Tortuga Lodge. Tortuguero.** Contact P.O. Box 6941-1000, San José. Tel: 57-0766; Fax: 57-1665. Three-day, two-night package, $305 per person, double occupancy, AP.

THE PACIFIC COAST

By Tony Tedeschi

If Costa Rica is an eco-tourist's dream come true, the Pacific coast of the country provides the real-life fantasy world to accompany that dream, a kaleidoscope of colorful fauna and flora that is almost dizzying in its variety and abundance. From Guanacaste just south of the Nicaraguan border to Corcovado just north of Panamá, the Pacific shore is a collection of national parks, preserves, reserves, wildlife refuges, beaches, marshes, swamps, gulfs, bays, tributaries, estuaries, and tiny offshore islands. Many of these are protected areas, each with a personality of its own. These areas share enough wildlife in common to have you searching for one more glimpse of yesterday's great sighting while you scan the canopy overhead for today's possibilities.

The port city of Puntarenas, due west of San José near the mouth of the **Golfo de Nicoya**, is the arbitrary dividing point between the northern and southern Pacific coast areas, a good place to cut the deck, simply because sea traffic exiting the port on voyages of exploration can't go both ways and must choose a northern or southern route. To the south are the great rain-forest preserves. North is a more climatically diverse terrain that covers both rain and dry forest areas. Both demand a sense of adventure and a suspension of your need for the sort of pampering found on other, more resort-oriented vacations.

This is not an area of interesting towns and cities. Puntarenas and, to the south, Quepos, the principal coast towns, are little more than jumping-off places to other areas. And it is not a venue of resorts, although the beaches here rival those anywhere else in the hemisphere. It is an area where the human species is at its best when it blends in. The stars of this show are not a health-club-honed couple strolling along the beach. The standouts here are the resplendent quetzal of the Monteverde Cloud Forest Preserve, the turtles of Tamarindo, the squirrel monkeys in the canopy above Manuel Antonio, the scarlet macaws of the Carara Biological Reserve, the harpy eagles of Corcovado, the crocodiles beneath the Tárcoles bridge, and iguanas sunning on tree limbs just about everywhere.

In the national parks of Costa Rica's Pacific coast you will get wet and muddy, sweat your brains out, nurse scrapes, massage bumps, soothe bruises, then fall asleep so soundly your tired muscles will bless you for finally giving them some relief. You will trek *through* rivers, slide down slopes, squat motionless under a bush and try to ignore the swarms of mosquitoes homing in on you—all just for a chance to see a collared ara-kari on a leafless limb, a chartreuse iguana in a patch of sunlight, or a leatherback turtle flippering its way up the beach. And you may not even get close enough to get the photograph you want, but you will carry the memories of these experiences with you for the rest of your life.

MAJOR INTEREST

South of Puntarenas
Carara Biological Reserve
Manuel Antonio National Park
Corcovado National Park
Caño Island Biological Reserve
Bird-watching, monkey-watching
Hiking, trekking

North of Puntarenas
Monteverde Cloud Forest Preserve
Palo Verde National Park and Dr. Rafael Lucas Rodríguez Caballero National Wildlife Refuge
Santa Rosa National Park
Casona Santa Rosa battle site
Guanacaste Conservation Area
Tamarindo National Wildlife Refuge
Bird-watching, monkey-watching, turtle-watching
Nicoya Peninsula's beaches

Touring the Pacific Coast

There are three principal methods of touring the natural wonders of Costa Rica's Pacific coast:

- A seaborne itinerary
- Day trips from a central location
- A continuous overland journey from point A to point B to C to D, etc.

In many respects, the seaborne method is the best way to see the most of Costa Rica's Pacific side, with the least amount of time expended in getting from place to place. The central-location method of visiting via overland routes (staging out of Puntarenas or even San José, for example) allows you to return to the comfort and convenience of a hotel each night, but limits you to areas within a few hours' drive. The third option involves long, rugged overland journeys along the coast, which, of course, allows you to tour the area at a slower pace and affords more opportunities to examine the landscape in detail. However, if you do not have a lot of time to spend, the A to B to C method of touring will not work. Important connecting segments of roads along the Pacific coast are unpaved and take hours to travel, even when their distances are short. Overland access to the most scenic sections of many of the parks is often difficult, sometimes limited, and occasionally downright impossible when roads are inundated by high tides or by flooding during the rainy season. (See "Getting Around," below.)

CRUISING THE COAST

The best seaborne tours of the national parks and reserves of the Pacific coast are offered by Temptress Cruises. The voyages embark from Puntarenas and cover the coast from Bahía Santa Elena (Santa Elena Bay) near the Nicaraguan border to Corcovado, down toward the Panamanian border.

Accommodations aboard the 60-passenger *Temptress* are a bit tight but quite comfortable. All cabins are air-conditioned and include two single bunks, a sink, and a separate shower stall. The dining salon serves standard

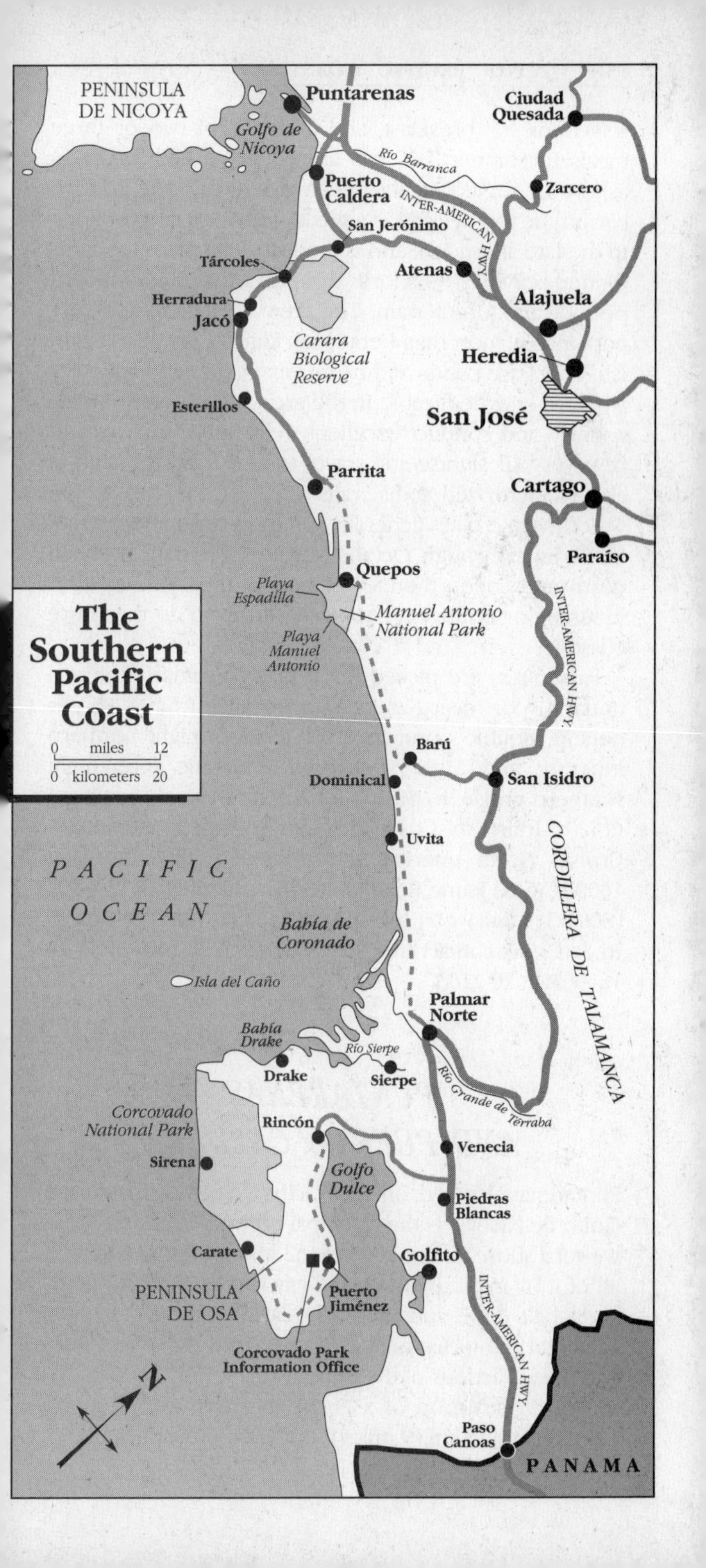

The Southern Pacific Coast
0 miles 12
0 kilometers 20
PENINSULA DE NICOYA
Puntarenas
Golfo de Nicoya
Ciudad Quesada
Río Barranca
Puerto Caldera
Zarcero
INTER-AMERICAN HWY
San Jerónimo
Tárcoles
Atenas
Herradura
Jacó
Alajuela
Carara Biological Reserve
Heredia
Esterillos
San José
Parrita
Cartago
Paraíso
Quepos
Playa Espadilla
Manuel Antonio National Park
Playa Manuel Antonio
INTER-AMERICAN HWY
Barú
Dominical
San Isidro
Uvita
CORDILLERA DE TALAMANCA
PACIFIC OCEAN
Bahía de Coronado
Isla del Caño
Palmar Norte
Bahía Drake
Río Sierpe
Drake
Sierpe
Río Grande de Térraba
Corcovado National Park
Rincón
Venecia
Sirena
Golfo Dulce
Piedras Blancas
Carate
Golfito
PENINSULA DE OSA
Puerto Jiménez
INTER-AMERICAN HWY
Corcovado Park Information Office
N
Paso Canoas
PANAMA

selections for breakfast, and a choice of two or three meals for dinner. Lunches are either packed for hikes ashore or served on the beach at mid-day. The alfresco bar on the top deck aft is a great place for a tall, cool one in the late afternoon, and is the gathering place for after-dinner activities. Folkloric troupes are brought aboard periodically to entertain. The crew is efficient and very personable; most members speak English as well as Spanish. Tours are conducted by university-trained naturalists who are knowledgeable in the great biodiversity of their country and conduct excellent treks into the parks and reserves. All sightseeing travel to and from the ship is aboard motorized Zodiac rafts.

Southern cruises generally run from November to May. From June through October, cruises alternate between north and south; therefore, you can then chose either itinerary, or arrange a back-to-back trip to do the entire coast.

Passengers are picked up at Juan Santamaría International Airport near San José. Rates range from $795 per person, double occupancy, for the four-night northern itinerary, and $1,595 per person for the seven-night southern cruise, to $2,100 for the north/south combination. (Airfare to Costa Rica not included.) Temptress Cruises' North American marketing and sales office is at 1600 N.W. Le Jeune Road, Suite 301, Miami FL 33126; Tel: (800) 336-8423 or (305) 871-2663; Fax: (305) 871-2657. In San José, contact them at P.O. Box 1198-1000; Tel: 20-1679; Fax: 20-2103.

PUNTARENAS AND PUERTO CALDERA

Puntarenas, located on the Pacific coast just inside the Golfo de Nicoya, is the principal port city on Costa Rica's western shore. About 100 km (62 miles) west of San José, all of it by major highway, the city is only about an hour-and-a-half drive and therefore easily accessible to Juan Santamaría International Airport (northwest of San José) and the attractions of the Central Valley.

The construction of a cruise-ship terminal at Puerto Caldera, just 15 km (9 miles) south of the city on route 73, has not diminished tourist traffic to Puntarenas; Caldera is little more than the terminal facility itself, so passengers arriving there and wanting to "go into town" are taken to Puntarenas anyway. However, they won't find much when they get to Puntarenas, either, at least not in the way of what you typically find in resort areas, such as fancy restaurants and fashionable boutiques or jewelry stores.

A town of fewer than 40,000 citizens, Puntarenas grew as a cargo port during the 19th century, principally to launch locally grown coffee and bananas on their journeys to consumers east and west (the eastern voyage was a very long trip in the days before the Panama Canal). With the development of Puerto Limón on the Caribbean coast during the latter half of this century, Puntarenas lost its trade with the east coast of North America and markets in Europe. Today the town seems little more than an embarkation point for visitors heading out on journeys of exploration through Costa Rica's Pacific coast parks and reserves (touring vessels still dock at the port) or for the beaches that line the coast.

Puntarenas (Spanish for "sandy point") is a finger of sand sticking out into the Golfo de Nicoya. The skinny peninsula that holds the town is as narrow as 100 meters at its thinnest and only six avenues across at its widest point. All the water and the sandy beaches on either side of the peninsula may beckon to travellers, but the waters that brush the shores of Puntarenas are not clean and should be avoided, despite what the locals may tell you or the lack of concern on the part of the gaggles of children who play in the waves.

However, Puntarenas is a good place to use as a base if you've decided to set out on daily overland visits to the natural kingdoms of the coast. You are only about a half-hour's drive from the Carara Biological Reserve, for example, and in a position to make day trips to the Monteverde Cloud Forest Preserve, Manuel Antonio National Park, and Palo Verde National Park.

A spin about the town will reveal the typical Catholic church surrounded by a central plaza (Calle 7 between Avenidas 1 and Central) and the local market (Calle 2 on the estuary of the Río Barranca), but neither is worth more than a cursory look. There is a tourist center near the small lighthouse at the very tip of the peninsula, just west of Calle 37, with some very basic brochures and information, but nothing you could not have gotten from the tourist authorities before your trip or at the tourist offices in San José.

STAYING IN PUNTARENAS

If you would prefer to base yourself on land, but do not want to spend the time it will take travelling from point to point, the hub-and-spoke method is, as we have suggested, an excellent option for seeing much of the Pacific coast. You can fan outward each day and return to the comfort of your hotel each night, and you will not have to lug all your gear around with you.

If you would like to trade your muddy boots and wet hiking clothes for a lovely room and some creature comforts each evening, then unquestionably the best place to do that in the Puntarenas area is at the ▶ **Fiesta Hotel Resort & Casino**. The resort is located on the coast about 2 km (1¼ miles) south of Puntarenas, at the mouth of the **Río Barranca** just off route 73, the principal coastal road. A sign on the highway will let you know you're there.

The Fiesta, opened in 1990, features 190 rooms, including some impressive suites, all of which include pleasant, breezy furnishings, air-conditioning, and color television with satellite transmissions from the United States for those who need a regular fix of CNN.

The hotel has the requisite gourmet dining room with the typical array of high-end beef and seafood dishes. And it includes a casino for that touch of formality that makes a resort a resort for those who feel the need to dress up every night, dine in high style, then hit the gaming tables. The hotel's real attraction, however, is the informality of the open-air **Restaurant La Macarela** and **El Mastil Bar**, where live music can really liven up the mix of tourists and locals in the evening. In La Macarela you can enjoy local fish soups and spicy seafood, chicken, or meat dishes, garnished with squash and beans and rice. There is no wall or room divider between the restaurant and the bar, so after dinner you can sit back and enjoy a drink and watch the revelers at El Mastil, or, of course, you may join them. Try a *cucaracha*, a flaming coffee liqueur served in a small brandy snifter, which you swill through a straw before the flames extinguish while the waiters cheer you on.

The best part about the Fiesta is that it understands its

raison d'être as a place for relaxation between forays into the forests, marshes, mountains, and assorted hinterlands (all of which can be arranged by the hotel's tour desk). There are also pools, tennis and volleyball courts, and a gym. Fishing excursions to the bountiful waters of the Pacific billfish haunts, just offshore, can also be arranged.

While the Fiesta is on the coast, it is near the mouth of the Río Barranca and the water along its beach is silty, especially during the wetter months. If your objective is only to catch some sun, and you prefer a sandy beach, you can drop a blanket here or stretch out in a lounge chair. A location by the pool, however, is a much better option if you want to swim.

Other hotels in Puntarenas are smaller and more modest in their accommodations, but also more moderately priced. The ▸ **Hotel Porto Bello** features cool, air-conditioned rooms and private hot-water baths, a combination not universally available in the area and a pair of great blessings after a day in the rain forest. The rooms are comfortable, if not memorable, but in this part of the country you will not be spending a lot of time in your room. Porto Bello also has a seafood **restaurant**, featuring daily fresh catches from the Pacific. The hotel is on Avenida Central about 3 km (2 miles) west of downtown. Avenida Central is known as route 17 here, although there are no signs for either designation.

The ▸ **Hotel Tioga**, on the other hand, is in the heart of the "tourist district" on Calle 19 and Paseo de los Turistas. A longtime favorite for Pacific coast vacationers, the Tioga has 46 air-conditioned rooms that come with hot- or cold-water baths (appropriately priced) and a serviceable **restaurant** on the premises. The hotel is four stories high, so most rooms afford a view of either the Golfo de Nicoya out front or the estuary of the Río Barranca across the narrow peninsula behind the hotel.

The ▸ **Hotel Yadrán**, one of the newer properties here, has a freshwater pool that's small but that works for cooling off if you prefer a liquid cool-down. The 42-room (all air-conditioned) hotel also offers bicycle rentals. The Yadrán is at the far western end of the principal boulevard, Paseo de los Turistas, near Calle 35.

Of the smaller, less-expensive properties, the ▸ **Hotel Las Brisas** is the best. The hotel, which has a small pool and a decent, if unimaginative, **restaurant**, was renovated a few years back and now offers hot water in all its rooms. It too is on Paseo de los Turistas, just west of Calle 31.

DINING IN PUNTARENAS

You will not discover anything in the gourmet category here, nor will you experience a culinary "find" or encounter great local cuisine for a ridiculously low cost. Nonetheless, there are some good restaurants where you can get your fill for a reasonable price.

The **Aloha**, just west of Calle 19 on Paseo de los Turistas, is an open-air restaurant where you can get a typical Costa Rican *casado:* rice and black beans served with either meat, chicken, or fish. They also prepare a wonderful ceviche. A full meal costs about $20. Tel: 61-0773.

Just west of Calle 21 on Paseo de los Turistas is **La Caravelle**, perhaps the nicest restaurant in town. Its specialty is seafood; the menu includes four different fish soups, a half dozen seafood dishes, shrimp, and lobster, with prices ranging from $10 to $25. Two nice choices are the *camarones a la mantequilla y limón* (shrimp with butter and lemon) or the *langosta* (lobster) prepared the same way. The wine list includes some very good Chilean and Argentine varietals. Tel: 61-2262.

If you want to experience some of the less-expensive local seafood, **La Casa de Mariscos**, on Paseo de los Turistas and Calle 6, is as good a choice as any. Here a meal of fried fish and vegetables runs about $5.

There is a collection of "international" restaurants, particularly along the Paseo de los Turistas, but the fact that they have designated themselves French, German, or Italian will not cause you to imagine yourself in Paris, Munich, or Rome. You might want to pop into **Bierstube**, however, which offers a decent selection of beers. It is more a local bar than a restaurant, and you can hobnob with the townspeople. It is just east of Calle 23 on Paseo de los Turistas.

SOUTH OF PUNTARENAS

It is not possible to see all of the southern Pacific coast if you are using Puntarenas as a hub for day trips. While the Carara Biological Reserve is a short trip of less than an hour, Manuel Antonio National Park, near Quepos, is several hours away. It can be done as a day trip if you start early, but if you want to give yourself a fair chance at seeing some of the animal attractions, you should overnight in Quepos. The attractions closest to the Panamanian border, such as Gorcovado National Park, cannot be accessed as day trips, partly because they are too distant, but principally because the road that runs along the coast is unpaved and an extremely slow-go for more than 90 km (56 miles) of its length. On the other hand, staying overnight in Corcovado, down near the Panamá border, is only for those who enjoy camping in hot, humid conditions.

The alternative strategy of hopscotching down the coast will also eat up days. If you have the time, a continuous trip down the coast route will allow you the most detailed look at the area. There are lovely beaches scattered down the coast, most reachable only after an arduous trip down unimproved roads. The most accessible are those between Dominical and Uvita, south of the village of Barú about 35 km (21 miles) west of San Isidro off the Inter-American Highway. Through this area, you will have to endure accommodations that are modest at best; in the national parks you will have to make do with dormitories where available, campsites where not.

Seaborne itineraries usually include both Manuel Antonio and Corcovado, and this option should be given strong consideration because you take your accommodations with you. (See above, Touring the Pacific Coast.)

Carara Biological Reserve

Forty kilometers (25 miles) southeast of Puntarenas and about 25 km (16 miles) from the cruise-ship dock at Puerto Caldera is the Carara Biological Reserve. This is a quick trip along paved highway. From Puntarenas, proceed along Avenida Central, which becomes route 17. About 10 km (6 miles) east of the city, route 17 intersects with route 73, a two-lane highway that runs right by the cruise-ship dock at Caldera. From Caldera, take route 73 for 16 km (10 miles) southeast to San Jerónimo, then take route 84 (another two-lane highway) south toward Tárcoles, another 9 km (5½ miles). The administration building at the reserve is about 5 km (3 miles) beyond the

Tárcoles bridge, on the left; there is a small admission fee. The cab fare from Puntarenas is about $80, from Caldera about $70. Cabs line up at the cruise-ship dock and you can negotiate the starting price downward.

The road to Carara runs through a great deal of pastureland, cleared by ranchers to raise cattle. Trees are generally clumped around water holes or line the rivers and creeks. When you begin to see the signs for Tárcoles, you are getting close. If you are not driving yourself, tell the driver you would like to stop at the bridge. He will probably know why; if not, tell him you want to see the *caimanes* (crocodiles).

TARCOLES BRIDGE

The view from the Tárcoles bridge is a poignant comment on the battle for Costa Rica's environmental future. If you look closely, you are apt to see dead fish floating belly up in the slow-moving current, evidence of ranches and farms upstream. Fertilizers and insecticides poison the river, killing fish, and ultimately destroying the food chain for the crocodiles.

Compared with other countries, Costa Rica has one of the highest percentages of land set aside for natural preserves; paradoxically, it also has one of the highest deforestation rates on earth. The country is desperately trying to strike a balance between farmers and entrepreneurs on the one hand, and environmentalists on the other. Reasonable people on both sides realize the importance of achieving the balance.

The country has a huge foreign debt, one of the highest per capita on earth, so there is strong pressure to commercialize to generate foreign revenue, and that places the rain and cloud forests in the path of encroachment, otherwise known as progress. While setting aside land for national parks, reserves, and refuges is the immediate, stop-the-bleeding solution, reconciling business and preservation is the long-term answer. And it is all summed up in the view from the Tárcoles bridge.

Study the edges of the river for any movement. What first appears to be a sandbar may well be a caiman enjoying a bit of sun on the part of its back that appears above the waterline. Also scan the tops of the trees rising from the bank before you. Iguanas are plentiful here, and one may well be resting on a limb just a few feet in front of you. If you hear a piercing squawk in the air above, take a quick look; nearby Carara is a refuge for the scarlet macaw, and you may be lucky enough to spot a pair flying over.

ENTERING THE PARK

On the way up the highway to the administration building (about 5 km/3 miles south of the Tárcoles bridge—go there first to pay a small admission fee) note the large iron gate at a turnoff to your left, about a kilometer (½ mile) past the bridge. This is the best place to enter the reserve. It is a good spot to park as well, and provides easy access to the wonders of Carara. As long as you have your admission receipt with you, you may enter at this point. If the gate is not open, you may slip around it easily; it is meant only to restrain vehicles. While there is no manned checkpoint at the gate, you may be stopped along the dirt road or on one of the paths by a park ranger, who may ask to see the receipt.

Before you enter Carara, or any of the parks in Costa Rica, you should be aware that there are some unwritten rules of conduct; following them will help you maximize the experience, while minimizing your impact on the environment: Keep talking to a minimum, do not interact with the animal life, try to disturb the plant life as little as possible.

If you are unfamiliar with tropical forest reserves such as Carara, you will find a visit more rewarding if you tour the refuge with a local guide. The universities in Costa Rica have some of the hemisphere's best biology programs, and many of the young people who have graduated from these programs become naturalist guides.

For example, if you have a chance to book the services of Rodolfo Zamora of Geotur, by all means do so. Rodolfo has made Carara a specialty, and he will guide you to some of its greatest natural treasures. He is fluent in both Spanish and English. Geotur, based in San José, specializes in natural history tours; Zamora's services can also be arranged through Costa Rica's Temptations (see "Touring Costa Rica" in Useful Facts).

TREKKING IN CARARA

Carara is one of the beneficiaries of Costa Rica's position between North and South America: An abundance of wildlife flows into this transition zone between the continents. But rain forests such as Carara are also important to the health of the rest of the planet, supplying a significant percentage of the world's oxygen supply. During the rainiest period in this area—October to December—the path you are walking is under water; these heavy rains are, of course, important to the growth of the plant life.

You can see a graphic example in the width of the bands on the trunk of a palm tree at the road's edge. Their spacing indicates the years when there has been a good amount of rain as opposed to when it has been dry: wide bands of growth for the wet years, narrow for the dry. You should also note the difference between primary- and secondary-growth forests, those sections that have been there for hundreds of years versus the newer growth, often the result of man's intrusions. If the trees have no vines, the forest has been disturbed.

This "trail" through Carara is really an access road for vehicles, but vehicular traffic is extremely limited. Trekkers, therefore, can penetrate the Carara reserve along a wide path without having to battle the underbrush, for the most part leaving the forest thickets undisturbed.

If the canopy begins to shudder and shake, you should immediately stop and stay as still as possible. Do not point up; follow the unfolding drama just with your eyes. Soon there will be a whole community above you. The leading players are white-throated capuchins, who swing through the date trees, gobbling fruit and shaking the canopy. The monkeys stir up the trees, things fall, and terrestrial animals follow along the ground, foraging.

These New World monkeys are distinguished by their prehensile tail. Along with fruit, the capuchins eat insects—one of the few species of monkeys that do—and occasionally leave the sanctuary of the treetops to come down for water, where they may play another role in the food-chain hierarchy and become a meal for a jaguar.

Wait to see if you can spot a peccary or an anteater crossing the trail. It is rare that one obliges, however, as they are generally aware of your presence. If you have a true sense of adventure, and no fear of the jungle at night when the animals are less skittish, a trip down this trail under a full moon may reward you with a sighting.

A good guide with a trusty unocular will be able to point out such once-in-a-lifetime sightings as a young spectacled owl perched on a tree limb, its white head rotating left and right, its black-circled eyes blinking in the direction of the lens. Or he or she will lead you off the roadway and down a narrow path to see the ants.

But even without a guide, you'll see your fill. Keep an eye trained on the trail for a parade of leaf-cutter ants, carrying their green harvests. If you spot a line of them or a straggler or two, follow where they lead. One such trail may take you to a large ficus tree, where, along an entomological superhighway, the ants move—thousands of them—carrying thumbnail-size cuttings of leaf in one direction, returning in the opposite direction for another load. The insects' course is an engineering marvel. It includes land bridges over such obstacles as rutted rain gullies and tunnels beneath larger obstacles such as tree roots. And they don't even eat those leaves. These ants are farmers. They take the leaves to their farms below ground, chew them into a mulch, then spread it over subterranean fields, where it serves as fertilizer for mushrooms, the food the ants actually eat. As many as 25 million ants have been estimated to dwell in one of these communities.

Along the trail, you should notice the beautiful heliconias, hanging in clusters that appear like blood-drenched spearheads. Alighting here and there you will see the brown-and-yellow heliconius butterfly, whose nine-month lifespan is the longest of any lepidopteran. Watch a red-billed hummingbird—stopping here along its 19,200-km (12,000-mile) migratory route—home in on a sweet flower.

There are tiny bird nests, huge brown termite nests. There are carnivorous beetles that eat ants and carnivorous birds that eat beetles. Then there is the symbiotic relationship between ants and the bullhorn acacia plant. The plant provides shelter for the ant, which in turn attacks wasps that would otherwise defoliate the plant. You will recognize the plant by the shape of its thorns, like the bullhorns affixed to the grill of a Texas Cadillac. Ping the plant's stem with your finger; instantly a squadron of ants will converge at the spot to ward off a perceived impending attack.

The Carara trek is a comfortable walk in every respect, but you should never lose sight of the fact that man can be a target here, too. If you are walking with others, keep an eye out for potential problems. For example, that bright-yellow caterpillar on the backpack of the trekker in front of you may look pretty, but you don't want it to touch your skin; it produces a very painful rash.

The Quepos Area

Named for the Indian tribe encountered here by Spanish colonial leader Juan Coronado, the town of **Quepos**, south of the Carara reserve and adjacent to Manuel Antonio National Park, was little more than a sleepy seacoast town until the 1930s. Its growth encouraged by the presence of the Costa Rica Banana Company, which settled into this area of the country's Pacific coast at the time, the town lapsed back into a quiet near-nonexistence with the demise of the banana plantations 30 years later. During the last two decades, however, tourists drawn to the beautiful local beaches have brought some new, much-needed revenue to the town. Nonetheless it still remains little more than a tiny village, here to support beach-goers, sport-fishermen, and the area's palm-oil plantations.

You get to Quepos from Puntarenas via route 73, a two-lane highway that about 10 km (6 miles) east of Puntarenas turns south toward Puerto Caldera. Once on route 17, drive 21 km (13 miles) southeast toward San Jerónimo, where it intersects route 84, the principal highway from San José. Here, you head south past Tárcoles and the Carara Biological Reserve, and on through the towns of Herradura, Jacó, and Esterillos to Parrita. Along the way, you will note a predominance of grazing lands with only patches of forest.

As you pass the small farms that make up the bulk of Costa Rica's landholdings, you will notice a great variety of skin tones and hair colors among the locals working the fields and gardens and among the children bouncing along the roads. The fair-skinned, tow-headed children are the descendants of British, German, and Italian immigrants who have come to the country over the past 150 years.

It is 77 km (48 miles) south on 84 from San Jerónimo to Parrita, all smooth going. At Parrita the pavement ends abruptly and turns into a gravel road. Buy some fresh fruit at the makeshift stands where the road turns to gravel;

you may want to stop now or later for a sweet, tasty interlude. The next 25 km (16 miles) of no-name road to Quepos will take a couple of hours. During the rainy season it will be muddy; during the dry season it will be so dusty you will marvel that much of this area has been designated rain forest.

Finally, about 5 km (3 miles) before you reach Quepos, the road does a dogleg left, but you want to go straight. You break out onto a stretch of coastline just before you hit town. Here the road is paved and runs adjacent to a long stretch of beach into Quepos. The town is tiny and its principal streets are paved, but after the torturous trip in it will not seem like much of a consolation.

There are actually five beaches in the area, numbered one through five and named (in the ascending order of their numbers) Espadilla, Espadilla Sur, Manuel Antonio, Puerto Escondido, and Playita. Espadilla is just outside the entrance to Manuel Antonio National Park and within the town of Quepos. The beaches are lovely and, if you have the time, a great place for a cool dip, especially after the trip in.

DINING AND STAYING IN THE QUEPOS AREA

By this point most likely you will be famished, and fortunately there are some nice places to eat in Quepos. Your best choices are a trio of restaurants along the road to Manuel Antonio National Park after you reach Quepos.

Plinio is a wooden building of tropical design, set in a garden of banana trees and tropical flowers, about 1 km (½ mile) from Quepos on the road to Manuel Antonio, on the right-hand side. Italian food is the specialty of the house, including the usual assortment of pastas and meat or fish dishes. One unexpected specialty is the vegetarian lasagna, which is quite tasty. The wonderful breads here are homemade. A full meal costs about $25. Tel: 77-0055.

Charrúas is a Uruguayan steak house about 1½ km (1 mile) from Quepos on the way to Manuel Antonio; it is in a white building on the right-hand side of the road. The alfresco restaurant has a very limited menu: one chicken, steak, or seafood entrée each day. They will prepare a box lunch, including a sandwich—usually ham and cheese—a salad, and a fruit juice, which, while not the world's greatest gastronomical experience, may be just what the doctor ordered about halfway through a day in the hot sun. Tel: 77-0409.

The **Barba Roja**, about 2 km (1¼ miles) from Quepos, just before the park on the right-hand side, serves good food at reasonable prices. It's a favorite among knowledgeable locals. There are daily specials, the best being grilled tuna or lobster. They also serve grilled meat dishes and chicken, and their homemade nachos are out of this world. Portions are large, and tropical drinks, such as margaritas, punches, and piña coladas, are served in large mugs. A complete meal runs about $25. Tel: 77-0331.

The combination of beautiful beach and a high potential for wildlife sightings may tempt you to stay in the area for a few days. Should you decide to do so there are a handful of small hotels, offering a range of accommodations.

▸ **La Mariposa** is the best place in town, but also the most expensive. It is built onto a bluff just off the road between Quepos and Manuel Antonio, and set in beautifully landscaped tropical gardens. The units here are two-room villas, each with living room and bedroom. Each suite also has a huge, greenhouse-like bathroom that includes a small indoor garden.

The ▸ **Kamuk Hotel** offers little more than air-conditioned rooms and hot baths, but at less than half the price of the Mariposa and about the same distance to Manuel Antonio beach it is a viable option for the sand-and-sun crowd. The ▸ **Karahé Hotel & Villas** offers 32 cabins with kitchenettes and private baths with hot showers, just a short walk from Espadilla beach and about a 20-minute walk from Manuel Antonio beach.

Manuel Antonio National Park

Manuel Antonio is the tiny-but-mighty jewel in the national park system's crown. It is literally next door to Quepos; drive south on a nameless, numberless paved road for about 2 km (1¼ miles) to the entrance to the park. Just ask anyone or follow your instincts; it is very easy to find.

The park was created more or less to keep the land from falling prey to developers. Although less than 1,500 acres, what there is of Manuel Antonio nonetheless makes it one of the most beautiful places in all of Costa Rica. Hotels would rim the beach here if it were not off-limits to such development—and, indeed, such a resort strip would rival anything in the hemisphere. But when you visit here you will understand why we really cannot improve upon nature.

Part of a Pacific coastal area of white-sand beaches, Manuel Antonio is perfect for bathing, and you can do that just as well in this rustic setting as you could with a lounge chair, a towel attendant's hut, and a bow-tied waiter pushing piña coladas. Here, instead of a trip over to the sail-board concession, you can go animal-watching. A sweaty but rewarding trip down the trails can be counterpointed with refreshing dips in the sea.

The fact is that you can't even get to Manuel Antonio without taking a dip. If you approach by sea it is a wet landing. If you approach from the land side you must wade across a small estuary to get into the park.

At an administration and information office near the park's entrance you will be charged a small fee to enter. The office, and the park, are open from 7:00 A.M. to 4:00 P.M., at which time visitors are expected to leave. This is one of the few national parks that does not permit camping, a rule that is enforced by guards who make a sweep of the park. The park is too small and its environment too susceptible to the deleterious effects of human traffic to permit people to stay for extended, uninterrupted periods.

What can you see in an area so small and so confined? If you are quiet, light-footed, and cautious, the answer is quite a lot.

More than 180 species of birds have been recorded in the park and more than 100 species of mammals sighted. Chief among the sighting prizes is the squirrel monkey, one of the rarest of the New World primates, which, it is feared, is headed for extinction. Sightings of this active, climbing, branch-running monkey, with its distinctive red back, are not frequent but do occur from time to time, creating the hope that enough of them will be around for long enough to reinvigorate the species. If you are not likely to see a squirrel monkey, your odds are much better with the white-throated capuchins, whose communities travel the treetops of Manuel Antonio, while earthbound peccaries, tapirs, and armadillos trail below, scrounging for the fruits and nuts with which the capuchins litter their wake.

A dozen islands that dot the waters offshore near Manuel Antonio are havens for the usual gaggles of pelicans, boobies, and frigates, among other birds. An elaborate reef system has developed between the islands and the beach. Within a few dozen meters from the shore, you can wade, then dogpaddle to the closest reefs, which provide for a fair snorkeling experience.

Because there are no accommodations in the park and camping is not allowed, if you intend to stay longer than a day in this area you will have to get a room in Quepos (see above).

Corcovado National Park

There are several things that make Corcovado National Park special. Its 100,000 acres account for about one-third of the **Península de Osa**, which juts out into the Pacific just north of the Panamanian border, and comprise perhaps the best example of Pacific coastal rain forest left in North America. Its incredibly diverse assemblage of flora and fauna offers one of the most rewarding opportunities for bird-watching and animal-sighting concentrated in a single, defined area. It includes a range of geography and variety of habitat that extends from lowland swamp, mangrove, and alluvial plain to mountain cloud forest, where the annual rainfall averages more than 500 cm (195 inches) per year.

Some 400 species of birds have been counted atop, around, and beneath the 500 types of trees that stand within the confines of the park—nearly half of the total bird species found in Costa Rica. Some 140 species of mammals make their homes in the area, 120 varieties of amphibians and reptiles. In the lakes, ponds, rivers, and streams 40 kinds of freshwater fish have been counted. Corcovado, however, is anything but a collection of statistics, although the numbers suggest the magnitude of the natural life here and the incredible beauty it represents.

Over the millennia Corcovado has assembled its diverse biology, until recently undisturbed by man. In the 1960s, loggers began to penetrate the park to harvest some of its many varieties of trees. Partly to put a stop to that, the area was declared a national park in 1975. Then gold was discovered in its systems of streams, which brought an influx of panners during the 1980s. The miners were evicted in 1986, but a tension developed between the naturalists and the local citizens, who could not understand why they were not allowed to pan for gold. The two groups have been meeting to work out compromises ever since. For now, the miners work the periphery of the park. But here, as in other places in Costa Rica, long-term ecological solutions will require understanding the importance of the natural environment to a population that needs to earn a living. There is a tendency on the part of the dispossessed locals to resent the tourist traffic in the park, so it is most important that visitors be careful in their treatment of the environment.

GETTING TO CORCOVADO

There is no easy overland route south from Manuel Antonio to Corcovado. The coast road is unpaved from Quepos south to Palmar Norte (where you can pick up the Inter-American Highway), a distance of about 90 km (56 miles), with portions of it passable only in the dry season. You can also follow this unpaved road 67 km (41 miles) to Barú, then take the paved road northeast to San Isidro and get on the Inter-American Highway there, but that stretch of dirt road will take you hours and will be a nerve-racking journey in wet weather. The only other option is to circle back toward San José, pick up the Inter-American Highway 14 km (9 miles) east of Atenas, then take it south to the access route to Corcovado. But this is a trip of more than 500 km (300 miles)! (For more details, see Getting Around, below).

The most pleasant way to see the best of the Pacific parks and preserves, as we have stressed, is from the sea, which allows you to cherry-pick the coast and lets someone else do the piloting. Many of the logistical headaches of getting to and into Corcovado, in particular, then locating a place to bed down, can be eliminated if you approach the park by sea. Temptress Cruises includes Corcovado as the southern terminus of its southern Pacific itinerary, and the half-day "hard nature" tour of the park off the cruise ship includes a tandem of benefits: the best nature has to offer, combined with creature comforts not available to those who choose to drive and hike overland. Costa Rica Expeditions offers transportation to Corcovado to guests of its tent camp within the park. (See "Touring the Pacific Coast," above; "Staying at Corcovado," below; and "Getting Around," at the end of this chapter.)

TREKKING IN CORCOVADO

During the pre-trek briefing aboard *Temptress,* the ship's resident naturalist guides will inform those taking the hike the next day that 45 minutes to an hour of the route will be "in" a stream, water that's sometimes waist deep. You are advised that the jaunt will require the "suitable clothing" you were encouraged to pack when you received orientation literature: all-weather hiking sandals and shorts or old clothing, plus plenty of insect repellent.

After the initiation of a wet landing from the rubber Zodiacs that usher the party ashore, the hikers are issued walking sticks, then led off into the rain forest, where they immediately pick up the trail beside a slow-moving stream. The pathway is hilly and muddy, a slick, reddish clay. There are slips, stumbles, grabs for tree limbs and vines, carefully placed steps with the invaluable support of the walking sticks, while the guide continues a monologue, sotto voce so as not to spook the animals most of the hikers have come to see.

If you have a choice of guides, ask for Margherita Bottazzi, one of the breed of young Costa Ricans who have been trained at the University of Costa Rica for careers in biology, zoology, or botany. It is, after all, in the natural sciences that their country has so much to teach the world. For years the experts have been trooping in from outside the country; now Costa Rica is producing its own crop of experts. When Bottazzi joined Temptress, she was instrumental in selecting the trails that would provide the best opportunities for passengers to experience the most the rain forests had to offer, without disturbing the environment in the process.

If you are guided by Margherita Bottazzi or any of her contemporaries, you will get a sense of how much these young ecologists love the natural wonder of their country, in its totality, and the relationships among all the plants and animals that make up its ecological fabric. You begin to understand the sensitivity in Bottazzi's light touch as she gently picks a tiny land frog from a leaf of grass and pronounces it "insect control" before she lowers her index finger and lets the frog hop off into a pile of wet leaves. She will not so much as strike any of the flying pests that accompany you through the Corcovado, preferring instead to leave the environment to its own devices. These young people of Costa Rica provide a lesson that in and of itself is worth the trip.

Along the trail, you must be extremely attentive or you will miss the less-obvious attractions, such as a sloth clinging to the underside of a tree limb. And you must be alert to the fact that out here the show changes quickly. For while you are noting the relationship between the trees and their various clinging vines, you may miss the quick pass of a violaceous trogon, or a red-legged honeycreeper, or the harpy eagle, a huge bird of prey that inhabits the forest here. If you do get to see a harpy eagle, you will find yourself holding your breath, for it almost appears the creation of a Steven Spielberg or George Lucas science-fiction movie, with its huge gray head and ominous hooked beak. While sightings of the bird are extremely rare (one has not occurred for several years), there is still hope that some harpy eagles are alive and breeding in the more remote reaches of the park, so you never know.

A squawk overhead should alert you to one of the park's real treats. If you hear it, crouch low beneath the huge leaves of a fishtail palm (they're everywhere), then direct your gaze to the sky. Chances are good that a pair of scarlet macaws is flying over. They are just a red crayon-swipe across a patch of blue—gone in an instant—but an unforgettable image.

At a wide point in the stream, where the water moves slowly over flat rocks and large, rounded boulders, the trail comes to an end. You enter the river here; before you do, perch on one of the rocks and make sure that your footwear is properly positioned and secured. You should continue to wear your sandals or tennis shoes because some rocks are slippery, and others are sharp and may cut your feet.

While you may have some reservations about entering the river, you immediately will feel the soothing effects of the cooler water. The hike up the stream will soon become the high point of the trek. It terminates at a waterfall, where there is time to rest, take a dip, and enjoy some of the fruit juice or water you have been hauling for several hours.

By the time you are led out of the rain forest to a clearing on the beach, the crew from *Temptress* will have assembled there, placed chairs beneath a grove of shade trees, and set up tables of food and tubs of cold drinks on ice. It will seem an amazingly civilized way to end a trip through a gloriously uncivilized environment. The crew understands the need for the transition—otherwise they might have trouble coaxing the passengers back on board. The afternoon is then given over to swimming, snorkeling, and assorted other water sports.

BAHIA DRAKE

One other option of the tour is a visit to Bahía Drake (Drake Bay) and the tiny village of Drake. The village is little more than a school, a general store, and a series of huts, but it provides an idea of how people live in an isolated portion of Central America. It is very difficult to reach by land. To do so you have to come all the way around the Península de Osa, from northeast to northwest, mainly on unimproved road, a distance of about 125 km (78 miles) that is passable only in the dry season, and a very rough ride even then. It is hardly worth the trip. However, if *Temptress* has a Zodiac running over there—and often they do when they are in the area—you should take a look. If there is time, take a swim in the bay: lovely, clear, warm water, bordered by a beautiful beach the color of café con leche.

Not far off the beach at Bahía Drake is **Cocalito Lodge**, a cluster of cabins and a restaurant run by a Canadian brother-and-sister team. The restaurant is the reason to call here. The owners have planted and nurtured a garden of vegetables and herbs, which accompany their tasty selections. You can enjoy any of three daily meals here, ranging from a delightful breakfast of French toast (covered in honey and coconut) to a dinner of seafood stuffed with the fruits of the garden. Guests who would like to spend a few days can stay in the cabins. The proprietors will pick you up at the airport at Palmar Norte and drive you the 10 km (6 miles) to Sierpe, on the Río Sierpe, from where they take you by launch to the dock at the property. Tel: 75-6291. Temptress Cruises will arrange for you to have dinner at the restaurant; after dark the crew takes you ashore, leading the way by torchlight and adding a touch of adventure in this wildly beautiful area.

STAYING AT CORCOVADO

Costa Rica Expeditions, one of the largest tour operators in Costa Rica, has built its ▶ **Corcovado Lodge Tent Camp** right on the beach. The site includes 20 walled tents, a screened, thatched-roof dining area, common bathhouse, and toilets. While this is more than do-it-yourself camping, it is still roughing it for most people. The heat and humidity are both very high in Corcovado, and if you are spending the night there is no escaping them. For those who decide to give it a try, the camp makes available its 10-meter (32-foot) pontoon boat for guided tours along the coastline of the park and access to areas almost impossible to reach on foot; staffers will also organize guided hikes into the park. They will also take you over to Caño Island (see below).

The tent camp is booked through Costa Rica Expeditions, which can also arrange air or land transportation. (See the Accommodations Reference at the end of this chapter.)

Campsites and bunking accommodations are also available at the ranger stations in Corcovado, as they are in most of the country's national parks and reserves, for minimal cost: less than $1 per day for campsites to about $10 per day for accommodations with a roof over your head plus meals in the park dining area. To stay and eat requires arrangements in advance with the information office in Puerto Jiménez (see Getting Around).

Caño Island Biological Reserve

Seventeen kilometers (11 miles) west of the Península de Osa is Isla del Caño, a biological reserve renowned for its seaside natural attractions and its man-made relics, including ancient sculptures of unknown origin and mysterious significance.

The small (750 acres) island is noted for its pre-Columbian cemetery and curious spherical stones hewn by a long-vanished people. A number of the trails lead past the stones, which are the subject of conjecture on the part of tour guides, as archaeologists have thus far failed to come up with conclusive explanations for either what they are or who made them.

The short hike up the sides of a mesa from the beach affords dramatic views of the surrounding sea. Aside from a handful of mammals and the standard assortment of seabirds, however, Caño Island itself has little to distinguish it. Beneath the glass-clear, lusciously warm waters that surround it, however, lives a rich assortment of sealife. A half dozen reefs harbor more than a dozen species of coral and colonies of inhabitants that range from tiny jacks to giant rays, an assortment of sea turtles, and even an occasional passing pod of whales.

The island's stretches of beach are silk-smooth light-brown sand, with charcoal swipes of black that change length and direction with each receding wave. Jetties and piles of black rock mark off the beaches and act as natural breakwaters for the riptide. Tiny rivulets empty fresh water from the morning rain on the plateau into the sea, providing miniature feeding estuaries for stiff-legged seabirds.

A beach here is a lovely place to park for a day, haul out the picnic baskets and a cold beer or a chilled bottle of white wine, and get a touch of sun. You can punctuate your periods of uninterrupted stress-relief with an occasional drift above the reef and a closer look at the amazingly brilliant colors darting about the coral beneath you.

There are no places to stay on the island, and camping is not permitted. The *Temptress* generally calls here as part of its southern itinerary. Costa Rica Expeditions also includes trips to the island as part of its southern Pacific packages and makes day trips over for those staying at its Corcovado Lodge Tent Camp.

NORTH OF PUNTARENAS

Most people exploring the Pacific coast will begin their journey—whether by sea or land—from Puntarenas. At the very least, visitors are likely to pass through the port on their way north or south. Using Puntarenas, then, as a launching point, we will explore the coast north of the city, where the diversity of terrain, the wide range of plant and wildlife species, and the accessibility of most of the area to Puntarenas combine the best of sightseeing with manageable logistics.

Each of the principal wildlife areas in the northern Pacific region of Costa Rica can be explored on a day trip or a longer excursion, depending upon your interest in the local flora and fauna. Suffice it to say that the longer you stay the more you are likely to see, but you can also encounter some of the resplendent wonders of this area through a series of single day trips. To maximize the effectiveness of your journeys into the wilds here, local guides are important. They know the effects of season, changes in weather and terrain, time of day, and method of approach. Making arrangements for a guide in advance of your trip is a good idea. (See "Touring Costa Rica" in Useful Facts.)

Monteverde Cloud Forest Preserve

The access road to the Monteverde Cloud Forest Preserve is off the Inter-American Highway, about 33 km (20 miles) north of Puntarenas. It is the right turn that heads northeast toward Sarmiento and Guácimal. On maps it looks like a short haul, perhaps another 25 km (16 miles) to the village of Monteverde, adjacent to the preserve. But maps also indicate that it's a gravel road, and that is treating it kindly. Locals will tell you that you can make it in an ordinary vehicle in dry weather but will need four-wheel drive when it is wet. The truth is that the latter is the best bet no matter what the conditions; much of the way is boulder-strewn, rutted, and potholed. It is teeth-rattling, spine-jarring, and bladder-busting, with no place for relief of the latter except the cover of a stand of trees here and there. Whatever you do, don't give up. The trip from Puntarenas will take two to two and a half hours in decent weather.

The end of the road will deposit you at the information center and gift shop, where you can make arrangements for a guide. Then you will have the privilege of sinking calf-deep into muddy ooze, sliding down slick clay slopes, parading through the low-hung clouds until your clothes feel as if they are moldering before your eyes. But this *is* a cloud forest. In a cloud forest it is not rain you are feeling but literally the undersides of clouds resting directly on

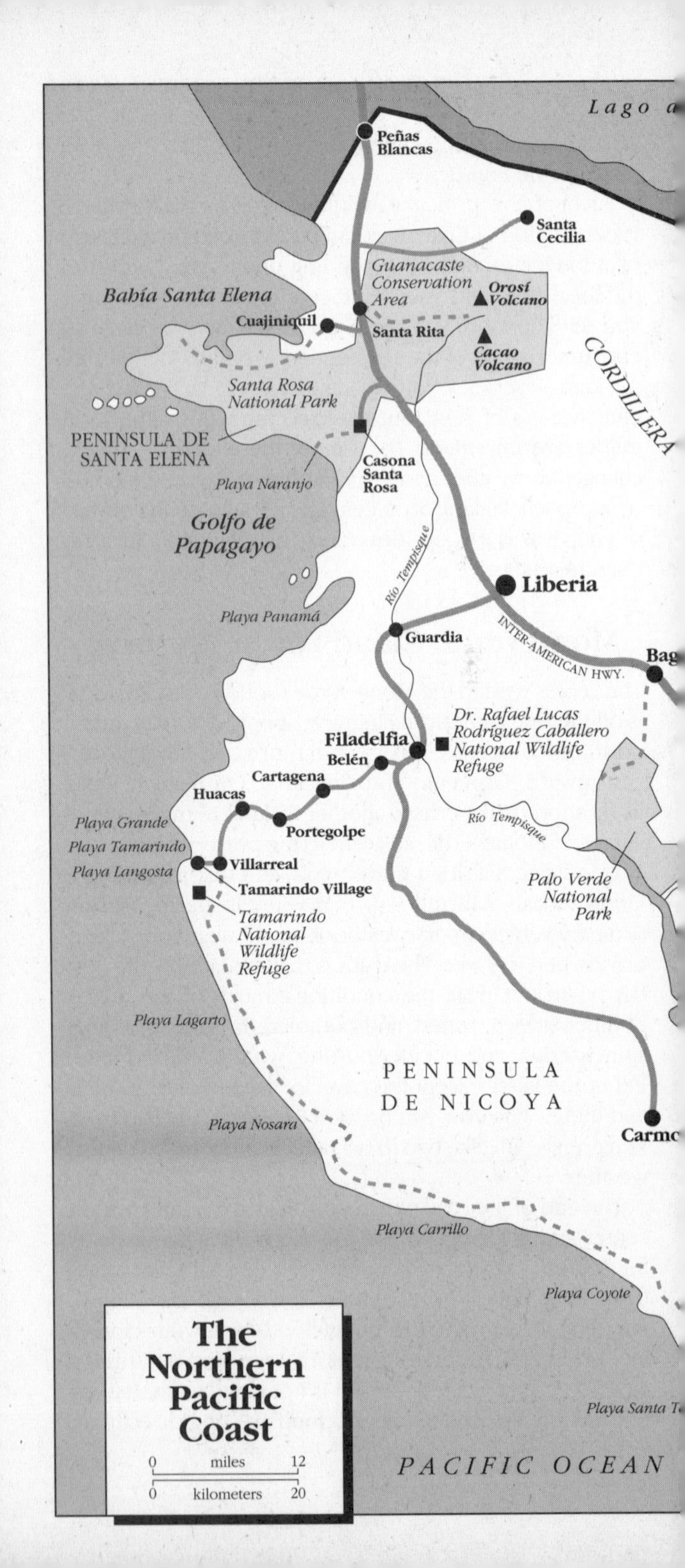

Lago
Peñas Blancas
Santa Cecilia
Guanacaste Conservation Area
Orosí Volcano
Bahía Santa Elena
Cuajiniquil
Santa Rita
Cacao Volcano
CORDILLERA
Santa Rosa National Park
PENINSULA DE SANTA ELENA
Casona Santa Rosa
Playa Naranjo
Golfo de Papagayo
Río Tempisque
Liberia
Playa Panamá
Guardia
INTER-AMERICAN HWY.
Dr. Rafael Lucas Rodríguez Caballero National Wildlife Refuge
Filadelfia
Belén
Cartagena
Huacas
Playa Grande
Portegolpe
Río Tempisque
Playa Tamarindo
Playa Langosta
Villarreal
Tamarindo Village
Palo Verde National Park
Tamarindo National Wildlife Refuge
Playa Lagarto
PENINSULA DE NICOYA
Playa Nosara
Playa Carrillo
Playa Coyote
The Northern Pacific Coast
0 miles 12
0 kilometers 20
PACIFIC OCEAN

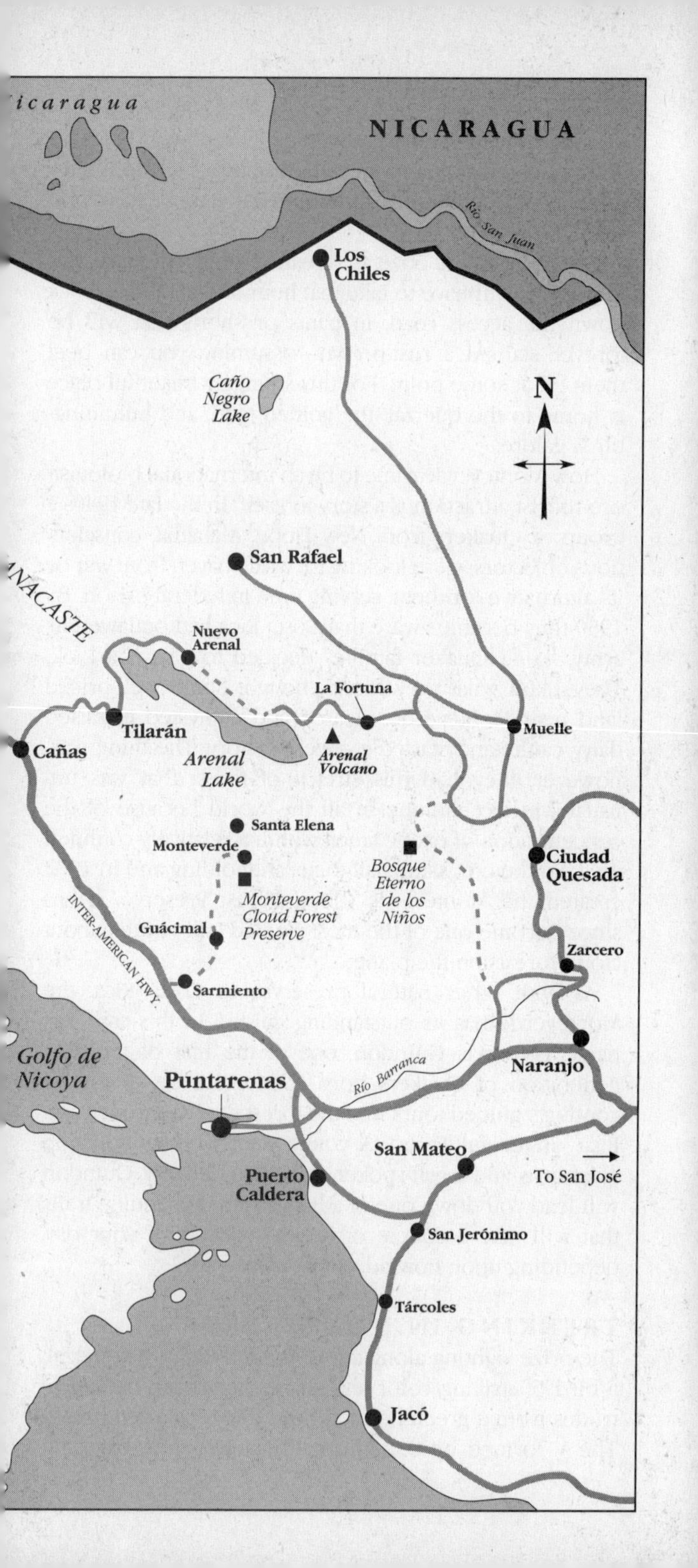

icaragua
NICARAGUA
Río San Juan
Los Chiles
Caño Negro Lake
N
San Rafael
NACASTE
Nuevo Arenal
La Fortuna
Tilarán
Cañas
Muelle
Arenal Lake
Arenal Volcano
Santa Elena
Monteverde
Monteverde Cloud Forest Preserve
Bosque Eterno de los Niños
Ciudad Quesada
INTER-AMERICAN HWY.
Guácimal
Sarmiento
Zarcero
Golfo de Nicoya
Puntarenas
Río Barranca
Naranjo
San Mateo
To San José
Puerto Caldera
San Jerónimo
Tárcoles
Jacó

the hilltops. Here there is a whole different world of flora and fauna—plants and animals that thrive in the incessantly damp, sometimes chilly landscape *above* the cloud line.

Out there in the ooze are creatures that will make you forget you will have to take that hour-and-a-half trip back down the access road, in pants or shorts that will be forever stained a rust-brown—assuming you can peel them off at some point. For this strangely beautiful place is home to the quetzal, the golden toad, and hummingbirds galore.

How Monteverde came to be an international biologist/eco-tourist attraction is a story in itself. In the late 1940s a group of Quakers from New Hope, Alabama, conscientious objectors, were looking for a safe haven from war or its alternative for them: serving time in federal prison. By 1950 they became aware that Costa Rica had outlawed its army, so 44 Quaker families decided to give it a look. They liked what they found, bought some well-priced land near Monteverde, cleared and cultivated it, raised dairy cattle, and started a cheese factory. The thing was, however, they had this stretch of forest that was unusual—in fact, unique in all the world because of the concentration of exotic fauna within a relatively confined area. So they set aside half their landholding and in 1972 created the Monteverde Cloud Forest Preserve. It has since become one of the most studied and written-about cloud forests on the planet.

As with other natural preserves in Costa Rica, the Monteverde has its outstanding guides. In this case, his name is Tomás Guindon, one of the first of the new generation of Quakers born at Monteverde. Today he conducts guided tours into the forest (see "Touring Costa Rica" in Useful Facts). A young man with muttonchop sideburns and a soft-spoken, bilingual delivery, Guindon will lead you down one of a half dozen demanding trails that will take a couple of hours, or most of your day, depending upon how adventurous you are.

TREKKING IN MONTEVERDE

The prize sighting along any of these treks is the quetzal, a bird of striking color and shape. Its golden beak protrudes from a green-hooded head that tops a red breast. The V formed by the split tail feathers—gray-black on top, white underneath—gives the appearance of a silk-lined tuxedo jacket. The quetzal is endangered because of its ever-shrinking habitat and the increasingly predatory strikes of weasels and snakes that like to dine on its eggs.

A shy bird, the quetzal will have you hoofing off the trail, across fields, over fences, then craning your neck and straining your eyes just for a glimpse, unable to give up after hours of anticipation. Guides like Guindon, tripod-mounted unocular at the ready, will do whatever it takes to produce a sighting. They know where the quetzals roost and what times of day they are likely to be there.

And when you do finally spot one, high in a laurel tree, pecking away at the fruit of this avocado relative, spitting out the seeds to assure more laurels and more fruit... when you've seen this, the great prize of the Monteverde forest, then your guide will tell you about the golden toad.

More treasured even than the quetzal, the golden toad is a tiny creature that appears to be a piece of orange porcelain. The problem is that the guide will only be able to show you a picture in a trail guide. None has been seen since 1988, and the fear is that the golden toad is extinct. No one is quite sure, however, so a trek through Monteverde could conceivably produce a sighting that will create the memory of a lifetime.

Even without the golden toad or the quetzal, Monteverde is worth the trip.

Just beyond the information center and gift shop at the starting point for the preserve's network of trails, in the cool shade of a stand of pines, hangs a hummingbird feeder, filled with a 15 percent sugar-water solution and surrounded—mostly mornings and evenings—with a variety of species, including the incredibly iridescent black and green long-billed variety. While this may smack of the artificiality of a controlled environment, it is an effective appetite-whetter. For once you duck beneath the moisture-laden branches at the mouth of the trail, the only thing contrived about the trek is the narrow, trodden path and the occasional terracing of the steepest, slipperiest inclines. On either side of the trail is a great assortment of bromeliads, each with a cup-like core that is a catch-basin for an entomological universe in miniature.

The clomp of your footfalls against the irregular surface of the trail or the sucking sound of your withdrawal from the mud is counterpointed by the song of the wren or the hum of the wind in a giant, ancient oak, its lee side bearded with tangled strands of dark-green moss. There are definite distinctions between the various forms of plant life that take hold of the trees: pythonic vines with elephantine leaves and tiny orchids that spot color along a trunk or limb. Some are epiphytes that draw their moisture and nutrients from the air and live in symbiotic relationship with the tree; others are parasites that suck away their host's life to serve their own ends. Most are beautiful.

Three quarters of the way up the Sendero Río (the River Path), which skirts the ravine above the Cuecha Creek, you will be standing on the continental divide. There is a notch in the tree line on either side, man made, but in fantasy it creates the appearance of a natural swath to mark the divide. The clouds usually clear away for brief periods, as if they, too, want you to mark the spot and note the view. The sound of the wind is overpowered, on occasion, by the deep-throated call of a distant bird: the three-wattled bellbird, a bizarre-looking creature with three flaps of flesh hanging from beneath its beak. The bird will likely hang back in the trees somewhere, however, make no appearance, and let his sound die beneath the breeze.

From the continental divide, the trek on the loop back to the information center slopes mostly downward, is planked along considerable stretches, and seems more . . . civilized. While it is a relief to aching muscles and mud-caked limbs, the return lacks something: the unpredictability of the hike up. The dual personality of the trail seems a metaphor for Monteverde itself, its attempts to balance civilization and the wild without allowing them to blend into the blandness of some middle ground. Monteverde does seem to be struggling with its definition of itself. Lodges and small inns now sprinkle the perimeters of the park, and the procession of visitors into the preserve grows steadily.

At the information center/gift shop area you will be able to hose off your boots or sandals, but your body will need a hosing as well, and that will have to wait.

Bosque Eterno de los Niños

The Monteverde preserve has grown larger over the past several years and has even spawned a kind of satellite preserve called the Bosque Eterno de los Niños, also known as the First International Children's Rain Forest. The idea for the Children's Rain Forest originated with a group of schoolchildren in Sweden who decided to do what they could to help save the tropical rain forests. They raised money—through recycling projects, bake sales, and contributions—to buy 15 acres to be set aside as a wildlife preserve. Within five years El Bosque's protected lands, adjacent to the eastern borders of the Monteverde preserve, had grown to almost 50,000 acres.

Efforts at preserving the environment in this area are overseen by the Monteverde Conservation League, a local nonprofit organization of concerned citizens and international biologists. The Conservation League is also working with the local community to help build a viable economy and to devise ways to integrate conservation with development.

For information on the Bosque Eterno de los Niños and the possibility of arranging a tour of part of the area, write to the Monteverde Conservation League, Apartado 10165-1000, San José.

STAYING AND DINING IN THE MONTEVERDE AREA

Small hotels and lodges have been popping up around Monteverde in ever-increasing numbers, spurred on by the growing interest in the area's biological wonders. However, there is still no "strip" per se, and most of the accommodations here tend to be tastefully integrated into the surroundings. Most of the hotels and lodges also incorporate a restaurant, but don't expect to be dazzled. Food at Monteverde tends to be very basic: meat or chicken, potatoes or yams, and green vegetables or corn. Remember, too, the area was founded and many of the establishments are run by Quakers, so there is little evidence of alcohol and no nightlife.

The ▸ **Monteverde Lodge** is in the adjacent town of Santa Elena. Make a right, per the sign, just before the access road intersects with the road to the preserve, and travel about 500 meters. The lodge has 27 rooms with private baths, and there is also a 15-person Jacuzzi for soaking out the day's caking of mud and relaxing cramped muscles. You can also commune with your contemporaries (or fellow sufferers, as the case may be) around a roaring fire; it can get cool at night up here, and it certainly is damp. From the lodge it is less than 5 km (3 miles) to the preserve.

The ▶ **Hotel de Montaña Monteverde**, along the road to the preserve, a few hundred meters beyond the Santa Elena town gas station, has 26 rooms with private hot-water baths. The **restaurant** serves basic family-style meals, but the view from the dining room of the surrounding forests is quite nice, and the fireplace makes for a comfortable gathering area, particularly on a damp, chilly evening.

A similar operation is the ▶ **Hotel Belmar**, a chalet-type construction of 25 rooms with private, hot-water baths and a simple, family-style **restaurant**. If you're not staying at the hotel, a meal from salad through entrée—generally a basic chicken or meat dish, with rice and beans—to dessert runs about $15, including a soft drink and coffee. It is a few hundred meters along on its own access road, a left at the gas station on the main road to the preserve.

The ▶ **Pensión Flor Mar** is in the village of Monteverde on the road to the preserve, about 2 km (1¼ miles) from the entrance. It is owned and operated by one of the Monteverde community's original Quakers, who will regale you with stories of how he and his contemporaries struggled to farm the mountain, and then to build the cheese factory that serves as a focal point for the area's dairy farms. Some rooms have private baths, others share them.

The best place to dine in Monteverde is **La Cascada**, on the access road to the preserve, about 200 meters short of the town's gas station. The menu includes a modest assortment of Continental dishes and some of the local seafood, rice, and bean fare. The restaurant also includes a nice selection of Chilean and Argentine wines.

SHOPPING IN THE MONTEVERDE AREA

La Lechería, the cheese factory, is just off the road to the preserve, short of the bridge over the Río Guácimal. It's worth a peek if you've never seen such an operation. You can watch the cheese being made through a large window, or you can arrange a free guided tour. You can also get a sample or two or buy enough for a few meals. The store's hours are 7:30 A.M. to 4:30 P.M., except Sundays.

Of the local galleries worth stopping at, the **Crafts Cooperative**, on the road to the preserve, is the best choice. Here you can purchase some lovely handmade and embroidered blouses and other fabric items depicting the quetzal, the golden toad, and hummingbirds, among other creatures, with proceeds going to benefit the local community.

The **Hummingbird Gallery**, just short of the park entrance, is worth a stop, too. Here you will see some wonderful examples of the work of British wildlife photographers Michael and Patricia Fogden.

Palo Verde National Park and Dr. Rafael Lucas Rodríguez Caballero National Wildlife Refuge

Some of the widest variations in Costa Rica's extensive biological diversity are found in the Palo Verde National Park, which now also includes the Dr. Rafael Lucas Rodríguez Caballero National Wildlife Refuge. The park is due west of Monteverde and northwest of Puntarenas. It sits in the lowlands along the northern shoreline of the **Río Tempisque**, west of the **Río Bebedero** and just above the confluence of both rivers, where they empty into the Golfo de Nicoya. Here the terrain varies from marsh, grassland, and savannah to dry forest.

Palo Verde, like many of the national parks and preserves along the Pacific coast, is not easily reached by land. The access road is south off the Inter-American Highway at Bagaces, about 20 km (12 miles) north of Cañas and 90 km (55 miles) northwest of Puntarenas; it runs south another 20 km to the park. As the road is gravel and dirt, it is wet and muddy during the rainy season and very dusty during the dry season. Renting a four-wheel-drive vehicle is your best bet. It is a good one and a half to two hours from Bagaces to the park. The *Temptress* calls in here as part of its northern itinerary.

The trees wear a thick covering of green during the summer wet season, then thin noticeably during the dry season (December to April), which allows for much easier animal-watching. In the dry months, watering holes and small ponds also shrink or dry up, which in turn adds to the concentration of wildlife around the remaining sources of water, again affording wonderful observation points. In the dry season the mosquitoes, gnats, and other flying pests that swarm the area during the rainy periods are far less concentrated, driven off by the stiff winds that are prevalent during that time of the year.

Palo Verde has the usual Costa Rican complement of mammals, reptiles, butterflies, and other colorful insects, but the big attraction here is the great diversity of birds, a combination of the year-round residential community and migratory waterfowl. Some 275 species have been recorded, but it is not so much the number that is appealing here—there are more species in other areas—as it is the unusual variety.

Among the residents or regular transients is the jabiru stork, a magnificent creature said to be the largest stork in the world. Its coloring is predominantly white with a gray-hooded head, set off by a blood-red neckband. Only a handful of jabirus nest here, and you would have to be extremely fortunate to see any, but the other varieties of birds you will see will make the trip worthwhile in any event. There are the tiniest of wrens and hummingbirds, magnificent ospreys and carcaras, and a great collection of wading and water birds: ducks, storks, egrets, herons, spoonbills, ibis, and grebes.

STAYING AT PALO VERDE

There is a **biological station** at the terminus of the gravel road into the park, where accommodations plus food can be had for about $30 a day. As in most of the biological stations in the Costa Rican national park system, these accommodations are bare-bones operations, but they allow you to spend a few days in the area and exponentially increase your chances of having a memorable encounter with the wildlife, perhaps even a jabiru stork. For more information, contact the Organization of Tropical Studies, Apartado 676-2050, San Pedro Montes de Oca, San José; Tel: 40-6696; Fax: 40-6783.

Santa Rosa National Park and Guanacaste Conservation Area

It is perhaps a tribute to Costa Rica's long-standing aversion to military strongmen that the country's national hero is not a *conquistador,* a general, or a president/ex-warlord, but a young *campesino* named Juan Santamaría. Santamaría's moment of glory came in early 1856, when he was part of an all-volunteer army assembled to drive back American adventurer William Walker, who had designs on controlling most of Central America and enslaving a good deal of the population. After routing the forces of Nicaragua, Walker pushed south into Costa Rica and dug in at a hacienda called **Casona Santa Rosa**, in the far northwestern part of the country. Here, 9,000 Costa Rican volunteers met and defeated the band of mercenary raiders, driving them back into Nicaragua. Pursued by the Costa Ricans, Walker sought shelter in a fort at the town of Rivas. Santamaría volunteered to torch the wooden fort and was killed in the battle.

Almost 120,000 acres around the hacienda where the Costa Ricans met and defeated William Walker were set aside to commemorate the event and in 1971 were declared the Santa Rosa National Park. The hacienda where the famous battle took place is known as La Casona and has been restored to its 19th-century personality. A museum has also been installed in portions of the hacienda, and its adjoining and adjacent buildings.

GETTING TO SANTA ROSA

The main entrance to Santa Rosa is off the Inter-American Highway not quite halfway between the town of Liberia and the Nicaraguan border, a little more than 35 km (22 miles) north of Liberia. (The capital of Guanacaste province, Liberia is a town of less than 30,000, with little of interest to visitors.) It is 155 km (96 miles) from Puntarenas, or a good two- to two-and-a-half-hour drive, and about 65 km (40 miles) from Palo Verde. La Casona, the museum, and the administration center are about 5 km (3 miles) southwest from the Inter-American Highway, along a well-paved road.

Southwest of La Casona, a dirt road leads toward the

southern coast of the **Península de Santa Elena** to Playa Naranjo (where the olive ridley turtle nests; see below) on the Golfo de Papagayo. Access to the north coast is via the Inter-American Highway to a turnoff just south of Santa Rita, then 6 km (3½ miles) through Cuajiniquil by paved road, and finally another 20 km (12 miles) of dirt road to just short of the coast at Bahía Santa Elena.

The easiest access to Santa Rosa National Park, however, is from the sea; Temptress Cruises visits here for one day as part of its four-day northern itinerary. (See "Touring the Pacific Coast," above, for contact information.)

TREKKING IN SANTA ROSA

Perhaps unanticipated at the time by the park's founders, whose goal was to preserve the area's historical tradition, was the territory's significance as one of the largest examples of tropical dry forest in the Western Hemisphere. And this may be the most important legacy. The park comprises virtually all of the Península de Santa Elena and will help assure its maintenance as a natural forest and wildlife preserve.

Plant life that distinguishes the dry forest from its rainier cousin lines the trail here. Most favored of the arboreal sightings is the guanacaste tree, namesake of the province and the national tree of Costa Rica. The maroon-red trunk of the gumbo-limbo, or naked Indian tree, is another common sight. Endangered cedars and giant ashes spread their crowns to the more abundant light in these thinner forests. Tree-dwelling vines and other plants here are also representative of the climatic conditions; cactuses reach toward the usually dry, blue sky from their perches on the tree limbs.

Here, courtesy of natural selection and the survival of the fittest, one of the orchids assures its continued existence by playing a trick on the wasp species that it depends upon to pollinate it. The orchid has evolved to assume the appearance of the female wasp. As the male wasp approaches the flower, the deception is carried a step further: The orchid emits a chemical that smells like the pheromone emitted by the female. By the time the male wasp realizes his mistake, he is covered in pollen, which he then carries to other flowers.

In the air above the trails and paths inside the park you are apt to see many of the more than 250 species of birds that have been identified here, including the violaceous trogon, crested guan, long-tailed manakin, royal flycatcher, toucans (including the collared ara-kari), and many varieties of orioles, tanagers, and hawks. The song of the spotted-breasted wren may lull you into a post-lunch siesta, but just as you are about to nod off you may receive a squawky wake-up call from the white-throated magpie-jay, commonly seen and heard in these woods.

There is no paucity of mammal life here either, with more than 100 species identified. In the dry season, from January through May, you are likely to see them gathering around small ponds and water holes, or congregating in the nearby trees. Among the most common are the coatimundis, peccaries, tapirs, and white-tailed deer; occasionally a coyote stalking its prey makes an appearance. Spider monkeys and white-throated capuchins also populate the treetops, while the jet-black howlers will shout you out of their territory if you get too close.

Insects provide their usual variety show, entertaining with a vast array of colors, shapes, and patterns. Great clusters of beetles huddle together in large globs on the surface of a leaf to fool predators into thinking they are really one large animal, too big to get a beak around. You can watch a giant green rothschildia caterpillar gobble up a fan-size leaf as you take a breather from your trek to nurse a soft drink or a fruit juice. Above you in the fruit trees, bats lick the nectar oozing from mangoes, tamarinds, or cashews, then, toward evening, begin flying their zigzag patterns.

However, the stars of nature's circus in this corner of the world are the reptiles. A scaly gray iguana resting on a tree limb, or an immature green one sunning in a patch of light that bathes a pile of dry leaves, may arouse your interest in these cold-blooded inhabitants of this area, but it is the turtles that will capture your imagination.

TURTLE-WATCHING AT PLAYA NARANJO

Santa Rosa is one of the few remaining nesting places for the olive ridley turtle. While these sea creatures are in the area from August through December, it is during September and October that their activity along the sandy beaches is most concentrated. Great *arribadas* (arrivals) feature a cast of thousands of the creatures, as they emerge from the Pacific Ocean to lay their eggs. In the process they crowd Playa Naranjo on the south coast of the Península de Santa Elena, just over 15 km (9 miles) southwest of the administration center. Ask the rangers at the administration center to point you in the right direction. As this period is the rainy season, you will need a four-wheel-drive vehicle if you are to have a chance at getting to within striking distance of the beach. The road down is unimproved, and will be wet and very muddy. Also, you need permission to enter the area when the turtles are nesting, so you must check with the administration center before deciding to do so. Tel: 69-5598.

GUANACASTE CONSERVATION AREA

With the addition of the Guanacaste Conservation Area to the national park system in 1989, this protected area of Costa Rica more than doubled. On the east side of the Inter-American Highway, Guanacaste extends the dry forest system here to the point where it now can truly accommodate the needs of the indigenous animals who must have room to roam.

Two dormant volcanoes, Orosí and Cacao, help define the terrain here and extend the range of habitat from coastal dry forest to mountain cloud forest. Although Orosí is much closer to the Pacific than to the Atlantic, it lies east of the continental divide, its watershed flows eastward, and the environment here is more Caribbean than Pacific.

STAYING IN THE SANTA ROSA/ GUANACASTE AREA

There are only rough lodgings and campsites in the park or conservation area. The best place to pitch your tent in Santa Rosa is in the **campground** near the administration center. Here you have access to water, for both drinking and showering, and benches to sit at for meals. You can also make arrangements to take your meals with the park service for about $10 per day; Tel: 69-5598.

Within Guanacaste there are two biological stations approachable by vehicle (four-wheel-drive) where you can bed down for the night. ▸ **Maritza biological station** is in the shadow of the Orosí volcano, about 12 km (7 miles) east of the Inter-American Highway, on a road opposite the Cuajiniquil turnoff. ▸ **Pitilla biological station** sits on the northeastern slope of Orosí. Turn east 10 km (6 miles) north of Santa Rita and follow the road to Santa Cecilia. Here, ask someone to point you to the dirt road south toward Orosí. (The area's third biological station, Cacao, is very difficult to get to; the last hour of the approach is on foot). Dormitory-style accommodations—no electricity and only cold showers—are the extent of the amenities at these stations. However, the price is right; lodging plus three meals is less than $20 per day. Transportation to the stations from the park headquarters at Santa Rosa is about $12. Campsites are available for less than $1 per day. Horses may be rented for less than $5 per hour. The Guanacaste Conservation Area information office can provide details; Tel: 69-5598.

If you would like to stay closer to the Santa Rosa/ Guanacaste area than Puntarenas, but not endure quite-so-Spartan accommodations, your best bet is the ▶ **Hotel Las Espuelas** in Liberia, where you can get an air-conditioned room with private bath. The hotel has a **restaurant** serving the local spin on meat or chicken with rice and beans. The grounds include a pool. It's about 3 km (2 miles) short of the main road into Liberia, east off the Inter-American Highway.

Tamarindo National Wildlife Refuge

The **Península de Nicoya** juts out from, and runs parallel to, the northwest coast of Costa Rica, forming the western shore of the Golfo de Nicoya. About 1,000 acres of coastline on the northwest shore of the peninsula, at Playas (beaches) Grande, Tamarindo, and Langosta (plus their territorial waters), comprise the Tamarindo National Wildlife Refuge.

GETTING TO TAMARINDO

Unlike most of the other nature refuges along the Pacific coast, Tamarindo is *not* a day trip from Puntarenas. It is too far away for just a day at the beach or to spend any quality time observing the turtles. Accommodations, unfortunately, are sparse, and the hotels are often full. If you decide to spend a night or two, book a room in advance and get written confirmation.

To get here overland from Puntarenas, travel 120 km (74 miles) north on the Inter-American Highway to Liberia, then 20 km (12 miles) west on route 21 to Guardia, where the road turns south and in another 25 km (16 miles) narrows to a secondary road just south of Filadelfia. At Belén the road forks. Take the right, or west, fork and follow the signs for another 35 km (22 miles) through the tiny villages of Cartagena, Portegolpe, Huacas, and Villarreal, until you get to the village of Tamarindo. The coastline is about a 1-km (½-mile) hike from Tamarindo village. Just about anyone in town, local or visitor, can point you to the trail.

ANIMAL-WATCHING AT TAMARINDO

It is a relatively tiny piece of real estate, but along the wide beaches here, from October through March, the giant leatherback turtles come ashore to nest. These largest of sea turtles grow to five feet in length and can weigh more than 800 pounds. They are distinguishable from other sea turtles not only by their great size but by their green-black leathery backs, as opposed to the distinctive hard shell of other sea turtles. Their other distinguishing markings are seven raggedy ridges that line their backs from front to rear.

During nesting season as many as 200 females a night have been observed waddling ashore at Playa Grande, paddling up the beach to where they deposit up to 100 eggs apiece, each the approximate size, shape, and color of a Ping-Pong ball. The nests are a feast for predators, which range from other reptiles, birds, and mammals to that most destructive of all mammals, man. The baby turtles' struggle for survival begins in the egg and continues on land after hatching, especially during the vulnerable period of their furious ten-minute dash to the sea. The battle rages on in undersea flight from predatory fish and seabirds, which can spot the tiny creatures as they float near the surface or come up for air. About one-tenth of 1 percent of the hatchlings survive this ordeal.

It is difficult to see the nesting process without disturbing the environment, which may be why the wildlife refuge does not even appear on the official map of the Costa Rican Tourist Board. Perhaps the best way to observe any portion of the nesting ritual is from a boat. Local boat operators will take you offshore for a fee, which varies widely but can be negotiated. If you are staying at the Hotel Tamarindo Diría (see "Staying in

Tamarindo," below), ask the desk to help you arrange a boat. Otherwise, you will have to take your chances finding one at one of the three beaches. Temptress Cruises (see "Touring the Pacific Coast," above) also plies the offshore waters during the nesting season, and their knowledgeable guides will point out schools of the turtles when they are in the area.

If you are an ecologically conscious and environmentally sensitive visitor, this is a very rewarding trek. Aside from being the nesting place of the turtles, the area is a rich mangrove ecosystem, including five separate varieties of the tree: black, white, red, tea, and buttonwood. The red variety is often covered with wild orchids.

Egrets and spoonbills call the swampy area home, as do a variety of ducks and the great blue heron. Magnificent frigate birds patrol the skies above, and brown pelicans dive-bomb for tiny sea creatures. Caiman slither through the root-snarled rivulets and estuaries, while howler monkeys roar in the trees.

You are not permitted to camp overnight in the reserve, and most of the accommodations in the immediate Tamarindo area are small guest houses with minimal facilities. This is a trip for someone who is more interested in creature sightings than creature comforts.

The Nicoya Peninsula Beaches

The west coast of the Península de Nicoya is not just for turtle nesting, however. From Playa Panamá in the north near Guardia to Playa Santa Teresa near the southern tip of the peninsula, the shoreline stretches about 200 km (120 miles), much of it beautiful beaches. An all-weather gravel road runs along the coast, connecting Tamarindo to Playa Santa Teresa, a distance of about 150 km (90 miles). The beachfronts vary in type from thickly forested to wide stretches of sand that range from beige to coffee-colored. Most are lightly populated, even in the busy dry months.

STAYING IN TAMARINDO

The most popular hotel in the area is the ▸ **Hotel Tamarindo Diría** in Tamarindo village. It has 60 air-conditioned rooms, each with private bath. The hotel is a three-story building with lovely views of the beach from the top floor. The grounds are beautifully landscaped and appointed with pre-Columbian statues. Two swimming pools offer cool dips and relaxing lounging. The alfresco restaurant offers the usual seafood fare, but there is also a fresh catch-of-the-day special. The in-house travel agency can arrange tours, including night journeys to observe the turtles. You may also want to avail yourself of the water-sports equipment, which is rented separately, and spend a few hours windsurfing or snorkeling in the clear waters. These activities can be a nice counterpoint to a trek spent chasing after the sight of a nesting turtle or a glimpse of some other exotic wildlife.

GETTING AROUND

Puntarenas

Getting to Puntarenas and Puerto Caldera from Nicaragua to the north, or the capital district of the Costa Rican Central Valley to the east, is via well-paved highway, much of it two lanes in both directions. If you are coming from Panamá to the south, the access to the Pacific ports is by the Inter-American Highway through San José, then west to the Pacific coast. However, through the mountains even the Inter-American Highway—the principal route to and from San José—can be circuitous for significant stretches, and you should always be on the lookout for locals who, because they feel they know the roads, take more chances than unfamiliar drivers do. Also be aware that beyond any curve you may encounter an extremely slow-moving truck, or one that is stopped while its driver takes a snooze or has a bite to eat.

Major international car-rental companies are represented at the Juan Santamaría International Airport near San José and at downtown locations in the capital. Because any overland trip along the Pacific coast will place you, sooner or later, on "unimproved" road, a sturdy four-wheel-drive vehicle will offer the best possibility of making it to your destination. (But don't be lulled into a false sense of security; even with four-wheel drive some destinations are unattainable, especially during the rainy season.)

The two-hour bus ride from San José to Puntarenas costs about $1.50. The bus departs from the intersection of Calle 12 and Avenida 9 in San José. For schedules and other information, Tel: 22-0064 or 22-1867 in San José; Tel: 61-2158 in Puntarenas.

South of Puntarenas

Unless you are beach-hopping down the southern Pacific coast, sticking to the highways—principally the Inter-American Highway—as much as possible is the best bet for getting to the towns or nature preserves here. While trying to hug the coast is certainly more scenic, it will add hours if not days to your trip, since there are stretches of up to 90 km (56 miles) where the road is gravel, and some shorter stretches passable only in the dry season. Even the coast road between Puntarenas and Quepos, the other principal town on the southern Pacific coast, is a gravel road for about 25 km (16 miles).

The only way to **Carara** is by car, or taxi if you don't drive. It is an easy trip, however, from either Puntarenas or Puerto Caldera: 40 km (25 miles) from Puntarenas and about 25 km (16 miles) from the cruise-ship dock at Puerto Caldera along route 73, which heads southeast to San Jerónimo, then route 84 south toward Tárcoles. The refuge's administration building is about 5 km (3 miles) beyond the Tárcoles bridge on the left, just off the highway.

You can take the bus to **Quepos** and **Manuel Antonio National Park**, if you don't want to drive. The ride from San José (west and south on route 84, via San Jerónimo, Tárcoles, Jacó, and Parrita) takes between four and five hours, depending upon the weather and the condition of the roads during the latter part of the trip. The bus fare is less than $3. For schedule, departure, and other information, Tel: 23-5567.

SANSA has scheduled air service between San José and Quepos, generally six days per week. For rates and schedule information, Tel: 33-0397; Fax: 55-2176. Travelair also flies between the two cities; Tel: 32-7883; Fax: 20-0413.

Getting to and then into **Corcovado** is a demanding experience, typical of journeys to most of Costa Rica's reserves and refuges. The park takes up a substantial portion of the western half of the Península de Osa on the southern Pacific coast. Access overland is southwest off the Inter-American Highway between Venecia and Piedras Blancas. Forty-five kilometers (28 miles) of paved highway will get you from there to Rincón. Thirty-five kilometers (22 miles) farther south, along a gravel road, is Puerto Jiménez, where you will find the park's information office; Tel: 78-5036.

From Puerto Jiménez you still have a way to go. The information office can help you arrange transportation to Carate, where any semblance of road ends. Prices are about $5 if you choose to be part of a scheduled trip, about $50 for a special trip.

If you are driving yourself, you will need a four-wheel-drive vehicle for the 45 km (28 miles) around the southern tip of the Península de Osa to Playa Carate, from which you still have another two hours of hiking to get to La Leona ranger station, the first of the five that ring the park. The ranger stations are five- to six-hour hikes apart, and the trails can be all but impassable during the rainy season, while portions of those that run along the shore are impassable at high tide any time of the year. The hike from Playa Carate to the headquarters ranger station at Sirena takes eight hours. You can also make arrangements to fly into Sirena, on a space-available basis, via Aeronaves out of Golfito; for rates and schedules, Tel: 75-0631.

Costa Rica Expeditions will make travel arrangements to Corcovado for those who book at its Corcovado Lodge Tent Camp (see Accommodations Reference, below).

Getting to **Caño Island** is a major challenge. Costa Rica Expeditions conducts day trips for those staying at its Corcovado Lodge Tent Camp; Temptress Cruises includes it as a stop on its southern itinerary and conducts guided tours (see "Touring the Pacific Coast," above). Information on arranging private trips to the island can be obtained at the Corcovado National Park office, where you must also apply for permission; Tel: 78-5036.

North of Puntarenas

The first part of the trip from Puntarenas to the **Monteverde Cloud Forest Preserve** is easy, all 33 km (20 miles) of it along the Inter-American Highway. However, the final 25 km (16 miles)—turn off the highway and head northeast toward Sarmiento and Guácimal—is a trial. It takes 2 to 2½ hours for the whole trip, depending upon how confident you are in your driving, especially along the access road with its terrible ruts and boulders.

The bus from San José takes a bit more than 4 hours,

and costs less than $4. For schedule times and departure points, Tel: 22-3854.

For a day trip to the preserve, your best bet is letting Costa Rica's Temptations set it up for you. General director Marcos Crespo is one of the most knowledgeable all-purpose guides in Costa Rica, and he sometimes heads the tours himself. Crespo is a member of a number of naturalist organizations, was a guide for a half dozen years before starting his own company, and is well versed in the country's history, geography, geology, and biodiversity. To contact his organization, see the Useful Facts section "Touring Costa Rica."

It's a difficult drive of 1½ to 2 hours to **Palo Verde** on a dirt-and-gravel access road that runs south off the Inter-American Highway from Bagaces, which is about 90 km (55 miles) north of Puntarenas. Temptress Cruises calls in here as part of its northern itinerary.

The main entrance to **Santa Rosa National Park** is west off the Inter-American Highway 35 km (22 miles) north of Liberia. Four-wheel-drive vehicles are necessary to gain access to the **Guanacaste Conservation Area** biological stations, which provide the best locations for campsites but are reached only by rugged roads east off the Inter-American Highway.

Access to the **Tamarindo** shore area is on foot from the town, which is reached by some of the country's better roads as you head west off the Inter-American Highway at Liberia. You will not need a four-wheel-drive vehicle here; simply rent a car at the international airport or in San José. A 5½-hour bus ride also connects the capital with the beach area (Tel: 22-8229 or 22-2750).

If you want to cut hours off your trip, you can reach the town of Tamarindo by air. Both SANSA (Tel: 33-0397; Fax: 55-2176) and Travelair (Tel: 32-7883; Fax: 20-0413) offer service to and from San José.

ACCOMMODATIONS REFERENCE

Unless otherwise indicated, the rate given is the projected rate for a double room, double occupancy, and does not include tax. Price ranges span the lowest rate in the low season to the highest rate in the high season. As prices are subject to change, always double-check before booking.

Puntarenas

▶ **Fiesta Hotel Resort & Casino.** Apartado 171-5400, **Puntarenas.** Tel: 63-0808; Fax: 63-1516; in the U.S. and Canada, Tel: (800) 662-2990 or (305) 871-8501, Fax: (305) 871-2657. $65–$242.

▶ **Hotel Las Brisas.** Apartado 132-5400, **Puntarenas.** Tel. or Fax: 61-2120. $25–$45.

▶ **Hotel Porto Bello.** Apartado 108-5400, **Puntarenas.** Tel: 61-1322; Fax: 61-0036. $50–$70.

▶ **Hotel Tioga.** Apartado 96-5400, **Puntarenas.** Tel: 61-0271; Fax: 61-0127. $37–$57.

▶ **Hotel Yadrán.** Apartado 14-5400, **Puntarenas.** Tel: 61-2662; Fax: 61-1944. $62–$86.

South of Puntarenas

▶ **Corcovado Lodge Tent Camp. Corcovado National Park.** Contact Costa Rica Expeditions, P.O. Box 6941-1000, San José. Tel: 57-0766; Fax: 57-1665. $22–$28.

▶ **Kamuk Hotel.** Apartado 18-6350, **Quepos.** Tel: 77-0379; Fax: 77-0258. $40–$85.

▶ **Karahé Hotel & Villas.** Box 100-6350, **Quepos.** Tel: 77-0170; Fax: 77-0152. $40–$80.

▶ **La Mariposa.** Box 4-6350, **Quepos.** Tel: 77-0355; Fax: 77-0050. $100–$165, MAP.

North of Puntarenas

▶ **Hotel Belmar. Santa Elena.** Contact Apartado 10165-1000, San José. Tel: 61-1001. Fax: 61-3551. $40–$70.

▶ **Hotel Las Espuelas.** Apartado 88-5000, **Liberia,** Guanacaste. Tel: 66-0144; Fax: 25-3987. $45–$65.

▶ **Hotel de Montaña Monteverde. Santa Elena.** Contact Apartado 70, Plaza Víquez, San José. Tel: 61-1846; Fax: 61-3651. $40–$75.

▶ **Hotel Tamarindo Diría. Tamarindo.** Contact Apartado 4211-1000, San José. Tel. or Fax: 68-0652. $60–$85.

▶ **Monteverde Lodge. Santa Elena.** Contact Costa Rica Expeditions, P.O. Box 6941-1000, San José. Tel: 57-0766; Fax: 57-1665. $68–$90.

▶ **Pensión Flor Mar. Monteverde.** Contact Apartado 10165-1000, San José. Tel: 61-0909. $22–$28, AP.

NORTH-CENTRAL COSTA RICA

THE ARENAL VOLCANO REGION

By Buddy Mays

The north-central portion of Costa Rica—that segment of the country lying north of San José on the other side of Poás volcano, east of the Cordillera de Tilarán (Highlands of Tilarán), and west of the Río San Carlos—has been little affected by the 20th century. Undisturbed for the most part by logging or other destructive human endeavors, this land of pristine lowland forests and smoldering volcanoes is a mosaic of scenic terrain that will astonish even the most veteran travellers with its incredible beauty.

Only a small percentage of Costa Rica's three million inhabitants reside in this corrugated landscape, yet for the most part it is well suited to handle travellers. Points of interest here are easy to reach on roads kept in surprisingly good shape by ill-equipped but enthusiastic highway crews. Tap water is sweet and drinkable, restaurant cuisine—nearly all of it strictly traditional—is superb, and tourist hotels, though limited in number, are clean, comfortable, and pleasant.

You'll quickly notice, however, that the inhabitants of the region, free of cultural influences from San José and living within sight (and sound) of potentially deadly

Arenal volcano, differ dramatically from other Costa Ricans. Unlike the good-time-loving Ticos from the Central Highlands and Central Valley, the cheerful, quick-to-grin fishermen on the Pacific side, or the mañana-oriented Rastafarians along the Caribbean, these north-central people are a serious, sturdy folk, prone to shyness, quick to anger, and, though not unfriendly, certainly less than outgoing. If you know any Spanish at all, this is the place to use it. Few residents here speak anything else, and, like traditional people everywhere, most of them appreciate visitors who at least attempt to communicate in the local language.

The principal route for tourists in this part of Costa Rica is the Naranjo–Quesada–Arenal road, which at Naranjo turns right off the Inter-American Highway 44 km (27 miles) west-northwest of San José and runs in a northwesterly direction. There are other highways here—smaller, rougher, twistier, and less well maintained—but the Naranjo–Quesada–Arenal road is the most scenic and the easiest to navigate.

Rental cars are available at the San José airport and most of San José's hotels (there are no cars for rent in the north-central region itself); however, while exploring the attractions and countryside in your own vehicle gives you plenty of freedom, it also has some disadvantages. Decent road maps, for example, are simply not available in Costa Rica, and most roads, both primary and secondary, are unmarked. Becoming thoroughly lost is a frustrating but common experience for most nonresident motorists; no one stays turned around for long, of course, but who wants to spend several hours each day trying to figure out where they are? Don't be afraid to ask directions. It's the best way to avoid getting lost in the first place.

Another, more dangerous disadvantage to driving yourself is the fact that Costa Ricans aren't the safest drivers in the world and certainly aren't known for their courtesy. Strangely enough, this quiet little country has one of the highest auto-accident rates (and accident-related death rates) in the world, and no one likes tangling with a macho, intoxicated driver. In addition to the lunatic locals, Costa Rica's truck drivers also create a major highway hazard. Many, especially those in the north-central region, have the dangerous habit of parking their rigs, large and small, in the middle of the road *on a curve,*

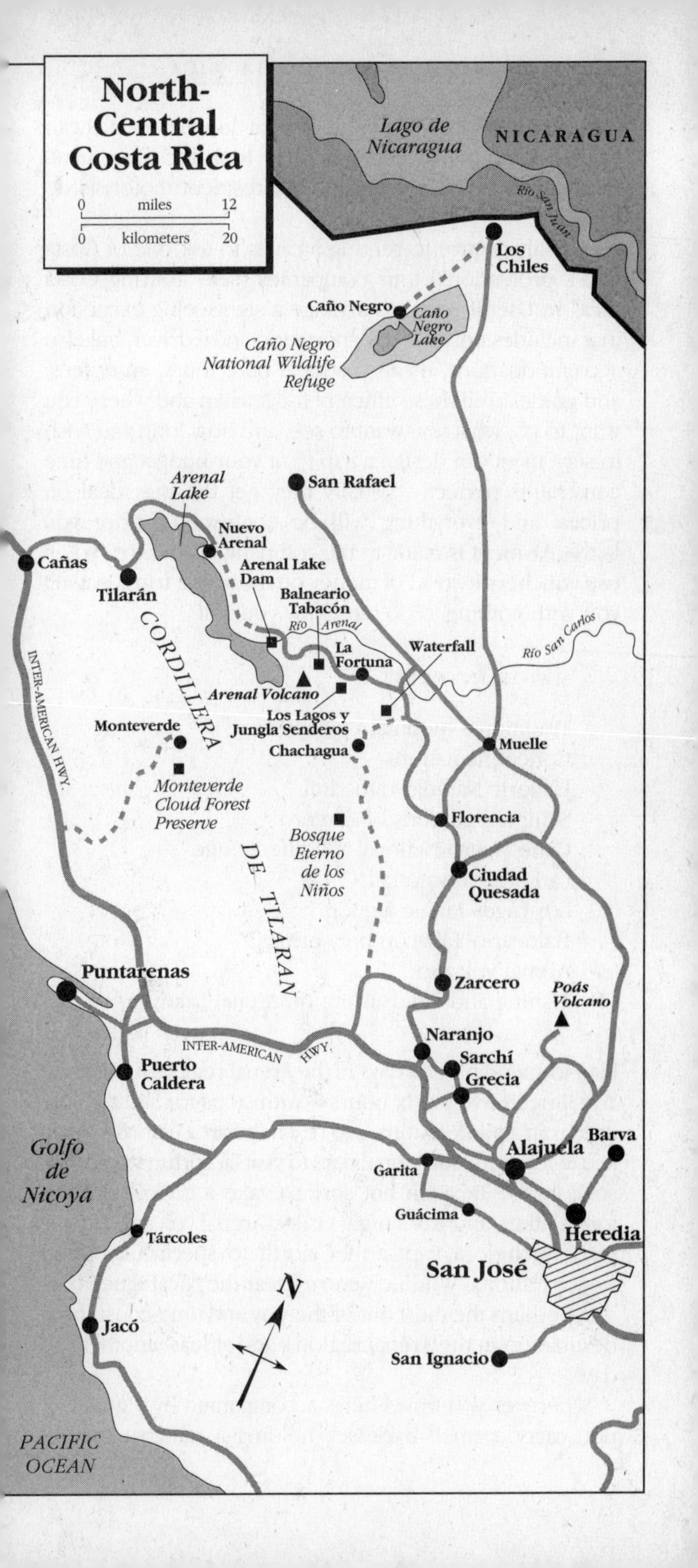

North-Central Costa Rica
0 miles 12
0 kilometers 20
Lago de Nicaragua
NICARAGUA
Río San Juan
Los Chiles
Caño Negro
Caño Negro Lake
Caño Negro National Wildlife Refuge
San Rafael
Arenal Lake
Nuevo Arenal
Cañas
Tilarán
Arenal Lake Dam
Balneario Tabacón
Río Arenal
Río San Carlos
La Fortuna
Waterfall
Arenal Volcano
Los Lagos y Jungla Senderos
CORDILLERA
INTER-AMERICAN HWY.
Monteverde
Monteverde Cloud Forest Preserve
Chachagua
Muelle
Florencia
Bosque Eterno de los Niños
DE TILARAN
Ciudad Quesada
Puntarenas
Zarcero
Poás Volcano
Naranjo
INTER-AMERICAN HWY.
Sarchí
Puerto Caldera
Grecia
Golfo de Nicoya
Barva
Alajuela
Garita
Guácima
Heredia
Tárcoles
San José
N
Jacó
San Ignacio
PACIFIC OCEAN

then leaving to take a siesta or eat lunch. Costa Rican drivers know when and where to look for these unattended vehicles; unsuspecting nonresident motorists do not.

One alternative to renting a car is to ask one of Costa Rica's professional tour companies (see "Touring Costa Rica" in Useful Facts) to arrange a sightseeing excursion that includes not only transportation and a driver, but also accommodations, meals, national park tours, entry fees, and guides. Tell these efficient folks when and where you want to go, what you want to see, and how long you wish to stay; most can design a trip to fit your budget and time constraints perfectly. Usually they get the best deal on prices, and everything will be confirmed before you leave. Payment is made to the company in advance (you'll use vouchers instead of money on the actual trip), leaving you with nothing to do but enjoy yourself.

MAJOR INTEREST

Traditional mountain villages
Coffee plantations
Historic Naranjo cathedral
Sculpted gardens of Zarcero
Caño Negro National Wildlife Refuge
La Fortuna waterfall
Los Lagos jungle lagoon
Balneario Tabacón hot springs
Arenal volcano
Fishing and windsurfing on Arenal Lake

Plan to spend several days in the Arenal region, if possible. You'll need five or six hours—with stops for sightseeing, lunch, and photographs—to reach the area from San José, and at least two additional days to visit La Fortuna waterfall, soak in the Tabacón hot springs, take a couple of rainforest hikes, and pay a night visit to Arenal volcano. If your plans include a trip farther north to spectacular Caño Negro National Wildlife Refuge (near the Nicaraguan border, perhaps the most out-of-the-way and time-consuming destination in the Arenal region), add at least another full day.

Wherever you travel here, accompanied by a guide or not, carry a small backpack holding a raincoat or umbrella, a jug or canteen of water, insect repellent, and a flashlight. And here, as elsewhere in Costa Rica, always be on the lookout for venomous snakes, poisonous spiders, and other hazards of the rain forest.

SAN JOSE NORTH TO NARANJO

The 44-km (27-mile) segment of the Inter-American Highway from San José west-northwest to the town of Naranjo and the beginning of the Naranjo–Quesada–Arenal road is an easily navigable, well-kept four-lane route. It begins in downtown San José as Avenida Central, becomes Paseo Colón as it travels west, then leaves the city in a northerly direction as Calle 42. If you're driving a rental car and get lost (almost everyone does), ask a local for directions to the Autopista Florencio del Castillo Norte, the Costa Rican name for the Inter-American Highway.

The Inter-American Highway is also the easiest route to many of the attractions discussed in the Northwest section of the Around San José chapter. On your way to the Arenal region, for example, you might want to make a side trip to the Butterfly Farm in La Guácima de Alajuela (about 35 minutes northwest of downtown), or include the city of Alajuela, Poás volcano, and the villages of Sarchí and Grecia on your route. For the villages, turn right off the Inter-American onto the Alajuela highway about 25 km (16 miles) northwest of San José, then follow the signs to Poás, Grecia, and Sarchí. To return to the main Arenal route from Sarchí, drive north on the main road through the village and you'll join the Naranjo–Quesada–Arenal road at the town of Naranjo.

Climbing slightly upward into the foothills of the Cordillera Central (Central Highlands) east of the Central Valley, the autopista carries motorists through an open, scenic landscape dotted with cattle ranches, ornamental nurseries, small truck farms, and sprawling coffee plantations (it's easy to understand why early Spanish settlers considered the land here—with its rich, black earth and abundance of water—to be far more of a treasure than gold or silver). Coffee, in particular, is of special interest to most Costa Ricans, and not just for its taste. Planted here initially about 1800 and exported commercially for the first time 40 years later, it quickly became the country's number-one cash crop. Today it has been nudged into second place by bananas, but hundreds of thousands of Costa Ricans still depend on coffee production and export for their livelihood.

According to local experts, the best-tasting Costa Rican coffee is grown at altitudes above 1,200 meters (4,000 feet) and at temperatures between 60 and 80 degrees Fahrenheit (15 to 27 degrees Celsius). Coffee berries, each containing two beans, are picked by hand, but because berries planted at the same time don't all ripen at once, a long harvest season is required (one of the reasons for coffee's high price). The picking season is from October to January in the Central Valley and from June to November in other parts of the country. If you're interested, coffee plantation tours are available at several places in the San José area (see Around San José for a detailed description of one).

Naranjo

The turnoff to the village of Naranjo and the Naranjo–Quesada–Arenal road is 4 km (2½ miles) beyond the government-operated highway toll booth (motorists have to pay a nominal toll to continue north). Well marked by signs, the junction is on the right.

Perched atop a ridge in the verdant foothills a five-minute drive beyond the autopista, Naranjo is a low-slung, bustling agricultural town that holds little of interest for visitors except for a beautiful **cathedral.** Dominating the southern side of the town square, which lies two blocks northwest of the main road (use the church towers as a guide), this huge white church with red towers and roof was built in 1924, badly damaged by an earthquake the same year, then rebuilt in 1929. Inside, the nave's ceiling is supported by thick limestone columns of Grecian type from main entrance to transept, and there is a fine collection of religious paintings, most of them from Spain, decorating the walls. Visitors are welcome to wander about as long as a Mass isn't in progress.

If you plan to visit the villages of Sarchí and Grecia from Naranjo, they lie 6 km (3½ miles) east and 13 km (8 miles) southeast, respectively. The Sarchí–Grecia access road turns right (east) off the main highway as you enter Naranjo from the south; a small sign on the main highway points the way, but it's easy to miss.

Most of Naranjo's streets are unmarked, so if you get lost heading north out of Naranjo, ask for directions to Zarcero or Ciudad Quesada.

NARANJO TO ZARCERO

The distance from Naranjo north to the village of Zarcero is about 21 km (13 miles), but the road, steep and narrow, snakes around. On a clear day views from the road of the Central Valley to the west and the sprawling hillside coffee plantations below are spectacular. For much of the distance the road is lined with living ornamental fences—colorful, manicured bushes (most of them formed from a plant called Indian cane), which not only keep cattle in their pastures and block the wind but also, because of a hyperactive chlorophyll-transforming metabolism, help to purify the air.

At the top of a hill 12 km (7½ miles) north of Naranjo, watch for a small, open-air café, **Soda El Mirador**, on the right. North-central Costa Rica is known for its tasty, traditional cuisine, and Soda El Mirador is a great place to sample some of its delightful delicacies. The menu here is fairly extensive, so if you're unfamiliar with Tico foods, try this: First, ask for a tall, cool fruit drink made of papaya, banana, and pineapple and called *fresco de frutas.* The fruit is chopped, not blended, and the concoction is undoubtedly one of the most delicious and refreshing cold drinks anywhere in the world. Next, order *gallo pinto* (a mixture of herbs, black beans, and white rice) and a platter of corn tamales and cheese tortillas. For desert try the fried bananas with cheese, which will melt on your tongue. Prices here are as delicious as the food; you can eat and drink till you nearly burst for less than $2 a person. You may never see another tourist at this tiny café, but the place is extremely popular with truck drivers, local farmers, and businessmen from Zarcero, 9 km (5½ miles) to the north.

Zarcero

The charming village of Zarcero, with its narrow, winding streets, cozy, tile-roofed homes, and small but attractive church, is nestled in the foothills of the Cordillera Central, which divides the Central Valley on the west from the

San Carlos plain on the northeast. There aren't any hotels in town, but, being blessed with clean, fragrant air and a cool invigorating climate (compared to the suffocating heat and often overwhelming reek of automobile exhaust that plagues San José and much of the Central Valley), Zarcero is one of the most attractive and popular communities in north-central Costa Rica.

Zarcero is famous for three things: a delicious strained white cheese known as *palmito,* locally made peach preserves, and gorgeous topiary gardens that adorn the main village square. You can purchase a hunk (eight or ten ounces) of *palmito* and a small bottle of preserves at nearly any store in town for very little money. Add to the cheese and peaches a loaf of fresh-baked bread or a basket of flour tortillas and the resulting picnic will be a delight.

Zarcero's famous **topiary gardens**, located in the main square in front of the church, can be easily seen on the right as you drive through the village on the main road headed north; you can park on the street in whatever space is available. Elephants with long trunks and huge ears, five-foot-high rabbits, bridges, castles, and towers are but a few of the dozens of designs sculpted from the lush shrubbery by talented local gardeners. Families with children come from miles around just to stand and gaze at these wonderful green images, and the garden is a favorite picnic spot for local residents.

Zarcero to Muelle

The fairly large agricultural hub of Ciudad Quesada (population 30,000), 28 km (17 miles) north of Zarcero, is known country-wide for its delicious white cheese. Where visitors are concerned, however, it has little to offer, not even a museum or pretty church. Streets here are narrow, unmarked, and congested, and it's easy to get lost as you pass through. If you lose your way ask for directions to Florencia.

Five minutes north of Ciudad Quesada by car, just where the road makes a sharp turn to the left, the lava-blackened cinder cone of Arenal volcano—usually spouting a spiral of steam and gas—comes into view on the right. There's a small roadside parking area here for stopping to gawk or take a photograph. Past the Arenal viewpoint the highway loops west, then slowly winds down out of the mountains and cloud forest into the hot, humid, tropical lowlands of the San Carlos plain.

At the stop sign in Florencia, 8 km (5 miles) northwest of Ciudad Quesada, you can go straight to reach Arenal volcano if you wish, but to stay on the Naranjo–Quesada–Arenal road (which is straighter and in better shape), turn right at the stop sign and go toward the village of **Muelle**.

Eleven kilometers (7 miles) farther north, just before you reach Muelle, you'll come to the junction of route 4 on the left, one of the few properly marked highways in Costa Rica. This is an important junction, so don't miss it. A left turn onto route 4 will take you to Tilajari Hotel & Resort, La Fortuna village and waterfall, Los Lagos y Jungla Senderos, Balneario Tabacón, Arenal volcano, and Arenal Lake. If you want to visit Caño Negro National Wildlife Refuge, however, instead of turning left on route 4, drive straight through Muelle and follow the Muelle–Los Chiles road north to Los Chiles, about 74 km (46 miles).

TILAJARI HOTEL & RESORT

Nestled on the west bank of the Río San Carlos 2 km (1¼ miles) west of Muelle on route 4, ▸ **Tilajari Hotel & Resort** is like a cool drink of water on a hot day. Among Costa Rica's most sophisticated and elegant resorts, this recently completed 30-acre country retreat is worth a visit even if you don't plan to spend the night. There are other accommodations in the area, but most visitors stay here.

Tilajari was designed for privacy and comfort. Forty-eight spacious guest rooms overlook the Río San Carlos just yards from the water. Bright, airy, and spotless, all the rooms have air-conditioning, a private terrace or patio overlooking the water (sunning crocodiles can often be spotted on the river bank), and a magnificent view of Arenal volcano to the west.

Tilajari's manicured grounds are dotted with ornamental shrubs, row upon row of orchids, and towering rainforest trees. The resort's common areas—restaurant, pool, racquetball courts, sauna, and discotheque—are connected to the guest quarters by flower-lined brick walkways, but sit by themselves about 200 meters upriver. The expensive first-class eatery here offers an excellent selection of Chilean wines, thick Argentine steaks, superb local seafood, and a peach Melba that will melt in your mouth.

Among Tilajari's long list of guest services (most of which are not included in the room cost) are horseback riding, jungle walks, and bird-watching expeditions into the nearby rain forest, and guided tours to Arenal volcano, Arenal Lake, Caño Negro National Wildlife Refuge, La Fortuna waterfall, and the hot springs at Tabacón.

Caño Negro National Wildlife Refuge

Located almost on the Nicaraguan border, this remote 20,000-acre jungle preserve surrounding Caño Negro Lake is difficult to reach if you're not with a local guide. The best way to see it, in fact, is on an organized and guided river trip, motoring slowly down the Río Frío in a *panga* (covered canoe), stopping every few yards to watch and photograph the wildlife. If you prefer to drive to the refuge, head north from Muelle to the town of Los Chiles, about 74 km (46 miles). From Los Chiles, turn southwest on the road to Caño Negro village and drive another 23 km (14 miles). Rustic camping sites are available for stalwart overnighters, but no other accommodations exist here.

Of all Costa Rica's nature preserves, Caño Negro probably has the largest viewable selection of indigenous wildlife. Among the larger animals commonly seen by visitors are crocodiles, tapirs, monkeys, river otters, white-tailed deer, peccaries, anteaters, and sloths. Jaguars and cougars also reside here, as do a number of species of rare butterflies and more than 200 kinds of birds.

If you haven't yet seen a three-toed sloth (known as the three-fingered sloth in some parts of Central America), you probably will in Caño Negro. Small and clothed in a dense, shaggy mat of mossy-looking hair, this docile, sluggish, tail-less mammal is one of nature's most interesting creatures. Its overall color is normally silvery-gray and its face—a wide-eyed mask covered with short hair—is white or cream-colored. Strangely enough, its fur is often infested with swarms of moths, which scuttle in and out of the dense hair like fleas. Basically tree animals, sloths spend most of their lives nibbling on fruit while hanging from the limbs or trunks of towering jungle trees such as the papaw or guarumo. According to scientists they leave their feeding tree only about once a month, at night, to defecate.

Another animal commonly seen in Caño Negro is the paca, a large rodent that resembles a bug-eyed, two-foot-long rat. Night animals (the best time to see them is at dawn or dusk), pacas spend much of their time feeding on jungle fruits that have fallen to the forest floor. Though shy and retiring, they are nasty fighters when cornered, chewing away at their attackers with long, sharp front teeth. In some areas paca populations are large—up to 50 animals per acre.

If you stay at Tilajari, the hotel will provide full-day trips to the reserve (transportation and lunch included) for less than $100 per person; even if you're not a guest, you can still sign up for the tours. Several local guides in Los Chiles offer a similar service, but they're hard to find and usually don't provide lunch. The best time to visit the refuge, simply because of better weather, is during the December to April dry season. Caño Negro is open all year long, however, and is a real treat during any month.

La Fortuna

West on route 4 out of Muelle, it's about 27 km (17 miles) from Tilajari Hotel & Resort to the small mountain village of La Fortuna. You must make two turns on the way: one to the left about 17 km (11 miles) west of Muelle, where you leave route 4, and another to the right 2 km (1¼ miles) farther on. If you get lost, watch for road signs directing motorists to La Fortuna and Tilarán.

La Fortuna, population 6,000, is the nearest community to Arenal volcano. Residents probably wonder when the mountain—just a few kilometers to the west—will again blow its stack and rain molten lava and hot ash down on the countryside (the last explosion was in 1968), but they don't live in a constant state of fear. Courteous and helpful, La Fortuna's inhabitants seem truly to appreciate the tourist trade. There's even a small downtown tourist-information kiosk that provides sightseeing and directional assistance. If you're heading out to the beautiful lagoon at Los Lagos y Jungla Senderos, 5 km (3 miles) to the west, you may wish to buy lunch supplies here in one of La Fortuna's small *tiendas* (grocery stores), so you can eat outside at the picnic area when you get there.

The village of La Fortuna is basically a support community for scores of tiny *haciendas* (ranches) and *fincas* (farms) in the Arenal area, and offers little in the way of accommodations for visitors. If you're desperate, there are a couple of small rustic hotels here, but neither can boast much in the way of comfort. There's an excellent restaurant in La Fortuna, however, **La Cascada**, easy to spot on the east end of the village. Specialties are *casado del pollo* and *casado del biftec,* savory combinations of white rice, black beans, fried bananas, tomatoes, and tasty chunks of chicken or beef. Customers can eat outside, but the street-side patio is hot and noisy. Most local diners prefer to sit inside, where they are cooled by fans and don't have to talk over the roar of traffic.

FORTUNA WATERFALL

To visit La Fortuna's famous *catarata* (waterfall) turn left (south) off the main highway in the center of town at the sign for Chachagua. Follow the rough, narrow road across a small bridge toward the mountains; about 1½ km (nearly a mile) up the road, turn right at the only intersection in sight, and keep going as far as you can. There are small, hand-printed signs in English all along the road on the right, so it's difficult to lose your way.

At the base of a steep hill about 5 km (3 miles) from the original turnoff, the road becomes too rough and rocky to negotiate, even for four-wheel-drive vehicles. From this point you'll have to walk another ten or fifteen minutes uphill. Stay on the road and keep the volcano on your right; the road ends at the waterfall overlook.

If you're afraid of heights, don't go too near the edge at the overlook; below, the hillside drops away steeply to a heavily forested valley floor, perhaps 150 vertical meters (500 feet) down. Directly opposite the overlook and surrounded by pristine rain forest is the *catarata,* a stunning, 75-meter-high (250-foot) cascade of Río Fortuna water spewing out of a narrow cut in the mountainside. The trail to walk to the bottom (a one-hour round-trip hike) begins a few feet to the left of the overlook. Where the trail forks, keep to the right; the left-hand trail is treacherously steep and leads only to the river, well downstream from the falls.

Los Lagos y Jungla Senderos

West out of La Fortuna toward Arenal Volcano the road meanders through segments of farm-dotted rain forest as it climbs onto the shoulders of the cinder cone. About 5 km (3 miles) past the La Fortuna village limits, watch for a sign on the left that points to Los Lagos y Jungla Senderos (The Lakes and Jungle Trails).

The entry fee to Los Lagos is less than a dollar, paid to either the farmer who runs the place or whichever of his children happens to be near the gate shack when automobiles or tour vans arrive. Once you've been waved through, follow the narrow but passable hand-made concrete track across a shallow stream and up into the forest for about 2 km (1¼ miles). Set in a valley at the end of the road just below Arenal volcano's eastern flank, Los Lagos is like a jewel in the jungle. About three acres in size and surrounded by primary (uncut) rain forest, this emerald-green freshwater lagoon is one of the area's prettiest sights. Along the lake's shallow southern shore there are thatched picnic shelters, a tiny boat dock, and a concrete ramp from which swimmers can enter the water without getting their feet muddy. If you brought a bathing suit, don't be afraid to use it; there is nothing dangerous in the lagoon, and the cool water is fantastic on a hot day.

In the forest surrounding the lake, brightly colored jungle birds glide from tree to tree like flying rainbows, and troops of howler monkeys often wander down off the volcano's slopes to feed. In addition to monkeys, visitors may also spot other rain-forest animals, among them pacas, deer, and tapirs. There are four *senderos* (trails) here, the beginning of each marked by a small sign. Three of the trails are less than a kilometer (½ mile) in length and lead to different observation points above the lagoon. A longer trail, about 5 km (3 miles) in length, meanders west through the rain forest to another lagoon farther up the valley. If you visit the lake on a weekday, you'll probably never see another soul, especially on the trails.

Los Lagos has no overnight accommodations and the owner doesn't allow camping, but there are several private campgrounds on the main road to Arenal volcano and Arenal Lake, about 2 km (1¼ miles) northwest of the Los Lagos turnoff. Watch for the signs on the right.

BALNEARIO TABACON

Balneario Tabacón (Tabacón Hot Springs) is a concentration of beautiful steaming pools and waterfalls at the bottom of a heavily forested valley about five minutes west of Los Lagos on the main road from La Fortuna to Arenal Lake. The bathhouse complex is adjacent to the highway on the left (west).

"Spring" is a misnomer in this case. The water is actually a thermal river that flows from the magma-filled bowels of Arenal volcano just a few miles away upstream. Straddling this hot, steamy waterway, the Tabacón facilities are surprisingly pleasant for being in the middle of nowhere. A lovely, tile-roofed Spanish-style villa, surrounded by fountains, pools, a water slide, and several acres of exquisitely manicured gardens, has both lounging and changing rooms. From most of the pools, bathers can see the huge cone of the volcano a few kilometers to the southeast.

On most days the water temperature at Balneario Tabacón is around 100 degrees Fahrenheit (38 degrees Celsius), and a half-hour's soak is guaranteed to relax and soothe tired muscles—at least momentarily. (Locals claim it is the best cure in Costa Rica for a hangover.) The bathhouse is open some days, closed others; there is no way of knowing when the manager will show up, so you have to take your chances. The cost is nominal.

Arenal Volcano

Arenal volcano, elevation 1,633 meters (5,358 feet), blew its top for the first time in recorded history in July 1968, blanketing thousands of acres of terrain (and one small village) with hot ash and lava, and killing 78 people. Most local residents were not aware that Arenal was a volcano, and no one suspected the mountain was alive and dangerous until it was far too late.

The rough road to the only "official" volcano-viewing area turns off the La Fortuna–Arenal Lake highway about 15 km (9 miles) west of La Fortuna. The junction, marked by a "Parqueo and Arenal Observatory Lodge" sign, is on the left. Two kilometers (1¼ miles) up this rocky track toward the volcano from the turnoff, and about 100 meters before another sign to the Observatory Lodge, turn left again. You'll reach the official *parqueo* (parking lot) on the volcano's lower slopes about 1 km (½ mile) farther along. The road is sandy in spots but passable.

The Arenal Observatory Lodge, about 16 km (10 miles) to the west at the end of a rough, dusty road, is used mainly by volcanologists from the Smithsonian Institution, and does not offer rooms to unannounced, nonscientist visitors. The lodge is open to public inspection, however, and if you don't mind the bumpy drive you're welcome to wander around.

As overheated magma is pushed slowly from the earth's bowels toward Arenal's numerous craters and fumaroles, the mountain belches a constant sonata of grumbles, groans, and roars. If the volcano is having an exceptionally active day it will explode every few minutes, blowing a huge cloud of ash and blue, black, or orange smoke hundreds of feet into the sky.

From the parking lot, visitors are welcome to hike up the lower shoulders of the mountain for a closer look at the steaming fumaroles. Unlike Poás and Irazú volcanoes to the southeast, however, Arenal is healthy and dangerous. New vents are opening constantly on the mountainside (usually with no warning), spewing poisonous gases into the air and spilling rivers of red-hot magma down the slopes. If you hike, don't go more than a few hundred feet from the parking lot. Several people are killed each year on Arenal, most of them tourists foolishly attempting to climb to the top.

Arenal is often cloaked in clouds and steam, but the vapors come and go rapidly, so hang around. Views of the mountain are magnificent anytime, but visiting the volcano at night—when bright, narrow streams of crimson magma can be seen cascading down the mountain and the clouds above the caldera turn bright-orange from the superheated lava—is an unforgettable experience. The Arenal Lake road is dangerous at night for motorists unaccustomed to local driving habits, however, so if possible arrange to take a guided excursion from your hotel. An evening tour from Tilajari Hotel & Resort costs about $35 and includes transportation, guide, driver, and snacks.

Arenal Lake

A few kilometers west of the volcano is Arenal Lake, a huge, multi-armed reservoir created in 1979 to provide hydroelectric power via the Costa Rican Institute of Electricity (ICE) for San José and other Costa Rican cities. Today, covering some 130 square km (50 square miles) and filled with a species of humpbacked, brightly colored game fish known as rainbow bass, it is one of Central America's best-known fishing lakes. Because of the 20- to 30-knot winds that, from December through March, sweep across the northwest end of the lake, Arenal has also become one of the most popular sailboarding lakes in the Western Hemisphere. Windsurfing experts say there is simply no other inland body of water like it anywhere.

The main road (the only passable road) along Arenal Lake meanders 15 to 30 meters (50 to 100 feet) above the water through stands of uncut rain forest, following the northern shoreline to the village of Nuevo Arenal, about 21 km (13 miles) northwest of the Arenal Lake dam, which is not far beyond Balneario Tabacón. Drive slowly enough to hear what seems like hundreds of different species of birds in the huge trees overhanging the road, chirping and singing like cicadas. Local residents are so concerned about protecting this undisturbed and wildlife-abundant environment that they have put up signs at most pullouts: *Recibimos turismo—no basura* (We welcome tourism—not trash).

STAYING IN THE ARENAL LAKE REGION

The majority of visitors to this part of Costa Rica stay at the elegant Tilajari Hotel & Resort because of its convenient location. For those who wish to spend a day or two fishing for rainbow bass or sailboarding on Arenal Lake, however, the area offers several out-of-the-way but pleasant accommodations.

Small and fairly rustic, ▸ **Arenal Lodge** sits at the end of a steep, 4-km (2½-mile) dirt road that leaves the main highway to the right (north) just past the Arenal Lake dam. The best thing about this isolated hostelry, perched on the side of a forest-covered hill about 300 meters (1,000 feet) above the lake, is its location. The unobstructed views from here of Arenal volcano, about 8 km (5 miles) to the southeast, are superb.

Arenal Lodge is primarily a fishing resort; it has a small staff of fishing guides and its own fleet of well-equipped boats. All-day fishing excursions for rainbow bass are expensive—about $175 per person—but the price includes a boat, guide, tackle, and lunch. Other activities offered here for an additional fee are bicycling trips, guided tours to the volcano, and escorted nature hikes into the nearby forest.

Accommodations at Arenal Lodge are adequate but not fancy: 14 cramped and unmemorable guest rooms, and a large and more congenial (and expensive) master suite with a tiled, walk-in tub. The restaurant serves typical Costa Rican food family-style, and guests can relax in an airy, brick-floored atrium-cum-common room.

If you're more interested in sailboarding than fishing, follow the main road around the western tip of the lake to the ▶ **Hotel Tilawa** and Tilawa Viento Surf (the hotel's windsurfing center), 15 km (9 miles) past the village of Nuevo Arenal. The pavement ends about 10 km (6 miles) northwest of Arenal dam; the remaining 10-km stretch to the village is extremely rough and rutty. Because of this unpaved part the drive from Arenal dam to the Hotel Tilawa takes about an hour.

Located on the side of a hill overlooking the lake, Tilawa is a modern copy of the Minoan palace of Knossos on Crete, complete with columns and frescoed walls. The hotel's exterior is painted in soft, natural shades of ocher, as are the patios, the swimming pool, and the floors of all 24 rooms and four junior suites. The comfortable furniture in each room was created by local craftsmen from rain-forest hardwoods; other niceties are handmade bedspreads from Guatemala and tiled bathrooms. Tilawa has its own **restaurant**, which serves both Costa Rican and American cuisine.

Many of the guests here are windsurfers (some of them fanatics), but for nonboarders the hotel offers horseback riding, escorted day and evening trips to Arenal volcano, and river-rafting expeditions down the nearby Río Corobicí, all for an additional fee. If you book a package tour (seven days), the cost includes accommodations, transportation to and from San José, all windsurfing equipment, and breakfasts.

Tilarán and Environs

If you're looking for a meal, head for the **Equus Barbecue**, located 5 km (3 miles) west of the Hotel Tilawa at the western end of Arenal Lake on the main road around the lake. The place is country basic but colorful; the chef prepares barbecued chicken and thick steaks over the chimney of the fireplace—after climbing onto the roof. The nearby village of Tilarán, 8 km (5 miles) south of the Hotel Tilawa on the main highway to the city of Cañas (which is on the Inter-American Highway), is basically a Costa Rican cow town, filled, particularly on Saturday nights, with rough-and-ready drovers from nearby cattle ranches. The town has a disco, movie theater, two or three noisy bars, and a handful of small restaurants.

From Tilarán, you can return to La Fortuna, Zarcero, and San José the way you came, or continue (now to the west) about 30 km (19 miles) to Cañas and the Inter-American Highway. The distance from Tilarán to San José via Cañas is about 200 km (124 miles). The distance from Cañas to Puntarenas and the Pacific coast is about 75 km (46 miles).

GETTING AROUND

Car rentals are available at the international airport outside San José and at most of the city's larger hotels. Worldwide rental companies such as National and Hertz have offices in Costa Rica, but there are also a number of local companies. Most San José travel agents recommend reserving a car at least one week in advance of your arrival; they also suggest that, if your driving plans include visits to Costa Rica's more remote areas, you rent a vehicle equipped with four-wheel drive.

Highways connecting principal towns and villages in the Arenal region are usually in good condition, though some roads in the Cordillera Central and the Cordillera de Tilarán are steep, narrow, twisty, and occasionally closed because of mud slides. The road from Zarcero to Ciudad Quesada, for instance, is often blocked by slides in the rainy season; if you hit a roadblock here, turn off your engine and wait it out. Highway crews generally clear up the mess within a couple of hours.

If you're driving a rental car, fill up with gasoline at every opportunity; in the north-central region service stations can be few and far between. Decent road maps of Costa Rica with properly marked highways and distances simply do not exist. If you get lost, ask for the road to the next village along your proposed route (*Donde está la carretera a* . . .). Keep an eye peeled especially for trucks that are parked on the highway while their drivers take a nap or have a picnic in the forest. Avoid driving at night (it's dangerous and you'll probably get lost), and wherever you are, always remember that Costa Rica has one of the highest rates of fatal automobile accidents in the world.

Allow yourself three or four days in the Arenal region, if possible. Driving time from San José to Tilajari Hotel & Resort is 5 to 6 hours with stops for lunch and attractions; considering the distance to be travelled, the possibility of unexpected delays, Costa Rican driving habits, and the need to leave yourself plenty of daylight, it's best to get an early start out of San José. If you plan to visit La Fortuna waterfall and Balneario Tabacón, hike in the rain forest, and spend an evening at Arenal volcano, you'll need at least two days, while a trip to spectacular Caño Negro National Wildlife Refuge will add another day.

Buses offer frequent and inexpensive service between San José and Arenal area towns such as Ciudad Quesada, Muelle, and La Fortuna, but they are usually antiquated, hot, crowded, and noisy. If you do ride a country bus in Costa Rica (it's quite an experience), don't be surprised if your seatmate is an unbathed and manure-splattered farmer holding a chicken or pig in his lap.

One excellent alternative to riding a bus or driving yourself is to let one of Costa Rica's excellent tour companies, such as Costa Rica's Temptations or Swiss Travel (see "Touring Costa Rica" in Useful Facts), organize a custom tour. They can arrange all accommodations, meals, transportation, guides, drivers, and entry fees in advance, leaving you free to enjoy the sights and attractions. These companies all have good contacts in Costa Rica's tourist industry, so usually you'll spend less money than if you went on your own.

North-central Costa Rica's rainy season lasts from May through November, with the wettest months being September and October. Rain usually falls during late afternoon or at night, while mornings are quite often clear. The best time to visit the Arenal region is in the dry season, December through April, but travelling in the rainy season has an advantage: Prices for accommodations, meals, and transportation in most areas are lowered by about 20 percent.

ACCOMMODATIONS REFERENCE

Unless otherwise indicated, the rate given is the projected rate for a double room, double occupancy, and does not include tax. Price ranges span the lowest rate in the low season to the highest rate in the high season. As prices are subject to change, always double-check before booking.

▸ **Arenal Lodge. Arenal Lake.** Contact P.O. Box 1139-1250, Escazú. Tel: 28-2588; Fax: 28-2798. $60–$80.

▸ **Hotel Tilawa.** P.O. Box 92, **Tilarán**, Guanacaste. Tel: 69-5050 or 69-5666; Fax: 69-5766. $46–$95.

▸ **Tilajari Hotel & Resort. Muelle.** Contact P.O. Box 81-4400, Ciudad Quesada, San Carlos. Tel: 46-1083; Fax: 46-1462. $60–$75.

CHRONOLOGY OF THE HISTORY OF COSTA RICA

- **Pre-Columbian Era**: Costa Rica is inhabited by indigenous Chorotega Indians. Chibcha Indians from the Colombia region and other tribes from areas that will become Ecuador and Brazil migrate here sometime before the arrival of the Spanish.
- **1502**: After weeks of battling stormy seas, Christopher Columbus—on his fourth and final voyage to the New World—lands on Costa Rica's Caribbean coast in the bay of Cariari near present-day Puerto Limón. Columbus names the region (Costa Rica and Panamá) Veragua.
- **1506–1508**: King Ferdinand of Spain sends Diego de Nicuesa and a small band of settlers to colonize Veragua. Because of the rugged terrain and hostile Indians the attempt is a failure.
- **1513–1521**: Veragua's Pacific coast is explored by mariners.
- **1522**: Spaniard Gil Gonzalez Davila lands on the Península de Nicoya and establishes friendly relations with the Chorotega Indians. Some inland areas are explored.
- **1524**: Francisco Fernando de Córdova starts the settlement of Bruselas on the Golfo de Nicoya (near present-day Puntarenas). It is abandoned within a few months.
- **1534**: Felipe Gutierrez becomes governor of Veragua and attempts to explore inland; he and his party nearly starve, and some of his men resort to cannibalism.
- **1539**: The Spanish crown officially divides Veragua into Costa Rica (Rich Coast) and Panamá.

- **1540**: Costa Rica becomes an official *gobernación* (territory) of Spain. Colonists under the leadership of Hernán Sánchez de Badajoz start a settlement (called Badajoz) at the mouth of the Río Sixaola. They are driven out a year later by Indians.
- **1561**: Juan de Cavallón, with 80 Spaniards and a complement of black slaves, founds the first permanent settlement in Costa Rica—Garcimuñoz, on the Pacific coast.
- **1562**: Governor Juan Vásquez de Coronado moves settlers inland from the Pacific coast to the Cartago Valley in the Central Highlands.
- **1563**: Cartago is established as the capital of Costa Rica.
- **1570–1572**. The Talamanca (southern mountain region) is pacified by Governor Perafán de Ribera.
- **1666**: English pirate Henry Morgan and 700 men march overland in an attempt to sieze Cartago. Morgan's expedition is stopped at Quebrada Honda by a contingent of colonial militia.
- **1700**: The population of Costa Rica reaches 20,000.
- **1706**: The city of Heredia is founded.
- **1709**: Money and cloth become so scarce in Costa Rica that cacao beans are designated as the official currency and many people are forced to wear fabrics made from tree bark and goat hair.
- **1723**: Irazú volcano erupts, virtually destroying the capital city of Cartago.
- **1737**: San José (originally known as Villanueva de la Boca del Monte) is founded.
- **1782**: The city of Alajuela (originally known as Villa Hermosa) is founded.
- **1821**: Costa Rica wins independence from Spain on October 29, but the news takes more than a month to reach the country. The official Costa Rican government declares the country a member of the Federal Republic of Central America.
- **1822**: Heavily armed government-backed forces from Heredia and the capital city of Cartago march on a rebellious San José (which did not want to join the alliance), attempting to force the city to become part of the Federal Republic of Central America. In the ensuing battle, the government

forces are soundly defeated by republicans from San José and Alajuela.

- **1829**: Coffee becomes Costa Rica's major source of foreign revenue, surpassing cacao, tobacco, and sugar.
- **1835**: Cartago, Heredia, and Alajuela form El Circuito de Ciudades (League of Cities); they raise an army of 4,000 to oppose Braulio Carrillo Colina, who has established a new capital at San José. The rebellion is crushed by loyalists under the command of Carrillo.
- **1847**: José María Castro Madriz becomes Costa Rica's first chief executive to bear the title of president.
- **1848**: Costa Rica declares itself an independent republic.
- **1856**: U.S. adventurer and self-styled president of Nicaragua William Walker attempts to invade Costa Rica from the north. In a battle that lasts only 14 minutes, Walker and his small army are defeated. In 1860 he is executed by firing squad in Honduras.
- **1870**: Tomás Guardia declares himself chief of state of Costa Rica and formulates plans for a railroad that will connect Alajuela to Puerto Limón. England loans him 3.4 million pounds sterling to complete the project.
- **1888**: Italian railroad workers, complaining of bad working and living conditions, organize the first strike in Costa Rica's history.
- **1889**: The country's first-ever popular elections are held. In San José, 10,000 armed citizens take to the streets to demonstrate their commitment to democracy.
- **1890**: The railroad from Alajuela to Puerto Limón is finally completed, costing the equivalent of $8 million and the lives of 4,000 workers.
- **1899**: The United Fruit Company (La Yunai) is founded. La Yunai acquires more land in Costa Rica than any other company and helps Costa Rica become the world's leading producer of bananas.
- **1900**: A decline in world coffee prices signals the temporary end of Costa Rica's coffee export trade.
- **1910**: Costa Rica's population reaches 360,000.

- **1913**: A strike by employees of La Yunai (who complain of unfair working conditions) is broken by the government. The main strike leaders are killed.
- **1917**: A military coup led by Federico Tinoco Granados displaces elected president Alfredo Gonzalez Flores. Two years later the threat of U.S. intervention helps bring about Tinoco's downfall.
- **1934**: A Communist-led strike against La Yunai finally brings better working and living conditions for employees.
- **1938**: Sigatoka, a plant disease that infects and kills banana plants, destroys huge numbers of them on the Caribbean coast.
- **1941**: Costa Rica declares war on Japan several hours before the United States does. The country also declares war on Germany and Italy.
- **1948**: To keep an opposition candidate from becoming president, congress annuls the presidential election. The country is swept by a civil war in which 2,000 people die. Later in the year the Costa Rican army is abolished; in 1949, a new constitution is introduced.
- **1955**: Eight-hundred well-armed rebels invade Costa Rica from Nicaragua. With the help of four fighter aircraft sent by the United States, volunteer Costa Rican forces drive the invaders back into Nicaragua within two weeks.
- **1968**: A major earthquake destroys scores of communities on the Caribbean coast. Shortly after that catastrophe Arenal volcano explodes, killing 78 people.
- **1978–1979**: Nicaragua closes its border with Costa Rica. Northern Costa Rica serves as a base for American-supported Sandinistas operating in Nicaragua.
- **1987**: Costa Rican president Oscar Arias Sánchez wins the Nobel Peace Prize. The Guápiles Highway, linking San José with the Caribbean city of Puerto Limón, is opened.
- **1991**: A major earthquake destroys much of Puerto Limón and the southern Caribbean coast, killing 45 people.

—Buddy Mays

INDEX

Alajuela, 15, 89
Alba Art Gallery, 70
Aloha, 142
Annemarie, 69
Archie Field's Río Colorado Lodge, 18, 128, 133
Arenal Lake, 195
Arenal Lodge, 196, 200
Arenal Volcano, 194
Around San José, 73, 74 (map)
Artesanías Biesanz, 72
Atlanta Dining Gallery, 62
Aviary of the Caribbean, 17, 114, 132

Babaloo, 65
Bahía Drake, 156
Los Balcones, 64
Balneario Tabacón, 16, 194
Barba Roja, 150
Bare y Cabinas Madre de Dios, 123
Bar Mexico, 67
Barra del Colorado, 128
Barra del Colorado National Wildlife Refuge, 128
Barva, 95
Barva Cloud Forest and Volcano, 15, 95
Basílica de Nuestra Señora de los Angeles, 79
Bellavista Fortress (Museo Nacional), 46
Bierstube, 142
Bon Vivant, 57
Bosque Eterno de los Niños, 165
Braulio Carrillo National Park, 15, 98
Bri Bri, 71
Bromelias Café y Grill, 61
Butterfly Farm (Alajuela), 14, 88

Cabinas Las Palmas, 110, 132
Café Britt, 15, 93
Café Ruiseñor, 71
Café del Teatro, 45
Cahuita National Park, 17, 115
Cahuita Village, 115
Calle Las Artesanías, 71
Caño Island, 19, 157
Caño Island Biological Reserve, 157
Caño Negro National Wildlife Refuge, 16, 190
Carara Biological Reserve, 18, 143
La Caravelle, 142
Cariari Hotel and Country Club, 51, 68
Caribbean Coast, 16, 105, 106 (map)
Carrecife de Cahuita, 116
Cartago, 13, 79
La Casa de Mariscos, 142
Casa Turire, 84, 85, 104
La Cascada: La Fortuna, 192; Monteverde, 166
Casona Santa Rosa, 169
Centro Comercial El Pueblo, 42
Charrúas, 149
Chaverri family factory, 92
Chavetas, 65
Chirripó River, 85
Cocalito Lodge, 156
La Cocina de Leña, 61
Continental Bar and Restaurant, 80

Corcovado Lodge Tent Camp, 157, 180
Corcovado National Park, 19, 152
Corobicí Hotel and Spa, 54, 68
Costa Rica Home & Host, 54
Crafts Cooperative (Monteverde area), 167

Da Pino Pizzeria Restaurante, 58
Dr. Rafael Lucas Rodríguez Caballero National Wildlife Refuge, 167
Del Río, 70

Equus Barbecue, 197
Escazú, 43, 72
La Esmeralda, 65

Fiesta Hotel Resort & Casino, 140, 180
Finca Rosa Blanca, 97, 104
First International Children's Rain Forest, 165
La Fortuna, 191
Fortuna Waterfall, 192
Fuji, 60

Galería Real, 71
Galerías Casa Alameda, 70
Golfo de Nicoya, 134
Gran Hotel, 44, 52, 68
Grecia, 15, 91
Guanacaste Conservation Area, 169, 172
Guayabo National Monument, 14, 83

Heredia, 95
Holiday Inn Aurora, 68
Hotel Ambassador, 53
Hotel L'Ambiance, 52, 62
Hotel El Atlántida, 114, 132
Hotel Belmar, 166, 180
Hotel Las Brisas, 141, 180
Hotel El Cypresal, 98, 104
Hotel Las Espuelas, 173, 180
Hotel Grano de Oro, 53, 59, 70
Hotel Herradura Resort and Conference Center, 51, 68
Hotel Ilan Ilan, 127, 133
Hotel de Montaña Monteverde, 166, 180
Hotel Porto Bello, 141, 180
Hotel Punta Cocles, 118, 132
Hotel Tamarindo Diría, 175, 180
Hotel Tilawa, 197, 200
Hotel Tioga, 141, 180
Hotel Yadrán, 141, 180
House of the Dreamer, 82
Hummingbird Gallery, 167

Infinito, 64
Irazú Volcano, 78
Irazú Volcano National Park, 78
Isla del Caño, 157
Isla Uvita, 112

Jungle Lodge, 127, 133

Kamuk Hotel, 150, 180
Karahé Hotel & Villas, 150, 180
Key Largo, 66
Kimbamba, 112

Los Lagos y Jungla Senderos, 16, 193
Lankester Gardens, 13, 82
La Lechería, 166
Limón, 132
Linda Vista, 78
Lukas, 61

Macchu Picchu Restaurant, 59
Malety, 71
Manuel Antonio National Park, 18, 150
Manzanillo-Gandoca National Wildlife Refuge, 17, 119
Maribu Caribe Hotel, 112, 132
La Mariposa, 150, 180
Los Mariscos Bar, 68
Maritza biological station, 172
El Mastil Bar, 140
Matama Hotel, 113, 132
Mawamba Lodge, 126, 133
Mazorca, 60
Mercado Central (San José), 69

Mercado Nacional de Artesanía (San José), 69
Monterrey, 43
Monteverde Cloud Forest Preserve, 19, 159
Monteverde Lodge, 165, 180
Moravia, 43, 71
Mordisco Restaurant, 58
Muelle, 189
Museo de Arte Costarricense, 48
Museo de Entomología, 49
Museo Franciscano (Orosí), 81
Museo de Jade, 47
Museo Nacional (Bellavista Fortress), 46
Museo Numismático, 46
Museo de Oro, 45

Naranjo, 186
Nicoya Peninsula, 20, 173, 175
North-Central Costa Rica, 181, 183 (map)
Northern Pacific Coast, 19, 158, 160 (map)

Orosí, 81
Orosí Valley, 13, 80

Pacific Coast, 18, 134, 137 (map: southern), 160 (map: northern)
Pacuare River, 84
Palo Verde National Park, 167
Paraíso, 80
Parque Cariari, 112
Parque La Sabana, 49
Parque Vargas, 112
Parroquia Las Mercedes, 91
Parroquia San José de Orosí, 81
Paseo Colón, 42, 43
Península de Nicoya, 20, 173, 175
Península de Osa, 152
Península de Santa Elena, 170
Pensión Flor Mar, 166, 180
La Perla, 67
Pitilla biological station, 172
Pizote Lodge, 118, 132
La Placita, 65
Playa Bonita, 112
Plaza de la Cultura, 42, 44, 68
Plinio, 149
Poás Volcano, 90
El Pórtico Hotel, 97, 104
El Pueblo, 64, 70
Puerto Caldera, 138
Puerto Limón, 111
Puerto Moín, 121
Puerto Viejo, 17, 116
Puntarenas, 18, 138
Punta Uva, 17, 119

Quebrada Gonzales ranger station, 99
Quepos, 148

Raba, 69
Recreo, 90
Restaurant La Macarela, 140
Restaurant Las Palmas, 110
Río Barranca, 140
Río Bebedero, 167
Río Colorado Lodge (Archie Field's), 18, 128, 133
Río Reventazón, 84
Río Tempisque, 167
Ruinas de la Parroquia, 80

Saints' Route, 14, 86
San Bartolomé, 95
San Bosco, 43
San José, 10, 37, 40 (map)
San Marcos, 87
San Pablo de León Cortés, 87
San Pedro, 43, 60
Santa María, 87
Santa Rosa National Park, 19, 169
Sarchí, 15, 91
Soda El Mirador, 187
Southern Caribbean Coast, 17, 109
Southern Pacific Coast, 18, 137 (map), 142
Spoon, 58, 60
Stanford's Caribe Restaurant, 117
Stefanel, 71
Super Taco Antojos, 58

Tamarindo National Wildlife Refuge, 173
Tango Bar del Che, 65
Tapantí National Wildlife Reserve, 13, 81
Tara, 55, 62
Tarcoles Bridge, 144
Teatro Melico Salazar, 67
Teatro Nacional, 44
Tilajari Hotel & Resort, 189, 200
Tilarán, 197
Tortuga Lodge, 127, 133
Tortuguero Channels, 18, 122
Tortuguero Lagoon, 126
Tortuguero National Park, 123
Tortuguero Village, 125
Turrialba Valley, 14, 83
Turrialba Volcano, 83

Villa del Este, 71
Los Vitrales, 57
Vogue Boutique, 71

Los Yoses, 43, 60, 70

Zarcero, 187
Zoológico de Aves (Zoo-Ave), 14, 89